I0083004

HONESTY IS EXPLOSIVE!

HONESTY IS EXPLOSIVE!

SELECTED MUSIC JOURNALISM

by

Ben Watson

Salvaged and Sorted by W. C. Bamberger

THE BORGO PRESS

An Imprint of Wildside Press LLC

MMX

The Woodstock Series
Popular Music of Today
ISSN 0891-9585

Volume Three

Copyright © 1985, 1989, 1990, 1991, 1992, 1993, 1994, 1995, 1996, 1997, 1998, 1999, 2000, 2001, 2002, 2010 by Ben Watson

All rights reserved.
No part of this book may be reproduced in any form without the expressed written consent of the publisher.

www.wildsidebooks.com

FIRST EDITION

CONTENTS

Introduction 7
Acknowledgments 10

Part I. CD and Book Reviews

1985—Arthur Blythe 11
1989—Tenor Saxophones 13
1990—Jack Nitzsche 14
1991—Ray Charles; Steve Coleman; Luc Ferrari, *et al.*;
  Mauricio Kagel; Joe Morris; Archie Shepp; Joe Turner; Joe
  Venuti and Eddie Lang; Ben Webster 16
1992—Pierre Boulez; Anthony Braxton; Cornelius Cardew;
  Ornette Coleman/Howard Shore; James Dillon; Malcolm
  Goldstein; Julius Hemphill; Joseph Jarman/Don Moye; Joe
  Morris; Paul Motian; Napalm Death; Max Roach; Giacinto
  Scelsi/John Cage; John Scofield; Michael Brook/Gary
  Lucas/Henry Kaiser/Romeo Vendrame; Frank Zappa 26
1993—Charles Brown; Devo; Bern Nix; Prince; Sun Ra 46
1994—John Coltrane; Tony Oxley/Derek Bailey/Anthony
  Braxton/Transient V Resident; Music Revelation Ensemble;
  Various (Classical) 53
1995—John Cage; Leo Ornstein/George Antheil/Henry Cowell;
  Rico/Kuubo; Kurt Schwitters 63
1996—Ascension; Eugene Chadbourne/Jimmy Carl Black;
  Anthony Coleman; Joe Maneri/ Mat Maneri; Katherine
  Norman; Iggy Pop; Various (Indian Classical) 69
1997—Andrew Balke (Book Review); Luther Thomas; Edgard
  Varèse 79
1998—Bassholes; Eugene Chadbourne; Charlie Feathers/Jenks
  'Tex' Carman; Roscoe Mitchell/Lake-Workman-Cyrille; Ed
  Palermo/The Muffin Men; Kurt Weill/Marianne Faithful/
  Loes Luca/Willem Breukeer Kollektief/Hanns Eisler 85
1999—Theodor Adorno (Book Review); Army of Ghosts;
  Autism; Bashful Brother Oswald; Carl E. Baugher (Book
  Review); Matt De Gennaro/ Alistair Galbraith; William

Hooker; Kevin Norton; Michael Prime; Various (British Jazz) 95

2000—Peter Brötzmann; Adam Clayson (Book Review); Christopher Delaurenti; Julius Hemphill; Billy Jenkins; Sonic Liberation Front; Various; Vienna Art Orchestra 113

2001—Derek Bailey/Eugene Chadbourne/Vertek Ensemble; Roger Beebe, *et al.* (Book Review); Nadine Cohodas (Book Review); Kahil El'Zabar/Billy Bang; Tony Glover, *et al.* (Book Review); London Improvisers Orchestra; Paul Minotto; Carl-Ludwig Reichert (Book Review); Daniel Sinker (Book Review); Wadada Leo Smith; Various; Thomas Wictor (Book Review); John Zorn (Book Review) 125

2002—John Wilkes Booze; Mike Osborne 158

Part II. Articles, Interviews and Events

Lawrence D. 'Butch' Morris *(1997)* 161

Ornette Coleman Plays *Naked Lunch (1999)* 169

Ornette Coleman Interview *(2001)* 172

When Worlds Collide *(2001)* 188

Madness and Music *(2001)* 191

Iain Sinclair's M25 London Orbital *(2002)* 203

Music, Violence, Truth *(2001)* 206

Index 211

About the Author 231

INTRODUCTION

THESE REVIEWS and articles were written between 1985 and 2002, mainly for *Wire* magazine and *Hi-Fi News*. In the early 2000s my career as a music journalist stuttered and began fizzling out, a painful and protracted process. Finally, with the birth of my daughter Iris in June 2005, and with a period of fulltime childcare looming, I asked *The Wire* to remove my name from its list of contributors, and retired. Ever since I'd read an older brother's copy of the Schoolkids' *Oz*, I wanted to be a music writer, and abandoning that ambition was a blow to my self-esteem, if not to my wallet.

What went wrong? Well, even during my heyday as a music journalist, BBC Radio voice and TV arts personality, nothing ever went quite right. I learned about music (1979-95) in Leeds, a tough industrial city in England's North, alongside music fans who spoke their minds: the F Club at Brannigan's, Rock Against Racism at the Poly and then at Roots in Chapeltown, the Termite Club upstairs at the Fenton, Leeds Jazz at the Trades Club and Irish Centre, the Duchess of York, the Huddersfield Contemporary Music Festival. As a newly-issued punk, I was the object of startled looks and barracking from passers-by, bus drivers, and shopkeepers. The cliché "aren't they nice up north?" never seemed appropriate. So I breathed the bluntness and honesty around me as if it was nothing unusual, unaware that it was shaping me as a writer and a critic. When I started writing for the *Wire* in 1987, I took a National Travel coach down to London and met the editors to see Naked City on a bill with Kronos Quartet. As we poured into the lobby after the Naked City set, I said something about Zorn needing a string quartet to make his own band seem transgressive, a somewhat artificial strategy: "What do you think?" "We're still making up our minds…" came the reply, giving me my first taste of the, um, *diplomatic* nature of music opinion in the nation's metropolis.

Nevertheless, I'm grateful to the late Richard Cook—he didn't found *The Wire*, but he made it something more than just another jazz magazine—for bringing me overground as a writer. I'd previously been limited to "avant-garde" publications circulated by contacts in the Cambridge Poetry scene, and to *The Leeds Other Paper*, a lone survivor from the agitprop '70s. Cook once told me he'd decided to promote me and Tony Herrington (a shelf-stacker from Manchester's best jazz shop) as new writers: a blast of bracing air from the North, or something like that. I loved writing for *The Wire*. Not everyone read it, still less bought copies, but everyone was aware of it. It gave me opportunities to talk to musicians: I wasn't just a fan, I was involved. As punks changed to yuppies during the '80s, I went with the flow, finding my first regular employment in computers, wearing a suit and sporting a ponytail (though I never missed an Iggy Pop or Cramps gig). Cook had come across to the *Wire* from *NME*. If you asked to see what was in his plastic bag, it was as likely to be LPs from the Pebbles series as rare Blue Notes or Atlantics. Unlike the moralists who swamped the local politics I was involved in, he didn't wince at my Zappa obsession, condemn him as a "sexist" or "capitalist". The "jazz fogey" pose Richard adopted at the end of his life was nowhere in evidence, and when I wrote about "Punkjazz" for the magazine, he and Mark Sinker applauded when I walked into the office. Happy days.

The only problem at the time was Andy Sheppard and Loose Tubes. I hated them, but they were stars in the firmament of the Jazz Revival, so my hostile reviews were bowdlerized. And Manfred Eicher was already using his considerable advertising clout to threaten writers who were sceptical about ECM's high-class muzak. But these were minor irritations. The real problems began for me after Sinker's (quite calculated) "reign of madness" finished ("Death to the Music Industry" etc), when Rob Young and Biba Kopf/Chris Bohn began centring *Wire*-taste around Zorn's concept of "avant". Music readymade for ascent to the South Bank (London's mausoleum of official musical culture), i.e. ghastly. One problem was that I'd researched the avant-garde. I knew what we were all talking about. I knew about Wyndham Lewis and Vorticism and I read *Finnegans Wake*. Every night! My interest began with finding Hans Richter's *Dada: Art and Anti-Art* in Kew Public Library, it flourished when I dropped in at a Kurt Schwitters show at the Marlborough Gallery on Bond Street in 1972, it went ballistic when I encountered the writings of Guy Debord and Asger Jorn and Theodor Adorno. When Cook enthused about Gene Ammons, even a Situationist couldn't sneer, but Rob Young on the "new" Nordic Cool? For fuck's sake! He didn't even mention Frode Gjerstad. You can't debate rationally with such people because they haven't got a straw of confidence. They don't actually know what they think, they're waiting to see what Thurston Moore or David Toop or the rich-kid owner of some boutique label will say. They're cringing at the next angry phone call from Evan Parker or Jon Hassell. You wear a t-shirt saying "Brian Eno Fuck Off" to the launch of David *Toop's Ocean of Sound* and *no one laughs*. In this cricked neck of the woods, a confident opinion is like a terrorist with a bomb: dangerous to life, flesh, career. Call in the cops! Music writing as trade-journal politics, not self-expression. These are the smoothies who merely raise their eyebrows when you say something they disagree with, but make sure your copy "goes missing" when it's time to print. That you're dropped from the next Arts Council bean feast. Cowards, philistines, feeble-minded tossers! Envious, vengeful nonentities. The squashy insidious bedrock, of course, of commercial business-as-usual—something avant-gardes worth their salt declare war on.

Should I ever have expected anything else? Probably not. "Avant"—a nauseating queue of art-college games awaiting your boring approval—is just the echo of a music industry which has adopted the shiny-teeth spasm-dance of celebrity over the insinuating power and majesty of Funk (and an "art world" which is just a branch of advertising). Nevertheless, despite the gruesome chains of sales teams peddling rotten fruit as the next hip taste, there are still a few true sparks around, people who make you think it might be worth re-entering the fray. People? Mainly Eugene Chadbourne, actually. Who's very around: portly, ubiquitous, universal music man. For real. Because Eugene has the *correct relationship* to jazz and country music, something no one in "avant" gets right (their trousers are too tight). Because even the ghosts of Hendrix and Zappa cannot snuff the experience and invention of Eugene's guitar-based project/object. He hasn't been bitten by the tick of commodity fetishism which makes Zorn sick: there are loads of releases with Eugene's name on them, but they're all spun off from the central intent, the dynamic fury, which is to tell the truth, to name and shame the abusers and idiots. Oh, and besides Eugene, there's David Murray. And Evil Dick. But where to write about such artists? Maybe there's nowhere to write simply because radical-music history has now been rewritten by David Keenan, so it's an inane void in which no one can hear you think…with actors prancing about in dark glasses pretending to play the blues. So: many, many thanks to W. C. Bamberger for rescuing these old writings from floppy-disc oblivion—we didn't leaf through old *Wire* magazines, we wanted my texts BEFORE editorial "wisdom" was applied. This meant dusting off dilapidated computers and reviving antique word-processing packages. I hope the work was worthwhile. Maybe someone out there wants to read a music journalist who remembers what it was like when Nick Tosches and Charles Shaar Murray were names to conjure with. Before reviews started to read like minutes from a media.com board meeting, or ingratiating text messages sent to a Facebook pal. Honesty is explosive? The ball is in your court, fact fanciers.

—Ben Watson
Somers Town
22 September 2009

Acknowledgments

I've already thanked W. C. Bamberger in the introduction, but here it is again: thanks, Bill! Otherwise, I'd like to thank Ed Baxter, Chris Weaver, and Richard Thomas at ResonanceFM radio, who keep something unique alive, and who (still!) allow me to sound off every Wednesday at 2 PM UK time with "Late Lunch with Out to Lunch" (www.resonancefm.com). If you're reading Bill's selective *Honesty Is Explosive!* in hardcopy, you might like to know that further Watson writings may be found on *militantesthetix.co.uk*, a website he runs with Esther Leslie, the noted Walter Benjamin scholar (and Iris's mum). Okay, Stefan Jaworzyn, isn't it time *you* did something to improve the state of things?

I. CD AND BOOK REVIEWS

~1985~

Arthur Blythe Trio
Spirits in the Field
Savant SCD2024

ONCE THE piano—that wood-and-metal contraption designed to mass-market the tempered system—has been hurled from the window, jazz improvisers step out into dizzying spaces of freedom. Vocalised, pliant, and lightning-quick, the alto saxophone makes best use of the possibilities of the piano-less trio (sax, bass and drums). No machinery to save you from your lack of culture or your dearth of imagination: as stark and stripped-down as a Supremacist canvas. Ornette Coleman showed the way, improvising melodies that continually modulate the key. Henry Threadgill's Air showed what compositional strategies can supply. Today, following this pioneering work, there is a plethora of alto-led, piano-less trios, though a sense of polish—of arch postmodernist simulacrum—tends to replace the punch and poignancy and joy of the innovators (the first cut is the deepest).

In this over-precious context, where the word 'downtown' lowers like a tawdry advertising slogan, Arthur Blythe's heady, soulful, gutsy blowing comes as a relief. The trio's drummer Cecil Brooks III—himself responsible for some seething organ-jazz on this label—puts it this way: 'When you hear Arthur, you're hearing the very essence of jazz, the blood and guts of the people who built this country.' Of course, without the artistic weight to back it up, such claims evaporate into the clichés used to flog everything from Levi jeans to Bruce Springsteen albums. The point is that Arthur Blythe's music really does hit the spot.

The bass parts for the trio are supplied by Bob Stewart's tuba. He establishes funky riffs, then allows them to cycle in the minds of the musicians and listeners while he contributes expressive smears and post-fusion coloration. He makes his elephantine instrument writhe and snarl. Cecil Brooks specializes in the complex, tricky rhythms that are the mark of New Orleans-sourced deep funk, but he is never phased by Blythe's sudden inspirations and tight-angled curves.

Arthur Blythe, meanwhile, is on a roll, unleashing lyrical storms leavened by passages of limpid reflection and sudden beams of impromptu humor. Blythe has not always been this untrammeled. The recent re-release of his 1979 *Lenox Avenue Breakdown* on Koch is a reminder of a period when he was attempting to shoe-horn harmolodics into unsuitable Latin formats. Here, though, traditional aspects emerge spontaneously, part of a great outburst of free music-making. Blythe makes the over-lauded work of more fashionable altoists seem prim and repressed: Glenn Millers to his Duke Ellington. The impact of *Spirit in the Field* is so immediate and uncontestable, one suspects it is only because the Savant label has been consigned to some 'authenticist' backwater that Arthur Blythe's name is not being shouted from the rooftops.

~*1989*~

Various
Tenor Saxophone on CD

'JAZZ IS a *lived* thing. It's not something that remains stationary and you play at a certain distance and that you clap at a certain time. It's about an interplay between people'. Cassandra Wilson talking after her performance at the Half Moon Theatre last year.

Jazz is indeed a lived thing. Whereas classical music eliminates individual tone—the musician reduced to a technician faithfully reproducing the composer's intention—in jazz it is prized. That is why the saxophone is so important, its combination of brass body and reed mouthpiece giving it both power and the capacity to vocalize.

It is also why records are crucial. Notation cannot capture individualized timbre: recording can. The record is the building block of black music, enabling it to have *history* (a privilege previously reserved for scored musics). Here are eighteen pieces of that history, tenor saxophones preserved on CD.

Coleman Hawkins' *Big Band* (*Jazz Anthology 550132*) is from 1940, recorded live at Harlem's Savoy Ballroom. This is the man who invented the saxophone as a jazz instrument. Before Hawkins, it was a novelty: he showed that it could be a vehicle for flights to equal those of Louis Armstrong. Thin, air-shot recording quality gives it a wartime-memory cast (as do cornball tunes like 'The Breeze and I') but Hawkins burns through, his gargling voluptuousness almost too much for theme Neubauten, this is the sound of emotions you dare not face. Crucial.

~*1990*~

Jack Nitzsche
The Hot Spot
Original Motion Picture Soundtrack
Antilles 422-846 813 CD

JACK NITZSCHE can call on heavy friends. Given his first break by Sonny Bono (of Sonny & Cher), Nitzsche helped Phil Spector create his Wall of Sound on the Philles label, working on such harbingers of hysterical pop as Tina Turner's 'River Deep, Mountain High' and the Crystals' 'He's a Rebel'. In 1963, twenty-six of his arrangements charted. Later he played keyboards for both the Rolling Stones and Neil Young. He scored the films *Performance*, *One Flew Over the Cuckoo's Nest*, and *Blue Collar*.

For Dennis Hopper's *The Hot Spot*—billed as '*film noir* like you've never seen'—Nitzsche has recruited Miles Davis and John Lee Hooker, the most irredeemably down-home, gutter-scrubbing proponent of amplified guitar blues. Hooker is notoriously hard to accompany (he is so goddamned lowdown he seldom sticks to twelve-bar formats) but Earl Palmer, Philles label house drummer in the '60s, manages to keep a heavy, simple blues thump that packs the heady rush of hemp smoke. 'Bank Robbery', a pounding train-time blues, has bassist Tim Drummond hitting a tremulous three note riff, the notes flexing like muscles. Hooker's guitar has an expressive depth of sound that makes jazz and fusion guitar sound anaemic, curling and burning and spitting with splintered anger. One hell of a rhythm section.

Over this blues boogie—caught in shimmering digital—Miles scribbles with his customary knife-edge nonchalance, bringing up the tension with the frosty hung blue notes of the 'Star People' solo, concluding his solos with a resigned logic that tears the heart.

Of course that is Miles being Miles: whether it was the claustrophobic sophistication of the *Birth of the Cool* sessions, the new open bop of the Original Quintet with John Coltrane, Gil Evans' light-music concoctions, the rock-funk of *Bitches Brew* or—most recently—Mulgrew Miller's synth-soul, his trumpet sound has always floated uninvolved, a cameo of alienation. Miles does not enter the music, doesn't act. He's a film star worrying about the look of his cheekbones under the studio lights.

After forty minutes it palls. The music keeps rubbing the same spot, like sex that never comes. You miss B.B. King's emotional peaks, Muddy Waters' get-up-and-use-me danceability, Johnny 'Guitar' Watson's narrative argument. Still, it's a great sound—unanticipated except perhaps in the strategies of *Blue Collar* —and that is what a soundtrack is supposed to deliver.

~1991~

Ray Charles
Genius + Soul = Jazz
Essential! Records

RAY CHARLES is an artist whose contradictions make the discords of modernism seem tame. Having made the epochal decision to bring church music onto the secular stage (thereby altering the entire relationship of black American music to the white-dominated market), he then recorded a country album and became an archetypal bow-tied figure in middle-of-the-road entertainment. This album (originally released by Impulse! in 1961) catches Charles at an interesting moment.

As the title indicates, this was a turn to jazz: R&B's prestigious but somewhat distant cousin. At this date, before Led Zeppelin made the blues a stairway to mega-buck success and with rock-and-roll retreating, jazz, with its connections to Frank Sinatra and Hollywood, looked impregnable. Charles had appeared with Milt Jackson at Newport in 1958 (later documented in *Soul Meeting*): this was his encounter with a crack big band.

The band is really the Count Basie orchestra without Basie, and it has the flagrant brassiness that characterized his sixties output. Occasionally the showbiz devices—'Stompin' Room Only' repeatedly ascends a note and begins again in the new key—sound tiresomely dated, but the power and ebullience of these musicians is a marvel. Phil Gilbeau's delicate trumpet underpins Charles' voice on the two vocal tracks with great effect. These feature Charles' cracked blues voice, a long way from the magnificent authority of his later style (illustrated here by the last three tracks, CD-only excerpts from *Genius Hits the Road*).

On Hammond organ, Ray Charles is a sparse and dexterous player, avoiding both Jimmy McGriff's over-powering extravaganzas and Jimmy Smith's warm flow. His stuttered intro to 'Moanin'' is particularly striking. A fine, socking album of vivid soul jazz.

* * * * * * *

Steve Coleman and Five Elements
Rhythm People (The Resurrection of Creative Black Civilization)
Novus PD83092 CD

IT HAS been claimed for M-Base that they are the most important realignment of the forces of black music since bebop. Steve Coleman, founder M-Base member and spokesman, has formed a distinctive *style* but whether he has shaken the foundations quite in the manner of Bird, Roach and Monk is less clear.

It is not the element of pop and funk that vitiates the claim: you only have to listen to the mid-forties hits of Joe Liggins ('The Honeydripper', 'Drippers' Boogie') to realize how close bebop was to the R&B ferment. And Coleman is not subduing his band's considerable chops.

The attractive part of *Rhythm People* is the way it popularizes without courting the petit-bourgeois academicism of fusion. As each tune begins, Reggie Washington's popping electric bass and Marvin 'Smitty' Smith's drumming—all stop-go funk and swirling energy—promise something special: shrink-wrapped Day-Glo funk.

Steve Coleman's hard, sinuous alto is overt and confident but it may be part of the problem. Though admirably free of Berklee School Coltrane-by-numbers ersatz-profundities, there is none of Bird's *pain*. The perpetual glibness gets wearing, a meal of candy floss. Modern alto *can* shine with the true grit: think of such dissimilar stylists as Bobby Watson or Pete McPhail.

Like Pinski Zoo, the Five Elements take their cue from Prime Time, insisting on a rhythmic interaction between players that opposes mainstream complacency. However, they do not take the separation of constituent parts into Ornette's prismic cacophony, instead involving each instrument in a funky fidget, a continual wriggle and thrust—smart but limited. It is almost *too much* fun, you miss the gutter grind of hip-hop, the linear drive of bop, the folk-howl of Jan Kopinski's tenor. The method abstracts the music from any social reference.

There are some lovely moments, like 'Blues Shifting' with Dave Gilmore's guitar full of bluesy twang and syncopated suggestiveness. Dave Holland's acoustic bass provides a much-needed sense of raw strain to 'Dangerous'. By the end, though, the obstacles and syncopations of the tunes resemble less the Dadaistic onslaught of original bebop than George Duke's 'funny funk' of the '70s or the humorous skips and dips of TV chat-show theme-tunes.

Cassandra Wilson's musty, enigmatic voice, with its intoxicating gleams and swoops, lends some much-needed direction to the last track, though even here it fades out in a Swingle Singers bossa worthy of a Martini ad. Listening to Dave Gilmore clamber his tidy, shiny way over the other's remorseless jolliness is not really that different from witnessing the up-and-down-the-harmony flexings of academic bop or fusion soloists (*i.e.*, it is tedious).

Steve Coleman's claim to what Anthony Braxton calls re-structuralism—a fundamental advance in the way music can be put together—seems pale in comparison to the wipeouts achieved in the last two decades by harmolodics, Chicago house or Braxton's own quartet music. Rather, this is penthouse funk whose busy good humour palls over the length of a CD.

* * * * * * *

Luc Ferrari
Petite Symphonie, Strathoven, Presque Rien Avec Filles, Heterozygote
BVHAAST 9009
Henri Pousseur
Scambi, Trois Visages de Liège, Paraboles-Mix
BVHAAST 9010
Konrad Boehmer
Aspekt, Cry of This Earth, Apocalipsis Cum Figuris
BVHAAST 9001/2

FOUR CDs of seminal classical electronics, sixties seed that fell on hard ground. BVHAAST is Willem Breuker's label, and he has evidently been involved with the project. He produced and annotated the Boehmer disk. A smart series: full background and bios, each cover sporting a different detail from Franz Deckwitz' oil painting

'Martian Landscape' (collection Boehmer). The style is Neon Park/ SciFi-paperback, dull red stones on an alien planet—views from a 1960s satellite.

The music is like that, too, simultaneously dated and erotically futuristic. Gottfried Koenig, born in 1926, worked at the Cologne Deutsche Rundfunk Studios in the '50s, helping Karlheinz Stockhausen realize 'Gesang der Junglinge' and 'Kontakte'. He is a pioneer in computer-aided composition. His were the purest electronics of all: 'Klangfiguren II' (1956) is clean, hard, unspectacular, wonderful. He softens: 'Output' (1979) is Webern from the hobbyist's PC, synclavier substitutions for the classical ensemble. The colour-coded 'Funktionen' (1969) is brilliant: witty, pithy exercises in stereo counterpoint.

Luc Ferrari, born in 1929, studied with Arthur Honegger and Olivier Messiaen, and was the founder of *musique concrète*, music achieved through splicing any recordable sound. 'Heterozygote' (1964) is a masterpiece, whizzing cuts and quotes inducing a glorious richness. Ferrari's interest in integrating recordings of lived life give his later works an episodic radio play flavour, but he achieves great moments. Essential listening for anyone seeking to merge words and sound (*i.e.* pop people).

Henry Pousseur, born 1929, has taught at Darmstadt since 1957 and collaborated with Boulez, Berio and Stockhausen. 'Scambi' (1954) is radical interference music strobed by silence. 'Trois Visages de Liege' (1961) is like watching a busy spaceport at night, a kinetic Kandinsky of bright, fizzing rockets and strange gleaming saucers. It was a sad day when Stanley Kubrick decided to associate SciFi with classical pomp rather than this kind of futurism (a regressive association John Williams' *Star Wars* cemented).

Konrad Boehmer represents a younger generation (born 1941), studying with Boulez, Pousseur and Stockhausen at Darmstadt in 1959, later working with Bruno Maderna and Luigi Nono. 'Aspekt' is a torrent of hard-ass abstract electronics with an undercurrent of fretboard strut—the music Mahavishnu never dared record. 'Cry Of the Earth' (1984) pitches huge slippery taped electronics against Chris Shultis' percussion—mighty. 'Apocalipsis cum figuris' (1984) is a great piebald macro-event that includes the (taped) voices of Dagmer Krause and Phil Minton singing Brechtian choruses, demonic belches and De Sade's *Justine*. It has not got the single-minded vision of the '60s pieces in the series, but has a breadth of reference that makes conventional opera seem antiquated and ornamental.

The music on these disks is not easy on the ear, but it fulfils the first condition of art: it is an index of human possibility.

* * * * * * *

Mauricio Kagel
Vox Humana?/Finale/Fürst Igor, Stravinsky
Accord 201262 CD

'VOX HUMANA?' for orchestra and female chorus sets songs by Isaac Levy written in Ladino, a language spoken by Spanish Jews in the middle ages. It begins in the religiose neo-medieval style favoured by contemporary Baltic composers, an innocent mass. Then it becomes demonic, discordant and percussive: the chorus sounds like a record slowing down, then erupt with shrieks. The composer himself recites the same text, his deep Argentinean tones dramatically contrasting with the turbulence around him. Busy and inventive enough to shrug off accusations of pastiche, even the peaks of nightmarish terror never manage to break the spell of theatricality. True surprise never arrives.

'Finale' is better. Conducted by Pascal Dusapin, it patchworks traditional orchestral devices: pulsing strings, luminous winds, flaring brass. The linear narrative, full of weirdly plausible disjuncture, is more interesting than the textures which—in the light of IRCAM and New Complexity advances—sound big-boned and old-fashioned.

'Fürst Igor, Stravinsky' frames Boris Carmeli's strong bass voice in varied percussion and Kagel's favourite low wind sounds: solemn and overlong at eighteen minutes.

Kagel has not lost his precision and wit, but the music does jump out at you like it used to. Performance—by the 2e2m Ensemble under Paul Mefano—is exemplary and recording at Radio France is excellent.

* * * * * * *

Joe Morris Sweatshop
Sweatshop
Riti 1 CD

WORKING OUT of Cambridge, Massachusetts, Joe Morris has developed a new kind of electric guitar music. He picks single notes and lets them hang, scrabbles runs, jumps to different pitch-areas. He has preserved the pure, incisive tone of '50s jazz guitar while pursuing Ornette's harmonic subversion.

The preceding album on this label, *Human Rites* (Riti 02 & 03), was a criminally neglected masterpiece: Morris' guitar chimed against Thurman Barker's drums with a weight and sense of pace unheard of outside Ornette himself—and his tunes have comparable strength. A hard one to follow.

Sweatshop, although it features the same trio as one record in the *Human Rites* double, is in a different vein: pounding high energy (merely number two of *four* different 'sets' Morris promises us!). He keeps it level and driving, Sebastian Steinberg's electric bass shaking out a delightfully rugged, almost cluttered beat, full of melodic warps. Jerry Deupree's drums have a beautifully physical resonance, a rubbery stick-on-skin feel. The guitar notes splay and fume under this rockpile drive like the sparks round the head of a drill.

'Oky Doke' has some of the hovering expansion that made the chamber trio music of *Human Rites* so magical, but in general that element has been hammered out on the industrial-rock anvil. Morris says in the sleeve notes that the each tune forces a 'different groove and different dialect'. I am not so sure: by 'The World Iz Big' the basic template seems a mite familiar.

Despite a thinner sound, the live tracks (also recorded direct to two track digital) let more space in, dance-music that moves the feet whilst intoxicating the head with harmonic transgressions. Whereas Jamaaladeen Tacuma streamlines his harmolodics with jet set-disco chicness, Morris informs his music with the impatience of punk (though recalling Hendrix in every rainbow lick!).

Human Rites showed that Morris is one of the great carvers of melody outside the tempered scale: this is not, as he calls it, '(God forbid) fusion', but a single-minded demonstration of thrasholodics. If he would only visit Europe and play Leeds Jazz, the man would be perfect. As it is, *Sweatshop* is a blast!

* * * * * * *

Archie Shepp
Freedom
JMY 1007 CD
I Know About the Life
Sackville SK-3062 CD
I Didn't Know About You
Timeless SJP370 CD

MUSIC FROM different eras. *Freedom* was recorded live in France on 15 December 1967 with two trombones (Roswell Rudd and Grachan Moncur III) and a mighty rhythm section of Jimmy Garrison (bass) and Beaver Harris (drums). They play a thirty-minute 'Portrait of Robert Thompson (As a Young Man)' and then Ted Joans reads a poem, 'Jazz Is My Religion' (six minutes). Recording is muffled but listenable. This was one of the heavyweight bands of all time, a seething ugliness that keeps breaking up into joyous jazz band exclamations. Shepp was orchestrating brilliantly and his choked, burgeoning tenor saxophone sounds fabulous. The band play blitzscape collective improvisations which swell into Shepp's patent romanticism with aching logic. Superb.

Shepp cooled off in the '70s and began behaving like some washed up tenor hero: gigs with pick-up bands, late arrivals, singing the blues, playing standards. Critics who had been affronted by the upfront politics and noise terrorism of his '60s band sharpened the knives. In *Wire* #93 Brian Priestley went so far as to argue that he cannot play at all, calling him 'a well-meaning amateur'.

'Professional' ballad playing sounds like something taught at Berklee to me, and Shepp is well free of it. *I Know About the Life* (live in Toronto 11 February 1981 with Ken Werner on piano, Santi Debriano on bass and John Betsch on drums) and *I Don't Know About You* (a Munich studio 6 November 1990 with Horace Parlan on piano, Wayne Dockery on bass and George Brown on drums) employ utterly conventional jazz formats, but Shepp's tenor still manages to sound like no one else, great blobs and gargles of livid expression, shockingly visceral, genuinely fascinating.

Maybe if you reduced the solos to student-exercise transcriptions they might look simplistic compared to, say, the lines Itchy Fingers play. But that was exactly Shepp's point in the '60s: black music is about the actual sound, not the notated abstraction. And

Shepp's saxophone still sounds *gripping*. How many jazz school clones can you say that of?

* * * * * * *

Joe Turner
Stormy Monday
Pablo (PA2310943) CD

A CD RELEASE of the twelfth record Big Joe Turner made for Norman Granz's Pablo label—sessions from the mid '70s. As usual, recording is immaculate, letting the swing and R&B veterans (Lloyd Glenn on piano, Pee Wee Crayton on guitar, Cleanhead Vinson on alto and, for the title track, an all-star trumpet line-up of Sweets Edison, Roy Eldridge and Dizzy Gillespie) whip up an irresistible storm.

It is like eavesdropping on a wonderful penthouse party. The tracks do not have the social relevance of Big Joe's '40s National and '50s Atlantic recordings (R&B classics which laid the basis for Rock 'n' Roll), but they are a treat nonetheless. Jimmy Robbins' Hammond organ is especially telling, riffing like a big band sax section behind the brass.

Big Joe Turner began his vocal career as a barman, shouting encouragement to the musicians whilst polishing glasses on a huge white apron. In order to be heard over the sheer volume of a big band's vast array (singers were issued with cardboard megaphones), Turner's song eschews consonants, discarding any obstacles to the glorious vocal outpour. Singing like a generous barman splashing big measures of gin into a glass. Fantastic. Dean Martin sentimentalized this sensual, sloppy-drunk shout of joy into a showbiz trick, but no one roars like the lion himself. Big Joe makes all the other voices sound underfed. Hear him soon.

* * * * * * *

Joe Venuti and Eddie Lang
Volume 1
JSP Records JSP309 CD
Volume 2
JSP Records JSP310 CD

PIERRE BOULEZ said recently that he preferred even the *schmaltz* interpretations of the 1920s to the current ideology of 'authentic instrument' recordings, because at least the latter were *of their time*. The onward march of instrumental technique has marooned jazz violinist Joe Venuti on the same charmed island as the *schmaltzers*: his aching skids and twinkling scrapes recall that emotionalism which had its last gasp with the delirious recordings the Hungarian Quartet made of late Beethoven in the mid-sixties.

Unlike the over-exposed Stephane Grapelli, though, Venuti does not rein in his hurt with coy dexterity. His threadbare, plaintive effects are startling premonitions of the soundworld of both *Pierrot Lunaire* and post-tonal improvised violin (Leroy Jenkins, Billy Bang). Stuff Smith certainly seems to have picked up on his *sing-zap-pling* application of *cadenza* virtuosity.

Of course this wonderfully thorough collection of sides cut for Columbia, Okeh and Victor between 1926 and 1928 (volume 1) and in 1928 (volume 2) was pop music of the day (though it is mercifully light on vocals). Hot jazz played by emigrant Italians (Joe's real name was Giuseppe): sentimental tunes ragged by blues guitar, swinging unlikely music full of humour and a freedom of small-ensemble arrangement that is breathtaking. 'I've Found a New Baby' has some maundering Jimmy Dorsey baritone and on-the-case guitar from Eddie Lang that fairly rattle the windows. Venuti's swooping cafe-terrace lyricism and finely-etched distortions are wonderful. Who cares if Frank Signorelli bungled his piano solo on 'Sweet Sue'? This is the sound of brilliant musicians shaking out a newfound music from the old sources.

Eddie Lang was a giant of the guitar. Born Salvatore Massero in 1902 (he took his favourite baseball star's name), he was known as Blind Willie Dunn on his 'race' recordings with the likes of Lonnie Johnson and Louis Armstrong. Stalwart of countless Okeh sessions, he contributed sterling blues guitar to many classic recordings of Western Swing (the cultural bedrock of Rock 'n' Roll). It is him, for example, with the Dorsey brothers on 'Lovesick Blues' by Emmet Miller & His Georgia Crackers. Here his cameo breaks and fresh-

24 * *HONESTY IS EXPLOSIVE!* BY BEN WATSON

plucked comping make even an old warhorse like 'Dinah' come alive. His thumbed solos, full of 1920s tremolo and unerring melodic invention, are an absolute treat.

The instrumental presence of these sides is exemplary: they throw Gypsy sweetness, academic virtuosity and folk abandon into a rhythmic matrix born of Africa. Unlike the retro-patronism of Trad, this music burns with New World hopes.

* * * * * * *

Ben Webster
There Is No Greater Love
Black Lion BL760151 CD

THIRTY-NINE MINUTES of the most sensual saxophone of all. Recorded in Copenhagen on 5 September 1965, a year after the veteran tenor player had moved there. Webster may not have had the curiosity (and ego) that made Coleman Hawkins investigate the beboppers and record with Monk, but in his later years he developed a glorious, tender style that is the epitome of caressing saxophone.

The recording is blessed with the presence of Kenny Drew, another American exile, whose uncluttered, stately style is always informed by the blues. He contributes some beautifully funky block chords to 'Close Your Eyes', the sole up-tempo number. Webster remains unruffled, his feathery ardour intact: he quotes a few R&B licks to show that he knows where the music is at, but expertly folds in his own whispered lines. On 'I Got It Bad', the famous tune he wrote with Duke Ellington, he milks sax subsonics—the excellent Alan Bates production lets us hear every breath.

Ben Webster's poignancy suspends time, but he has such a keen grasp of the melodies he improvises on that the effect is never directionless or impressionist. There is enough weight in his timbre to make sure the honey is never cloying. The rhythm section (Niels-Henning Orsted Pedersen, bass and Alex Riel, drums) is fine, Pedersen particularly lustrous on 'Autumn Leaves'. The cover amusingly demonstrates why Webster was nicknamed 'Frog'.

For sultry late-night listening, this music cannot be beat. Perfect.

~1992~

Pierre Boulez

Sonatina for Flute and Piano/First Piano Sonata/Dérive/
 Mémoriale/Dialogue de L'Ombre Double/Cummings
 Ist der Dichter

Erato 2292-45648 CD

FIGHTING THROUGH the slurry of new age fusions, pre-modernist old hat on designer labels, baroque revivals, Mozart-necrophilia, 'the shock of the old' and all the other accoutrements of yuppie lifestyle be-cool-and-be-background classical consumerism comes a taste of the real thing. It bites.

Sonatine for Flute and Piano (1946) benefits from the searing flute of Sophie Cherrier. She has a big sound, but also understands the convoluted melodies that spur the piece. Almost a *Pierrot Lunaire* mix-down, it has Schoenberg's rhythmic snap, leading to blatant peaks of tension. Cherrier produces fantastic, violent, pressured notes for these, almost vocal in intensity. Pierre-Laurant Aimand's aggressively precise piano provokes playing from Cherrier both saturated with her individual breath and faithful to Boulez's provocative blue-print. On *Mémoriale* she shows that she may well be playing the most exciting flute since Eric Dolphy.

First Sonata for Piano is an eight minute reminder that serialism, far from being an exercise in higher maths, is actually a technical device that, like William Burroughs' fold-in, puts a bomb under the usual emotional triggers. It is only inhuman to the extent that it explodes a fetishistic ordering of 'human' emotions: tenderness, violence, reflection, surprise and comfort are sliced up into new shapes, new possibilities, freeing us of what are in fact arbitrary Pavlovian responses. The salivary ducts recoil, startled, refreshed.

Pierre Boulez has been accused of 'selling out' by those who associate the avant-garde with economic deprivation—IRCAM is no garrett—and those who notice a late lushness. The segue to *Dérive* (1984) could not be a better demonstration: extreme '40s piano followed by music that basks in the timbral presence of flute, clarinet, cello, vibes and piano. The point is whether or not the instrumental forces are sweetening a compositional idea or constructing their own idea. The latter is true. It is great, situationist title and all.

When a score examines the particular sonority of an instrument as deliberately as *Dialogue de L'Ombre Double* (1982-85) and it is played with such transparent commitment (Albert Damiens on clarinet) then divisions between 'classical' and 'improvisation' become objective nonsense. This *is* the music of Eric Dolphy, more than Wynton Marsalis could imagine.

The CD finishes with *Cummings Ist der Dichter* (1970) (so named when the German promoters thought they were being told the title and Boulez was simply telling them who wrote the words—an amusing aleatorism the rather dry sleeve note omits). A choir singing such challenging intervals sounds modernist-primitive, as if you must be mad to organize so many people to sing so crazy. Long may the delirium continue. *Rose à Boulez!*

* * * * * * *

Anthony Braxton
2 Compositions (Ensemble) 1989/91
Hat Art 6086 CD
Duets Hamburg 1991
Music & Arts 710 CD

FIRST, TWO vast compositions (Nos 147 and 151 in the opus) played by ensembles from Frankfurt and Hamburg. In the shorter No 147, a mere sixteen minutes to No 151's seventy-three, improvised clarinets (John Corbett, Roland Diry and Joachim Klemm) are the fluid element in the structure, which is designed to invoke a ballroom's mirrors and chandeliers. Both pieces display a keen ear for instrumental colour and dispersed multiple events: apt to put Kandinsky on the cover, another magician of detail and vertigo.

Braxton suffers from his idol Stockhausen's gargantuan ambition: the news that No 147 is merely 'one component in a series of 36 one act operas' is distracting. The music also sports the glittering brightness of the later Stockhausen, but without his tinge of decadence (erotics out of Richard Strauss).

Braxtonians moan about the lack of recordings, but even as a composer he is not badly served (at least, compared to some). The Four Orchestra set (Arista, 1978) and No 96 (Leo Records, 1989) showed a similar style. On one level it is gorgeous, subtle, expansive; on another, one misses the sense of urgency and direction of his small group work. Luxuriant as it is, the music does not seem to push at any discernible limit: hard to find a *necessity* for it. Maybe all will be revealed, but how many endless operas must we sit through?

The duet album, tunes recorded with bassist Peter Wilson (also a participant in the other project), is more like it. Braxton's bass clarinet growls and rumbles like a somnolent dragon, his flute uniquely provocative. Wilson has a lovely woody sound and is very inventive. Braxton darts and dips in his Dolphy-plus manner, but also expands the harmonic parameters (something Coltrane did but the clones never do). Some of the tunes have Braxton's irritating habit of dressing up exercises (scales) as 'compositions,' but for the most part these steely duets sound like history being made.

Braxton wants to be recognised as a European-type composer, and good luck to him—his music is more interesting than ninety percent of the 'new' stuff in the current repertoire. If he'd focus his powers, if he'd face the pressing issues in orchestral music (microtonality, electricity, ethnicity, chance) rather than copying Stockhausen's megalomania, he'd be unbeatable. Until then, I'll go to Finnissy and Dillon and Scelsi for classical music that can measure up to the intensity of Braxton's group work.

* * * * * * *

CORNELIUS CARDEW
Piano Music
B&L

KILLED IN mysterious circumstances by a hit-and-run driver in 1981, Cornelius Cardew continues to be a focus for dissident voices in classical music. He premiered Pierre Boulez in England (1956) and worked with Karlheinz Stockhausen (1958-60). In 1966 he joined the improvising group AMM. In 1969 he founded the non-musicians' Scratch Orchestra and, on conversion to Maoism, denounced Cage and Stockhausen (and his own compositions) for serving imperialism. The CD arrives with a commendation from noted leftie Robert Wyatt on the back.

At the Huddersfield Contemporary Music Festival this year, Ixion revived works from Cardew's *avant-garde* period, works postmodern fashion is keen to forget. In contrast, the pieces on this CD were written as attempts at populism following Cardew's political 'awakening'. They are gentle and folky, reminiscent of Michael Finnissy's piano writing before the tensions erupt. Here, where things liven up, it is in a fairly predictable and 'classical' manner.

It is politics that make the music of interest and Cardew's Maoism deserves a proper critique (the sleeve note points out that he didn't support Communist regimes in eastern Europe—a disingenuous remark considering that as a Maoist he would have supported the recent butchery in Tiananmen Square). As any SWP member knows, Mao rode to power using a peasant army after the zigzags of the Stalinist Communist Party lost the revolution for the working class. Mao suppressed workers' democracy (the prerequisite for any Marxist transformation) and instituted state capitalism.

To serve up this tepid tea-room fare as 'communicative' betrays a patronising and pessimistic view of the potential of the masses. Genuine *avant-garde* art proposes a utopian critique of capitalism's treatment of subjectivity. Cardew's *Piano Music* therefore criticizes capitalism about as much as Mao actually opposed the economic exploitation of the Chinese working class—*i.e.*, not at all.

Still, for raising questions like these, this music is more important than the smugly entrenched elitism that passes for 'classical' music most of the time. So—this CD deserves to be a Wire Winner[1].

* * * * * * *

Ornette Coleman/Howard Shore
Naked Lunch
Milan 262732 CD

---

[1] This strange concept was an accolade given certain CD releases in *Wire* magazine. You could write a longer review, although you had (of course) to be positive. Unfortunately the *Wire*'s commercial imperative did not recognise that negative criticism actually requires more space to explain its "no."

SOMETIMES THE mass culture industry hands you a gift. In this case, inviting Ornette Coleman onboard for the soundtrack to a well-publicised film. Predictably, the journalists have all been my-thologising the biography of the man who wrote the original book: William Burroughs, junkie and homosexual. This is at the expense of Burroughs' material achievement, which is to extend the literary modernism of Wyndham Lewis, James Joyce and Samuel Beckett. Burroughs provides a further twist to the relationship of human be-ings to language. The technique of fold-in—the merging of disparate texts—results in prose which disassembles identity in shards of vul-gar effects. This extrusion beyond taste restores social issues to a modernist trajectory that was in danger of cancelling itself in man-darin aphasia. By 1972, Burroughs had broken through into proph-ecy. *The Wild Boys* was a terrifying anticipation of 1992's riots in Los Angeles.

The choice of Ornette for the film of *Naked Lunch* is brilliant, because Ornette's music—simultaneous voices pursuing different agendas—works just like fold-in. Neither Burroughs nor Ornette are at home in the art they inhabit; both speak for the fractured subject of late capitalism. Burroughs spent time in Marrakesh listening to the Joujouka Musicians of Morocco, theorising how their untempered, timeless music effectively abolishes reified western thought—Ornette recorded with them. A slice of that encounter (from *Dancing In Your Head*) reappears here, a palimpsest beneath Shore's strings.

David Cronenberg makes glossy Hollywood films. They re-deem their inevitable commercialism because they are pitched at the cutting edge of technique, special effects which interrogate how the body feels about itself (*The Fly*). Howard Shore supplies the big melancholic strings required for Hollywood horror, but refuses to build them up into any discernible symphonic argument: over these (excellently recorded) swathes of sound, Ornette plays his instru-ments (alto, trumpet, violin) with his unique waywardness. It's great.

On the recent Contemporary Music Network tour, Ornette was criticised for presenting too packaged a Prime Time, everything too polished and in-place. Had he lost his improv chops? There are four improvised trio tracks here (son Denardo on drums, Barre Philips on bass). These show he can still play the ass off any young alto contender: rattlingly fleet interactions. Ornette seems to bloom in a filmic context—*Chappaqua Suite* was likewise vast and surprising. Ornette also plays to Monk's 'Misterioso' alongside David Hartley's piano—utterly fascinating. The pliant, winsome oddness of Ornette's saxophone is still unreeling multiple possibilities.

* * * * * * *

James Dillon
East 11th Street
NMC

ACCORDING TO Richard Bernas, conductor of Music Projects/London, the percussion-only title piece here is structured by timbre rather than pitch and therefore connects back to Edgard Varese. An unfortunate comparison. Dillon's writing is pretty and detailed and he thinks in a linear, romantic way, so 'East 11th Street' lacks the vertical violence one associates with Varese. Improvising drummers like Shannon Jackson, Ken Hyder and Tony Oxley get closer to Varese's tight structure and keen sense of abruptness. The ensemble—who are no slouches—have to keep such an alert eye on the irrational metrics of the score that they cannot unleash the physical weight one expects from percussion.

Dillon's acute ear for texture is better served by winds and strings: the originality of 'Windows & Canopies' and 'La Femme Invisible,' the other two pieces on this CD, is nothing short of astonishing. It is as if the shimmer of an impressionist ballet has suddenly developed a life of its own, clotting into seething biomorphs in front of the eyes. 'Windows & Canopies' uses twelve strings, each playing an independent part: now the fine detail of 'East 11th Street' generates power rather than holding the players back, the percussion marking genuine notches on the music's unique evolution. It is like a gentle IRCAM study (*e.g.*, Tristan Murail) shot through with fiercer structure—girders spanning the wisps. There are passages of Xenakis-like objectivity, but these are thrown onto linear bass lines, are broken into by expressive violins, balanced, displayed. The sense of alchemical activity is palpable, a pleasure with the sounds of the orchestra that resembles Hitchcock's passion for the properties of film.

'La Femme Invisible' is more straightforward, the textures less tortured and strange. Its structural convolution—the music seems to submerge you at once in dense overlays and recapitulations of what has not yet been heard—has the reassuring ring of a strong piece of orchestral modernism. Pools of violin and simple piano offset the rest. Dillon manages to make the sounds of the orchestra melt and merge, spilling metallic chimes of bell and cymbal into piping strings like someone rolling silver balls in a puzzle.

Dillon's spontaneity—an ear for the sensual impact of instrumental sound, an utter disregard for the academic rules for symphonic deployment—gives the music an organic, breathing quality. One is used to finding this kind of presence in saxophones (Johnny Hodges, David Murray), voices (Nat Cole, Tammy Wynette) or guitars (Hendrix, Evert Brettschneider)—to hear this carnality in an orchestra is almost shocking. So much western classical use of orchestral colour has been manipulative or representational (Wagner, Strauss, Nyman) it is wonderful to hear it step out on its own. Breathtaking.

* * * * * * *

Malcolm Goldstein
Sounding the New Violin
What Next? WN0005 CD

MALCOLM GOLDSTEIN is an improvising violinist who obtains commissions from interesting people. Not many people can issue an album with pieces written for them by both John Cage and Ornette Coleman. He does not quite have the discrimination of Siegfried Palm, who does similar things for the cello, but his repertoire is still worth a listen.

'Eight Whiskus' has Cage's characteristic oriental feel, the brilliantly unpredictable silences, the undeniable oddness. Goldstein's own piece, 'Sounding the Fragility of Line,' explores the tension created by long, caustic, under-bowed sounds. In combination with the striking CD insert—metallic pages in purple and blue—it evokes a sensation of sparkling unease. I've never heard recorded violin sound quite so like horsehair on catgut. It makes you wince but you have to admit it's utterly original.

Pauline Oliveros' graphic score is realized in an irritatingly playful manner (references to Bach etc) and James Tenney's 'Koan' is the obligatory Minimalist nonsense: art as an endurance test (I failed). Ornette's 'Trinity' maintains both his sense of tumbling chaos and his freakish feel for melody. It would probably be more fun to hear Ornette play it himself, but the cleanness of Goldstein's technique does (I suppose) add a new dimension. Philip Corner's 'The Gold Stone,' full of glissandi and pile-ups, is a joy.

Goldstein stresses playing abrasion—the sound his instrument makes—over notes, an emphasis more familiar in jazz and improvisation. The net effect is intriguing, scratchy, extreme—and sure to clear the house at parties.

* * * * * * *

Julius Hemphill
Fat Man and the Hard Blues
Black Saint 120115-2 CD

MAIN COMPOSER for the World Saxophone Quartet, Julius Hemphill is an alto saxophonist who has not had the recognition he deserves. Born in 1938 in Fort Worth, he came to prominence in St. Louis in the '60s, a member of the Black Artists Group. His Texas blues and gospel background is reflected in a socking, immediate sound and supple lines delivered with swagger and an explosive sense of drama. He has an ear for the outreach pioneered by Eric Dolphy.

You get precious little of his alto on this album, though. The emphasis is his ensemble writing for an all-saxophone sextet. The sextet are good players. Andrew White, famous as Coltrane-transcriber (and own-label stand-up comedian), plays a gospel solo on 'Anchorman' which is a highlight: a refreshingly direct examination of Trane's harmonic legacy, the tenor tender and personal. Marty Ehrlich has previously played some outstanding alto with Richard Abrams and Bobby Previte. However, the net result seems less than its illustrious parts.

Hemphill leans on Ellington voicings without ever quite getting Duke's sense of experiment and collective fun. The textures—relieved on WSQ albums by the free exhortations of David Murray and Oliver Lake—get very samey. Investigate Jean-Paul Bourelly's *Jungle Cowboy* for what Hemphill is capable of as a soloist (check out his squealing solo on Jean-Paul Bourelly's sultry masterpiece 'Mother Earth'). The sextet have a welcome blues liberty with ensemble discipline, but Hemphill does not take enough risks as a composer: the music ends up polished but somehow dull.

* * * * * * *

Joseph Jarman/Don Moye
Calypso's Smile
AECO Records 008 CD

INTERESTING TO hear Jarman play a calypso on tenor (like most Chicagoans, he is an adept multi-instrumentalist), because it immediately begs comparisons with Sonny Rollins. He lacks that creaking greatness, the honeyed power, but unlike Rollins he plays with his peers instead of journeymen. His solos move and groove with a freedom Rollins seldom manages to fix on record these days.

Don Moye is a wonder drummer, busy yet unobtrusive, creating dancing spaces in the music. His chimes and bells (another Chicago trademark) are apt yet still surprising. Bassist Essiet Essiet always has a note when it's needed, too.

'Morning Desert Song' is a delightful ethnic number with Moye on African drums and clay bongos. Jarman's flute is maybe a touch anodyne—the duet doesn't threaten the David Murray/Kahil El'Zabar monopoly on duo ethnic jive. 'Treibhaus Tribal Stomp' pays homage to an appreciative club in Austria. Jarman is good, but his long Traneish lines lack intensity.

The real stars of this disk are the rhythm section. In England, where it seems you have to make a choice between tunes (retro-bop, fusion) and interest (improv), it's great to hear players who make both happen at once.

* * * * * * *

Joe Morris Trio
Flip and Spike
Riti 2 CD

JOE MORRIS is one hell of a guitarist. Keeping to a 'jazz guitar' tone of crystalline purity, he improvises melodies outside the chords. I was so excited I sent a tape to Derek Bailey. He said the phrasing reminded him of Albert Ayler. Sure, but it's Ayler played by Grant Green (as bizarrely logical as Frisell's juncture of Jim Hall and Jimi Hendrix). He's produced a conceptual infinite guitar with a single string. If he had his ear to the ground, John Scofield would be shaking in his shoes (a sight to see!).

Morris's touch is subtle, giving every song statement a note-in-the-air poignancy. Maybe harmolodics need not dwindle out in bar-room blues and half-baked disco. This, his fourth release, is not quite as delightfully out as *Human Rights* (no 2), and less hammer and tongs than *Sweatshop* (no 3) (where can I get no 1, *Wrap-around*?). Morris has played with the best (Bang, Barker, Cyrille, Nix, Redman, Hopkins), but his thing is so damn original it hurts.

'Itan' develops a lilting groove that resembles an ethnic forgery by Can, or some well weird house mix. 'Mnemonic Device' show-cases finger string effects—McLaughlin, Company-style. Like the leader, bassist Sebastian Steinberg can make his instrument evoke contrasting soundworlds with minute acoustic inflections. Drummer Jerry Deupree is fantastic, slap-happy and simultaneously fine. All three vary their attack on every note: they're always *there*.

Beneath the surface cool you sense a delirious funk. It creates a tension similar to the tumble-down-chaos-that-rocks in Beefheart. The publicity has a quote: 'it's nice to hear someone who just gets a little nuts'. And how! Nuts like Bird, nuts like Cecil! I've run out of superlatives. Get your ears round this, poor starved twangfans: hear what a guitar can make happen in the air. EeeeeOoooowwWW!!!

* * * * * * *

Paul Motian Trio
Motian in Tokyo
JMT 849154 CD

CELEBRATING TEN years of musical activity, this is an excellent re-cording of a set by Bill Frisell (guitar), Joe Lovano (tenor saxo-phone) and Paul Motian (drums). The basic musical form is for me less appealing than the piano jazz of Motian's trio with Geri Allen—the swelling, pastel romanticism of the opener, 'From Time To Time', for example, seems redundant. However, when there is more harmonic challenge, as on 'Shakalaka', the results are rivetting. Frisell leaps in with great grooving blues sounds, but the convoluted metre makes it all syncopated and knotty, keeping alive the teeth-gritting poise of blues guitar where otherwise it would be too pat. The stilted intensity—stasis within the onward rush—links back to Blood Ulmer, Derek Bailey and punk's puncturing of the soaring rock solo. Knife-edge excitement.

'Kathelin Gray', a theme from Ornette Coleman's collaboration with Pat Metheny, *Song X*, sounds heart-achingly lovely. On 'Mumbo Jumbo' Frisell tangles and then soars, rainbows over fist-fights. This trio are still surprising themselves—and us.

Almost forgot Joe Lovano (just as one tends to omit him from memories of the gigs). He is dogged and resourceful, a personal version of Coltrane's examination of harmonic steps—a smoothed out Frank Lowe. There is nothing inept or not apt but he never peaks or shocks like the other two.

Motian is a top rank drummer, but what makes him special is the flawed bridges and broken riffs. They seem to assert so definitely and yet the key is obscure. Just as you want to raise a cheer because you've got it there is always an extra variation. And yet, like Monk, it's still funky.

Here's to another ten years of this magic!

* * * * * * *

Napalm Death
Utopia Banished
Earache MOSH53 CD

IT'S BEEN said before, but say it again: Napalm Death are the best. They're so sussed, so righteous and so perfectly angry that they don't mind looking like a bunch of dumb clucks (always a good sign). Shane Embury and Mark Greenway write lyrics that move with the syntax of agonised thought, blunt resistance to the horror of the modern world that creates its own cadences, improvises its own rhetoric. Napalm Death are everything that anarcho-punks Crass promised but failed to be: they take on the limitations of their stance in the texture of their art, don't overreach themselves. Politics without pomposity. Try

I ABSTAIN!
SUMMON MY PRIDE?
WHAT? PRIDE BEHIND YOUR BLINKERED EYES?
YOUR VIGILANCE IS SHIT
'THE LADS TOGETHER'—YOU'LL FALL ('I Abstain')

or

PROGRESSION OR PROCESSION?
DO OPINIONS COUNT OR DO THEY MOUNT?
THE PILES OF SHIT,
(THAT THE) ALTERNATIVE PRESS DELIGHTS US WITH
CRITIQUE ELITE—ILL INFORMED.
NO WRONG CAN BE DONE, DEPENDING ON THE TREND AT
TIMES TO BE UNTRENDY
UNEXPIRED EXILE,
RELUCTANTLY WE ALL INDULGE THEIR TASTEFUL HYPE
('Exile')

The very punctuation is technically innovative. It compares to BLAST's Vorticist assault of 1914. In case you suspect this might entail sympathy for Wyndham Lewis's subsequent political direction, 'Aryanisms' is a minutely observed anti-fascist polemic. The intelligence and quick-swivel honesty of their lyric is only equalled by the nerve-slice vibrancy of their musical acumen. New drummer Danny Herrara is amazing: speed and precision become terrifying and beautiful. Napalm Death are also really funny, precisely because they have no truck with 'humour' or 'irony' or scare-quotes, as if their utterness will burn a hole in social reality.

A DREAMLIKE NOTION THAT LIFE EASES BY,
CUSHIONING THE BLOW OF IMPENDING REALITY,
AIMLESSNESS IS FLOGGING US—AWAKE!! ('Awake')

The 'you' they rail against is the socially constructed persona of civil and juridical fictions: they want to bust the bourgeois ego's membrane through, slog beyond, not float in appalling distances. On the back of the CD, they crouch round a slab from the Berlin wall planted in the forecourt of the Imperial War Museum in South London. It's painted with the slogan: CHANGE YOUR LIFE. They crouched there for the photo because that slogan struck a chord. They meant it. Napalm Death help, they really do.

* * * * * * *

Max Roach with Chorus & Orchestra
To the Max!
Enja NJ702122 CD

A DOUBLE CD, room for bebop's founding drummer to unfurl his many current involvements: jazz, choral and string composition and his percussion group M'Boom.

The resonance of a choir is inevitably religious, but the John Motley Singers are sharply professional, their buttoned-down discipline and nobly-articulated vowels reminiscent of Carnegie Hall Mahalia Jackson or the chorus of Gershwin's *Porgy & Bess*. Tyrone Brown's bass is recorded well upfront and the results are surprisingly attractive, Ronnell Bey's solo voice sinuous and flamboyant.

The choral piece is part of a suite in three sections called 'Ghost Dance'. M'Boom performs part two: with percussionists as heavy as Roach himself, timbales legend Ray Mantilla and Joe Chambers (a dazzling thirdstream composer in his own right), M'Boom has to be a treat. In the '90s, world music trappings have replaced rock sonorities as a way of disguising musical conformism, but M'Boom prove that Afro-centrism was always part of bebop's modernity. Linear and limpid, Roach's elegance and clarity make it all seem simple. Then, for some reason, a nuclear bomb goes off (I couldn't get much sense out of the libretto). Part three is the hard bop quartet, a briskly swinging vehicle for Odean Pope's tenor (he's more at home here than with his harmolodic trio, where he falls back on Tranisms) and Cecil Bridgewater's lovely bright trumpet: sterling, authoritative hard bop.

The Uptown String Quartet, led by Roach's daughter Maxine, integrate beautifully with the improvisors on 'A Little Booker'. Roach is combining known quantities in *To the Max!*, but he does it with such neatness and spirit that the results are exceptional. No waste and no fuss, just care and sparkle. Each disk ends with a beautiful drum solo, models of wit and economy.

* * * * * * *

Giacinto Scelsi
Bot-Ba
Hat Art 6092 CD
Giacinto Scelsi
Music for Cello
Etcetera KTC1136 CD
John Cage
Music for Trombone
Etcetera KTC1137 CD

WHEN GIACINTO Scelsi's music is good it has a penetrating intensity that gives the illusion of unmediated presence. Sound appears to be eloquent in itself. Since his death in 1988, however, his mystical beliefs and reclusive lifestyle have been used by supporters to set up yet another straw saint in the increasingly nauseous pantheon of new age composer-gurus.

Despite such hagiography, Scelsi's music is not retrograde medievalism or twinkly-dink piety: like Ennio Morricone and Alvin Curran (other members of his circle) he interrogated sound with a keenness that is both beautiful and terrifying. He started doing that seriously in the '60s. Before that he was floundering around in inept gestures borrowed from Webern. *Bot-Ba*, which has Marianne Schroeder play piano pieces from 1939, 1952 and 1978, contains little of value. Despite her excellent touch, Schroeder'd piano is physically incapable of the microtonalism that is Scelsi's trump card. The music seems arbitrary, flighty and vacuous. *Music for Cello* features Frances-Marie Uitti (like Schroeder a collaborator) with recordings supervised by the composer in 1978. Pieces from 1957 seem turbulent and misdirected, but 'Ygghur' from 1961 is suddenly gripping and intense.

The Scelsi myth is in danger of obscuring what is good about him, which is close attention to sonic production and microtones—creating the kind of in-yer-face performances we expect from improvisation. Prior to these experiments, his music was rhetorical and pointless. Performers would do well to stop flogging the myth and exercise some discretion in choosing which pieces to record.

Scored music worth its salt interrogates performance procedures and is therefore often worked out in conjunction with virtuosic players. Whatever John Cage's declared use of chance—on 'Ryoanji' he was measuring the distance between stones in a Japanese rock garden for musical proportions—trombonist James Fulkerson makes of it something really fabulous: against clinking percussion from Frank Denyer he breathes like a somnolent dragon. 'Solo for Sliding Trombone' puts the trombone part of 'Concerto for Piano' with the tape of 'Fontana Mix', a streaming rubble of different sounds: varied and very pretty. The piano part of 'Two5' (forty minutes for piano and trombone) makes Scelsi's efforts seem hopelessly mired in romanticism. Long trombone notes tremble between irritating persistence and horn-in-fog lyricism. If this is the sound of chance, it is preferable to the intentions of ninety-nine percent of contemporary classical composers. Recorded at Keele University in June 1992, *Music for Trombone* contains some considered and evocative music.

* * * * * * *

John Scofield
Grace Under Pressure
Blue Note 798167 CD

IN A seminal (if little read) article in the obscure underground freebie newspaper *Jazz in the North*, I once wrote 'Derek Bailey is a watershed for guitar modernism. You can distinguish Bill Frisell's playing, with its abrupt turns and blasted cul-de-sacs, from John Scofield's coherent blues rapture precisely because of Bailey's influence'. If only criticism could contemplate itself in endless perfection. It can't. Why not? Musicians. Scofield invites his polar opposite to play on his album!

Scofield starts with a perfect example of his whole-tone coherence, expert 'blues' guitar runs etc. Frisell counters with a Bailey-like stutter that links modernist aphasia back to chamber-jazz reticence. They play together as might Eddie Lang and Lonnie Johnson, smart solo following smart solo on an efficient but anonymous bass/drum canvas (provided by Charlie Haden and Joey Baron).

On 'Scenes from a Marriage', Frisell suddenly cuts loose, but it goes against the grain of Scofield's concept. On 'Pretty Out', Frisell has another try at making it a Frisell record, but Haden and Baron are so ill-suited—or misdirected—they can only supply a muddled tradbop backdrop. With Frisell as out as this, Scofield's attempts at ripostes are sad.

I suppose the idea was to compare guitar styles by recording a 'straight-ahead' date, but unfortunately jazz is not a *lingua franca* for these two guitarists. Post-rock guitar cannot merely use acoustic bop to emulate the intimacy or logic of Wes Montgomery and Kenny Burrell. Here Frisell is so far ahead in terms of harmonic imagination and textural expression that he can't fit the mainstream mold (Scofield supplies all the tunes). Presumably the Frisell's need for commercial exposure explains the pairing—there certainly isn't much of musical sense in it.

* * * * * * *

Toru Takemitsu
Visions
Denon CO79441 CD

IF YOU'RE interested in Takemitsu as a composer—and he is the grand old man of the Japanese establishment's post-war adoption of European music—this is an excellent introduction. There's a piece from each part of his career: *Requiem for Strings* (1957), *November Steps* (1967), *Far Calls, Coming, Far!* (1980), and *Visions* (1989).

In 1957 Gustav Mahler was utterly underrated—Leonard Bernstein's campaign of rehabilitation was not yet underway, let alone the mass showcase that was the movie *Death in Venice*. Takemitsu's *Requiem for Strings* uses Mahler, mining a similar area of heartache as the slow movement of Mahler's Fifth—vast, overlapping strings. There are eddies of aspiration, but they rise up only to disperse into the anguished wasteland. Igor Stravinsky was impressed, and so should you be: it's sumptuously emotional, but telling in the way only innovative art can be. Some of the string writing simply sizzles with invention.

November Steps is a concerto for traditional Japanese instruments: the biwa (a kind of sitar) and the shakuhachi (a wooden flute). Takemitsu declares he's after contrast, not integration: hearing these evocative instruments twang and rasp amidst Darmstadt-style modernism is a gobsmack experience. The playing is semi-improvised. It's as if Pierre Boulez had written a concerto for Derek Bailey (*i.e.*, fantastic). In confronting European and Japanese musics, Takemitsu incidentally abolishes the distinctions that keep our most valued modernists in separate boxes.

In the 1970s Takemitsu became a nationally recognised composer and a less interesting one. *Far Calls, Coming, Far!* deploys late romantic clichés to build an exceptional climax, but the focus and strangeness of *Requiem For Strings* is lacking. *Visions* is sweet and glittering and reminiscent of Messiaen—but then so was John Williams' score for *Close Encounters*. A brilliant orchestrator, Takemitsu ends up seduced by his ability to create pretty sounds: the listener is scintillated but nevertheless misses the emotional engagement of yore. The music doesn't go anywhere.

The Tokyo Metropolitan Symphony Orchestra plays superbly throughout.

* * * * * * *

Various
Michael Brook
Live at the Aquarium
4AD tad 2011 CD
Gary Lucas
Gods and Monsters
Enemy EMY133 CD
Henry Kaiser
Lemon Fish Tweezer
Cuneiform RUNE45 CD
Romeo Vendrame
The Principle of Moments
RecRec Music ReCDec 35 CD

FOUR GUITARISTS charging out in utterly different directions. Our esteemed editor voted Michael Brook's previous album *Cobalt Blue* a 'winner' (*Wire* 100). I suspected at the time he was making a complex case for New Age banality. *Live at the Aquarium* was. Brook has invented an instrument called the 'infinite guitar'. So what? He's worked with Brian Eno and Daniel Lanois. Again, so what? Techno-romanticism listens with forked ear. *Live at the Aquarium* is the sound of TV commercials, and dated ones at that. Next.

Gary Lucas plays rock of various persuasions (psychedelic folk, heavy, Cajun, industrial, funk) full of rough-and-ready clutter and the occasional well-managed guitar freak-out. Heavy friends include Jon Langford (Mekons, Three Johns) and Keith LeBlanc (George Clinton, Adrian Sherwood). Nice moments, but nothing gets serious or nasty enough to imply Lucas means it. User-friendly and unkempt, which may be your cup of tea. I'd prefer something a bit more coherent. Whatever happened to Mallard?

At Company Week 1990 Henry Kaiser seemed to be a victim of his technology, walled off from musical interaction. This series of solo free improvisations, though, shows another side. Unlike Michael Brook, he does not rely on the fact that you probably forgot what he just played (infinity is a long time): his notes are tense with discovery. Kaiser uses many effects, sounding like drums, drills, orchestras—but there is always a guitarist's propulsion to see you through (what used to be called 'swing'). At twenty-four minutes, 'It's a Wonderful Life' nearly gets lost, but it is saved by some fast-stream inventiveness that recalls Conlon Nancarrow. Every improvisor has a harmonic world in which they live and move: Kaiser's expands as he plays, which is a great achievement.

Close attention to sonority is a rare and special thing. The mass-market example is Ennio Morricone, who scored soundtracks from buzzing flies, harmonicas and wind. The high art example is Giacinto Scelsi. Romeo Vendrame could be the example from free improvisation (though his 'events' are unrepeatable: the tape is the 'work'). This does not sound like guitar, it is slow and quiet like ambient, but it employs none of the dinky music-college kitsch usual in that area. The only people that compare in terms of achieving such longspan, near eventless tension are the Logos Duo from Amsterdam. Amazing. Go eat a sand dune, Brian Eno.

* * * * * * *

Frank Zappa
Playground Psychotics
Zappa Records ZAP55 CD
Shankar
Touch Me There
Zappa Records ZAP50 CD
Prazsky Vyber
Adieu C.A. Live
AP Records AP0001-2311 CD

IN 1970 and 1971 Zappa was much criticised for working with Flo & Eddie, vocalists from The Turtles. Actually, they were fantastic singers, ideal for Zappa's operatic concept. *Playground Psychotics* is a double CD from that period, equal parts documentary 'on the bus' recordings and music: a bunch of musicians being alternately amusing, obnoxious and thought-provoking. *The Great Rock 'n' Roll Swindle* without the media hullabaloo.

Zappa has rescued John Lennon and Yoko Ono's appearance with The Mothers at the Fillmore (June 1971) from the disastrous Phil Spector mix on *Some Time in New York City*. Yoko Ono's artless shrieking now sounds quite musical: instead of screaming spoilt-brat style over Zappa's solo on 'King Kong', she is now backed by the Mothers in full free-improvising splendour. She also calls Zappa 'the greatest'—Ono getting it right for once.

There is a thirty-minute bravura rendition of 'Billy The Mountain' and much *200 Motels* 'if Zappa hears us he'll steal it and make us do it in the movie' paranoia. If you go for the trip, it's an endless discussion of recording as power, the paradoxes of identity in showbiz and the cleavage of public and private in a commodity system. With their consummate part-singing, Flo & Eddie also bring out the full beauty of melodies from *We're Only in It for the Money*.

L. Shankar's *Touch Me There* is the CD release of a record Zappa produced in 1979. The notable track is 'Dead Girls of London', Zappa's jaundiced view of English maidenhood. Van Morrison originally recorded the vocal track but, according to Zappa, Mo Ostin of Warner Brothers scuppered the deal—here it's Zappa and Ike Willis. Their leering innuendo is actually better than Morrison's pained croak (available on sundry bootlegs for years). Otherwise, the 'top London session men' play a big-boned rock that cannot really rise to Shankar's scurrying, waspish violin.

Prazsky Vyber is a band led by Michael Kocab, the Czech rock musician and composer who rose from underground status to a seat in Parliament during the November 1989 revolution. It was Kocab who got Frank Zappa over to meet Vaclav Havel. Recorded during celebrations at the departure of the last Russian soldier in June 1991, the music is in the rhetorical heavy-rock-cum-cabaret style familiar from Bill Nelson, Killing Joke and Laibach. Zappa plays guitar on a reggae track, his unique sleazy sound still stirring after a three year lay-off.

~1993~

Charles Brown
Blues and Other Love Songs
Someone To Love

BORN IN 1920 in Texas City, Charles Brown was part of the mass immigration to the war-economy industrial boom that was '40s California. He had a massive hit in 1946 with 'Driftin' Blues,' a smoochy, bluesy track with a really arresting, grainy vocal. His bassist Eddie Williams described the singer-pianist's appeal like this: 'Charles at that time lacked the polish of the professional, but he had the technique...Nat [King Cole] never did that well in the black market. So we took Nat's sound back into the blues.' Call it supper-club blues then, or, 'sepia Sinatra' music, Charles Brown was the best (Dr John cut the exquisite *In a Sentimental Mood* as a tribute to Ray Charles—and to Brown). Magic stuff.

These are recent recordings and I'm pleased to report that Mr. Charles Brown has still got it. *Blues and Other Love Songs* is graced with Houston Person on tenor sax: laidback easy jazz blues with Brown's sleepy-eyed, honeyed tones right up against the ear. This is the real bottle-of-bourbon-on-the-piano stuff Tom Waits couldn't get if he paid for it—Johnny Hailstones meets Cecil Gant. Brown's clunking piano also has intriguing similarities to that of Thelonious Monk. *Someone to Love* has Bonnie Raitt guesting (one vocal, one slide guitar number) which is fine if you're not allergic to country singing or big names (I'm neither). Clifford Solomon plays tenor.

Charles Brown provides music that's perfect to unwind to, but is nevertheless full of intriguing felicities, a lesson in the generous scope of the blues. The simultaneous anguish and smile in his voice is like a hot bath for tired bones. Necessary.

* * * * * * *

Devo

Hot Potatoes: The Best of Devo; Q: Are We Not Men? A: We Are Devo/Devo Live; Oh No! It's Devo/Freedom of Choice; Duty Now for the Future/New Traditionalists

DEVO'S FIRST six albums now available on CD in pairs, plus a sampler, all at mid-price—surely a bargain? Not according to current opinion: 'their sophomoric philosophizing doesn't cover their lack of imagination' (*Rolling Stone Record Guide*); 'heartless, soulless techno-drivel made for nerds by nerds under the guise of prescience' (*Hi-Fi News*). Even at *The Wire*, Devo are hardly heroes; the editor had to make several phone calls before he could find anyone willing to take them on. Why such resistance to Devo, one of the truly GREAT bands of the '70s?

Like Frank Zappa, Devo are anathema to those who believe in the authenticity of 'passionate white rock.' Their cod philosophy of de-evolution—remarkably similar to the *Mad*-magazine-meets-the-Situationist-International of The Church of the Sub-Genius—amounts to deconstruction of the rock aesthetic. The current ubiquity of Jacques Derrida's buzz-word may make it sound like entertainment—the wacky art-installation at a shopping mall near you—but actually deconstruction *hurts*. Hear the rock ideologues whinge!

Old wave artists chafing at the restrictions of such ideology welcomed Devo in a way critics did not: Devo played support for Neil Young at his request; Iggy Pop covered their anti-religious 'Praying Hands'; Brian Eno produced their first album; George Clinton name-checked them on *The Electric Spanking of War Babies*; Moon and Dweezil Zappa guested on a Vandals record produced by Devo's Bob Casale, while Frank himself used their 'squared-off' style as one of the generic forms he triggers by hand-signals.

The *Hot Potatoes* collection lacks the intricate webs of idea and riff that tie Devo's songs together on the albums, but the material is brilliantly varied (a point well made by David Quantick in his notes). The packaging plunders old Devo images in Virgin house-style; a pity that the band weren't consulted on visuals. They did supply a 'Whip It' mix that boasts their contribution to House (it wasn't just Kraftwerk and Depeche Mode) and there is 'Be Stiff,' a song celebrating their first signing (otherwise only available as an expensively rare 7' single). Mark Motherbaugh's vocal on 'Working In A Coal Mine' by Allen Toussaint shows that boy-scout-on-heat hysteria can get as close to the blues as white bluesboom arrogance: political correction never sounded this funny.

The couplings are not chronological. *Are We Not Men?* (1978), the Eno-produced debut, comes with *Devo Live* (1981): it therefore contains their epochal version of 'Satisfaction,' a Dadaistic reggae beat subverting the swagger of the original and emphasizing instead the social critique contained in the lyrics; 'Jocko Homo,' the Devo anthem, and a monumental live 'Whip It.' *Oh No! It's Devo* (1982) and *Freedom of Choice* (1980) are prime Devo, sparkling with their self-conscious deployment of musical excitements. 'Peekaboo' (not the New Vaudeville Band's hit from 1967) has an unstoppable R&B riff made ridiculous by comic stops and starts—but like all Devo, you can still dance to it. *Duty Now for the Future* (1979) comes with *New Traditionalists* (1981). It's usual to play off early 'creative' Devo versus later exhaustion, but the latter's cover—plastic neo-classicism half a decade before the postmodern monstrosity which is Sainsbury's in Kensington—and words like 'If you live in a small town/You might meet a dozen or two/Young alien types who step out/And dare to declare/We're through being cool/...Eliminate the ninnies and the twits!' convey telling urban-realist advice.

All you need now is the Devo videos and you've got some of the best of what the twentieth century has to offer on plastic.

* * * * * * *

Bern Nix
Alarms and Excursions
New World Records 80437 CD

BORN IN Toledo, Ohio, guitarist Bern Nix was first inspired by the twang of Duane Eddy and the blues of Freddie King. Seeing Les Paul on television led him towards jazz. In 1975 he joined Ornette Coleman's Prime Time. His is one of the twin guitars—clear and ringing next to Charlie Ellerbee's fuzz and distortion—to be heard on the epochal *Dancing in Your Head*. In the early '80s he helped foment the No Wave punkjazz explosion in New York, playing with James Chance and Elliott Sharp.

This is a trio recording, with the unbeatable Fred Hopkins on bass and Newman Baker on drums. For all the horror with which Ornette's harmolodics is regarded by both record companies and music professors, Nix is a pretty player. His sins against conventional harmony (the earnestness with which such liberties are defended in the notes indicates the degree of conservatism in current jazz) give an open-ended, spacey feel that is never less than engaging.

Unfortunately, Nix is not a forceful composer: you miss the poignant melodies that provided him with a springboard in Prime Time. For a taste of how beguiling free jazz can be, though, (a form so often damned as an impossible racket), *Alarms and Excursions* is a useful disc.

* * * * * * *

Some Reflections on Prince
Dirty Mind (1980)
WEA K56862

OKAY, THE title track begins with a disco throb and fades out in a hi-energy tango, but not since the albums Mandré cut for Motown in the mid-'70s had black pop been so keyboard-based and hi-tech. This was dance music by someone who understood New Wave starkness and minimalism. Relentless synthetic chords provided a brittle surface to be penetrated by funky beats, Prince's falsetto squeezed to sexual yelps. News from the bedroom so recent you could practically smell the sweat, 'When You Were Mine' documents the attractions of non-proprietary sex with a lust that simply aches; 'Uptown' was an explosion of rage against racial and class restrictions. If all this seemed a little contrived, the contrivance was knowing and winning. Compared to Marvin Gaye, Prince's sexuality was a cartoon—but (as demonstrated a decade later by The Simpsons) cartoons are not necessarily devoid of critical power.

The Black Album (1988)
unreleased

PREPARED FOR release and then cancelled, this became *the* bootleg of the '80s. It was transmogrified into *Lovesexy*, which softened its rhythms and defused its obscenities. Prince is one of the few artists to follow up Jimi Hendrix's experiments with slowed and speeded tape. Here, his slowed-down voice becomes a parody of gangster macho psychosis while his falsetto begins to sound like a speed-up: gender is integral to placement of a voice's emotional pitch. Listen to a Little Johnny Taylor record as if it's a woman singing: it sounds assertive and empowered rather than broken-up with emotion. Here Prince plays games with *tessitura* (the natural pitch of his voice) like never before. Singing like Bootsy and indulging the infantile regression of George Clinton's 'Pot Sharing Tots', *The Black Album* cemented Prince's connection to the P-Funk underground (the next year Paisley Park signed Clinton). Urgent, sexual, plastic, funny—one even suspects Prince decided to make this occluded classic a bootleg item just to watch the accountants squirm.

Batman (1989)
Warner Bros. WX281

ROPED IN to give some class to a corporate master plan, Prince only lapsed with 'The Arms of Orion', a ghastly ballad co-written with Sheena Easton: a tune worthy of Andrew Lloyd Webber (there can be no greater dis). 'The Future' shows that Prince was as aware of Batman's retro-politics as the creators of the graphic novel *Batman: The Dark Knight Returns*: 'Systematic overthrow of the underclass/Hollywood conjures images of the past' (a critique initiated by Marx and Engels, natch, in their polemic versus Eugène Sue in *The Holy Family; or, Critique of Critical Criticism*, 1844). Sly Stone, Wild Cherry, Marc Bolan, Free all bounce around in the mix. It's all utterly silly, but you nevertheless want to dance down the street to it. Production is shinier and juicier than of yore, but still edgy and fresh. 'Lemon Crush' is sublimely regressive sex-fixated gibberish worthy of Little Richard (there can be no greater praise).

Graffiti Bridge (1990)
Warner Bros. WX 361

A CURIOUS and scrappy effort, saved by the devil-may-care creativity of Prince's production values. 'New Power Generation'—reprised at the close—huffs and puffs with all the stylistic repro-politics we expect of funk, while 'Love Machine' has Morris Day and Elisa coo sexual innuendo against Prince's future-soul layerings. On the fade Candy Dulfer's sax sounds completely disoriented, the party well out of bounds. As the double-LP proceeds, the groove becomes impossibly scattered, as if Prince wants his syncopations to tell every story at once: an instrumental like 'Tick, Tick Bang' is all over the place, yet works by virtue of Prince's king-of-the-fools let's-all-party dementia. 'Melody Cool' roots all this excitement in the gospel of soul with an appearance by the fabulous Mavis Staples. Each time Prince shakes up the ingredients they fall down a different way, which is why we love him. Only the vacuous sentimentality of the title track lets the side down.

Under the Cherry Moon (movie, 1986)

DISMISSED AT the time as a frivolous throw-away, *Under the Cherry Moon* is in fact the vital visual analogue to *Parade*, Prince's masterpiece. Shot in glorious black and white and set in a timeless retro-Riviera, all champagne and art-deco, it had Prince (Christopher Tracy) and Jerome Banton (Tricky) caste as two rascally gigolos-on-the-make. Christopher Tracy makes the mistake of falling in love, plays the game for real and is shot dead by the irate father (menacingly played by Steven Berkoff). Whereas *Purple Rain* had mythologised Prince's musical combination of black and white in Oedipal terms, *Cherry Moon* is untramelled narcissism. The scene where he plays piano to the enraptured dowagers—his eyes shining, ruff flouncing, camp to the max—is an excessive self-portrait that simultaneously celebrates and satirises his function as superstar. Mixing sacrificial lamb and Rudolf Valentino in a single parable, *Cherry Moon* teeters on a line of self-parody that is endurably fascinating. Note the self-conscious placement of Miles and Joni Mitchell album sleeves in the bedroom. The delivery of 'Kiss'—in a vintage car, after a lover's tiff—makes mincemeat of every other pop video, an artful parade of trembling emotion that brings tears to the eyes. Not since Frankie Lymon had the young male been simultaneously so devastated by lust and seductive in its expression.

Sun Ra & His Arkestra with Symphony Orchestra
Pleiades
Leo Records LR 210/211 CD

SUN RA is (*circa*) eighty years old and hennas his beard. His music is similarly incongruous. He records with a symphony orchestra, but close-mics Talvin Singh's tablas and India Cooke's violin, so that their expressive finger-on-instrument immediacy dispels any hint of classical formality. 'Pleiades' uses a banal three note figure that recalls 'Jesus Christ Superstar', but altoist Marshall Allan plays saxophone extremities that indicate where John Zorn is coming from. A

Chopin prelude lilts into alto-squeals worthy of Godzilla and absurdist fairground chinking from the synth. Sun Ra: oddness beyond reckoning.

Recorded at the Théâtre Carré Saint-Vincent on 27 October 1990, the sound is immaculate, suggesting a state radio broadcast (there is no producer listed and no notes to explain who financed this Arkestra/Symphony encounter).

If you like to fix on the single, perfect artwork Sun Ra is not for you. Like Duke Ellington, Sun Ra exfoliates a baroque fractal, the seething wake of intelligence on the move in unlit pastures. 'Sun Procession' is a typical Ra anthem, a march whose tawdry splendour suggests some historically-inaccurate Roman legion wending its way through the desert heat-haze. Bolted together out of the debris of the mass culture industry—cocktail tinkering, military fanfares, Miklos Rozsa film scores, free-jazz obstreperousness—Ra creates a junk epic that points to the precariousness of the spell of art.

Sun Ra's four-decade output has piled up into the Mount Eiger of discography (merely listing his record labels causes problems; some of the pressings consist of *single* copies!)—but this can nevertheless be recommended as a place to start. Confounding rumours that he went off the boil in the '80s, *Pleiades* is a triumphant compendium of Sun Ra's polymorphous ingenuity.

~1994~

John Coltrane
Live in Seattle
Impulse! GRP21462

FORGET THE arguments of the Vinyl Defence League (sub-atomic sound-storage, the necessity of surface noise, the smell of the cardboard...): this release *proves* the CD is a good thing.

Despite his much-hawked 'cosmic' image, John Coltrane was exceptionally aware of packaging, able to realise albums—*Giant Steps*, *A Love Supreme*, *Ascension*, *Sun Ship*—that could vie with a Beatles album for unity of vision and expert address to the format (as with Hendrix, posthumous scavenging/re-release schedules/box-sets of alternate takes can obscure the fact that Coltrane *only ever put masterpiece commodities on the market*). But *live* Coltrane was always a problem for record companies and other such commodity brokers.

Coltrane played to see what might happen, pushing the 'song' into lengths that were as unpredictable as they were (retrospectively) inevitable. In 1971 Impulse! issued *Live in Seattle*, seventy-seven minutes of an 'augmented' classic quartet (*i.e.*, Trane, pianist McCoy Tyner, bassist Jimmy Garrison, drummer Elvin Jones plus tenor Pharoah Sanders and bassist/bass-clarinetist Don Garrett), recorded in 1965 by bright spark Jan Kurtis, who just happened to be in a Seattle nightclub with an Ampex 350-2 and the know-how. Spread over four sides of vinyl, ludicrously programmed for an autochange (so both 'Out Of This World' and 'Evolution' were split between different discs), the music was hard to follow. My memory of the record (a cut-out costing £3.50 in 1977) could be summarized as 'the one with the shouting' (actually, the dreaded shouting is a brief moment at the end of 'Evolution', and beautifully done at that). Now, a double CD can handle an extra fifty-five minutes from the same gig ('Body & Soul', 'Afro-Blue') with ease.

Why is this music so marvellous? Why do birds sing? *etc*. When 'Body & Soul' recedes into a reflective Tyner solo and you hear nightclub sounds (clinking glasses, subdued chat), it's a shock to realize all this mightiness is in fact jazz. The power—an undeterred, confident assault on the citadels of the avant-garde from a jazz perspective—is gobsmacking. The weight and rawness Coltrane developed in his music makes it accessible to rock fans: the more he progressed, the more he drew on the exhilarating, vital chaos of the R&B he started from.

You can tell Trane from Sanders because the former is more lyrical, more modally compact, with a clarified muezzin uplift (a feature Sanders duplicates today with spooky accuracy). There's a fantastic sense of harmonic expansion: as soloists strut and stretch, the accompanists unwind acres upon acres of canvas for their spurts. Next to Trane's majesty, Sanders (the vinyl issue had 'featuring Pharoah Sanders' as big as the title) is a worrisome whinger; but in his stress and squeak (the equivalent of guitar feedback) you find new colours—trembling, blue, expansive. Towards the end of 'Evolution', Elvin Jones is particularly god-like, invoking an idea of rhythm as kicking about boxes in a darkened cellar.

Coltrane 'tribute' bands, however fine (Dudek/Oxley; Pharoah, Branford Marsalis etc), imitate the letter, not this pulverising, effortful glory. If I say this record reminds me of Hession/ Wilkinson/Fell, The Crusaders, Mieko Kanno playing solo violin, Rancid Poultry, all I mean is that it measures up to terrific live experiences still burning in the memory. *Live in Seattle* is simply the best recorded music that the twentieth century has to offer, no fooling.

* * * * * * *

The Tony Oxley Quartet
Incus 15 CD
Derek Bailey/Anthony Braxton
Moment Précieux
Victo 02 CD

Transient V Resident
Broken to Be More Beautiful
Discus 01 MC

THE LIST of drummer-led bands—Shelly Manne & His Men, The Dave Clarke 5, The Aynsley Dunbar Retaliation—is not exactly inspiring. But Tony Oxley is different. Born in Sheffield in 1938, he learned his rudiments in the Black Watch military band. In the mid-'60s, together with guitarist Derek Bailey (a participant here), Oxley developed the fiercely creative style of free jazz that came to be called free improvisation. In 1966, Oxley moved to London and became house drummer at Ronnie Scott's, backing such luminaries as Sonny Rollins, Stan Getz and Joe Henderson. In 1969, he played on John McLaughlin's *Extrapolation*, a record whose lite freedoms proved highly influential (Miles, Weather Report), and then moved to Europe to play free improvisation (though his quartet with Gerd Dudek showed that he could still play modal jazz better than anyone apart from Elvin Jones).

As this new release shows, there's a lot of humour in Oxley's trenchancy, an impatience with filigree which is paradoxical given the blatant sensitivity of his smallest sounds. Derek Bailey always shines when pitched against a good percussionist. Like Oxley, he has extended the scope of his instrument to become a resonant sound world. Like Oxley again, he favours a harsh, metallic attack. Keyboardist Pat Thomas provides a welcome fluidity among all this Sheffield steel abrasion, his post-Cecil flights trickling beautifully. Matt Wand is the joker in the pack—contributing a warped 'Death March' soundbyte (to which Oxley responds with gusto) and sly, funky bass notes redolent of rave-scene twoc-squad disobedience. This is committed music played by musicians who want to improvise at the very edge of their technique and understanding; go with it and it's wondrous—sensible jazz opinion calls it 'abstract' and 'inaccessible'. Sensible opinion always was stupid.

Moment Précieux was an instant classic when it was released in 1986. Anthony Braxton has an arrestingly raw sound on saxophone, a personal cry as indelible as a great singer's. He tangles up with Bailey's knotty conundra in simultaneous affection and recoil, a wonderful example of thought being true to itself whilst also admitting its object. Bailey contributes some of his most thoughtful-sounding notes on record. No CD extras, just the original pair of 23- and 24-minute pieces—and that's just fine.

Transient V Resident pitches two keyboard players against each other in improvised dialogues: Sheffield meets Bradford in forensic glitterbang. Transient is Martin Archer, third stream composer, Hornweb Quartet saxophonist and leader of the wonderful Ask (an improvising group that includes Matt Wand). Resident is a guy called Chris who has piles of electronic equipment but no car. Live (suffered in a defiantly non-ambient art-gallery setting) TVR came across as arduous and arbitrary; listened to at home, though, the variety of sounds—no Jon Hassell-style limitation to ethnic atmos-pherics—is impressively gratifying. It's also very funny. Transient's Second Viennese School atonalities question Resident's pump-and-riff future-pop effects like a monstrous parody of Radio Cologne seriousness. Resident replies with minimal idiocies dreamt by Tangerine Dream, infantile sniggers shiny with the sexpot mockery of Issy in *Finnegans Wake*. These people juggle the sounds that move you, and wonder about them. Preposterousness as an aesthetic: it really does promise to liberate the listener. Whereas Ask are providing urgent answers to questions about the relationship of musicianship to experiment, *Broken to Be More Beautiful* is more like weird wallpaper. But there's a place for that, too. It all depends on your taste in curtains.

* * * * * * *

Music Revelation Ensemble
In the Name of...
DIW 885 CD

JAMES BLOOD Ulmer is the most unpredictable of musicians. His last recording for this label, *Harmolodic Guitar with Strings*, had him declaring that he was going to separate out the strands of his music—blues, funk, classical, jazz—in order to make it clearer to the public what he was about. His sub-Bartókian string quartets did nothing to convince one this was a wise move (though one equally dreaded any more examples of his barren 'blues' stylings).

Now Ulmer delivers one of the most exciting albums he's ever made, giving hope to anyone who has perhaps contemplated abandoning jazz as a progressive force. He's dumped the idea of separating out his musics: in the past jazz combined classical, blues and Dixieland, now it's got to be just as ecumenical. Using his patented guitar sound—power chords that seem to summarise everything that ever made you thrill to Guitar Slim, Jimi Hendrix or Johnny Thunders—he provokes playing from Arthur Blythe (alto), Sam Rivers (soprano, tenor and flute) and Hamiett Bluiett (baritone) that must be their best for yonks. Too often people associate free jazz with denial of pleasure: on the contrary, Ulmer's wide-ranging chordal palette and lustrous sound provides an expansive, richly sensual environment for his hornmen.

When Ulmer played London's Dingwalls in February, he delivered a strong set of songs (it is not often pointed out, but Ulmer was as much part of New Wave as Talking Heads), but only on the encore did he hint at the amazing free jazz he's capable of. Organic, groovy, trusting and thrusting, the Music Revelation Ensemble trio mobilise everything that matters about amplified musicianship. They make most other group interactions sound one dimensional. Amin Ali plays Fender bass and drummer Cornell Rochester has the take-no-prisoners ferocity associated with the likes of Billy Cobham. Despite such high-tech impact, the trio do not paint themselves into the usual fusion corner of academic metres and conformist harmony: anything can happen, and it usually does.

Their deep musical knowledge sparked by instant improvisation, Ulmer and Ali and Rochester spin off ideas and spaces and felicities at such a rate of invention it simply staggers the attentive ear. Maybe this is what Charlie Parker sounded like to swing fans in 1942. Ulmer is aware of what he is about. Instead of fetishizing the external aspects of jazz history—standards, acoustic instruments, *suits*—he grasps its liberating, dialectical principle. Take all this stuff that's around and *play with it*—to the nth degree. From the sleeve notes:

> 'The purpose was in creating a sound that doesn't inhibit, to create a system where David Murray, Arthur Blythe, Julius Hemphill, Sam Rivers, Hamiet Bluiett could use their energy, like Wynton Kelly behind John Coltrane. [*Yeah, James! We hear you!*] Since Bud Powell there's been rock 'n' roll, R&B, funk and now hip hop, if you want to have jazz grow you got to incorporate all that music into jazz. To re-establish what jazz is. They established what jazz is too quick, and that's why they ended up with fusion. They did not know about John Coltrane and Bud Powell and Dizzy and all these brothers and whatnot. I play every kind of chord you can hear under the fucking sun behind the players so as to make sure that they list every territory that was ever played—and also fit their free sound.'

It's true. James Blood Ulmer turns to interactive, spontaneous musical account every advance in music that has mattered since the start of the century (a big claim, but then jazz always did know more than any other methodology). Forget the besuited neo-classicists, forget 'world music' and the way it flogs the parochial as surrogate globalism, forget hair shirt experimentalism, forget (especially) the intellectual hoop jumping required to make muzak sound radical (*i.e.* forget Ambient): *this* is the real deal—technically advanced as fuck, splinteringly inventive, blues-drenched and angry. This music makes history. Get down, get involved.

* * * * * * *

Various Classical

EUROPEAN ART music could be defined as concrete philosophy, the search for a non-verbal, sensual attitude towards the world, one which feels 'right' or 'true'. Magazines dedicated to classical music tend to take the word 'classic' literally, elevating scores beyond criticism. Reviews are reduced to judgements on the technical means of reproduction: a conductor's tempo, the skill of the players, the engineer's placement of microphones. The compositions themselves are all products of 'genius', guaranteed 'testaments to the human spirit'.

Such criticism is nonplussed by works that haven't yet been admitted to the canon. Because of the inertia of academic institutions, this usually means anything written this century. With the minimalists attempting to dump all innovations since atonality into the dustbin of history, the idea of a reliable canon for twentieth century music becomes still more problematic. Of course, that music should be riven by doubt in this century should come as no surprise. Break the certainties of faith (*i.e.*, progress beyond medieval plain chant), and it all depends on what you want.

In the 1910s, the internal development of the music demanded innovations that turned it into a specialist art, alienating an audience brought up on Mozart and Brahms. Whether you take this to be an indication of something wrong with society (Theodor Adorno) or a perverse 'creepiness' on the part of composers (Steve Reich), modern classical music is inevitably controversial.

Deutsche Grammophon spur one to think about history by yoking together Alfred Schnittke, Witold Lutoslawski, and György Ligeti (Classikon100 439452). Schnittke's reputation was established in this country at the Huddersfield Contemporary Music Festival in 1990, when, to celebrate Glasnost, a brace of Russians were presented under the slogan 'The Curtain Rises'. Schnittke's 'polystylism'—baroque, romantic and modernist modes all mixed together—was applauded for its populism and accessibility. The composer's association with a circle of dissident, anti-Stalinist intellectuals made lionization seem appropriate. Now, as the dust settles, Pierre Boulez's comment—that, deprived of contact with the global mainstream because of the Iron Curtain, Russians were bound to write parochial music—seems more apt. Schnittke's *Concert Grosso No 1* (1977) seems particularly weak, his jokes and 'irony' unable to hide an inability to make his orchestral sounds evolve (Morricone's ironic use of baroque arrives from avant-garde research into echo and sonics; it is not just a matter of cranking out pastiche Vivaldi). Schnittke's cracked bells and wistful violins are naively manipulative; compared to Lutoslawski, his orchestral palette is meagre indeed. The latter's *Chain 3* (1986) and *Novelette* (1979)—while unashamedly romantic—keep pushing the orchestra into unprecedented new zones of texture.

Ligeti's *Chamber Concerto* (1970), performed by Boulez and his Ensemble InterContemporain, leaps out of the classical soundworld with effects that could almost be electronic. His special ability to score streaming, horizontal textures puts one in mind of crystals, astral lights, seams in the earth's crust. Whereas Lutoslawski achieves authentic expression within the terms set by romanticism, Ligeti abandons the heaving of the human heart for something objective, thereby connecting to *musique concrète* (Schaeffer, Boehmer), avant-garde jazz (Abrams, Braxton, Threadgill) and free improvisation. Actually, Ligeti is a poet of those most human attributes: curiosity about the external world, desire to transform it. It's the most significant piece of music among these discs.

Lutoslawski's third and fourth symphonies are also available, with a setting of a (wonderful) surrealist poem by Robert Desnos (Sony SK66280). Twenty-bit technology helps the LA Philharmonic under Esa-Pekka Salonen sound terrific. Lutoslawski's pacing of effects—cello stomach rumbles, percussive palpitations, nervosities of high strings—gains coherence via grounded, in-the-body physicality, rather than formal/academic correctness. Someone on top of his tradition rather than sunk in it.

Toru Takemitsu seems to have abandoned the experimental intensity of his '60s/'70s music in favour of a role as 'Japan's greatest composer' (*Cantos* RCA/Victor 0902662537). As with Ennio Morricone, work on films (some classic Kurosawas, for example) alerted him to *timbre*, and some of his east-west fusions are stunning. Here, *Waves* (1977) and *Water-Ways* (1978) are beautiful mood studies, filigrees of held notes, overlapping tensions and eruptive surprises. Naturalistic elements—drums as thunder—derive from filmic practice, impressionism detailed enough to make most New Age/Ambient sound crude. But mark the dead hand of academia: *Fantasma/Cantos* (1991) may nod to Dukeish lushness, but it's way too conventional to justify its length.

Probably the only English composer to measure up to Lutoslawski for his combination of integrity and mainstream success is Harrison Birtwistle. His *Antiphonies for Piano and Orchestra* (Collins Classics 14142) was written for the widely-photographed pianist Joanna MacGregor (she's piled her magnificent hair atop her head for the cover shot, an unprecedented manoeuvre). She's ideal for Birtwistle, her touch vivacious, her structural command chillingly assured. Birtwistle's orchestral palette derives from Edgard Varèse, all martial horns, hieratic percussion and harsh strings. It's rather strident and ungiving for the living room; at first you feel that maybe he could have learned from Varèse's brevity too. There is a typically English 'mythological' feel to Birtwistle, reminiscent of the bronzed, Henry Moore-like structures favoured by opera-set designers. It's worth working at, though: his multifaceted constructions are impressive, if not revelatory. Whereas Boulez takes Messiaen's soundworld into delirious slithers, Birtwistle is epic and sturdy (the disc also includes new recordings of *Nomos* and *Imaginary Landscape*).

A good slice of Messiaen's music with *Oeuvres pour piano et orchestre* (Koch/Scwann 3-1123), recorded in 1985, Yvonne Loriod at the piano. Messiaen might have been a devout Catholic, but his music is worlds away from the 'gloomy piffle' of John Tavener and ECM's Hilliard Ensemble. The gamelan-derived chiming in 'Oiseaux Exotiques' is surely the missing link between Wagner's Nibelungen and Carl Stalling's cartoon chases (and John Williams should pay royalties to the Messiaen estate for his *Star Wars* chords). Maybe Messiaen is a little restricted in what he can do, but this is all so light and bright and finely detailed it is a joy. Steve Reich may call it 'creepy', but serialism is really just composition intoxicated with possibility.

That is also the claim made for Charles Ives, the 'father of American music'. The Orpheus Chamber Orchestra play accurately (*A Set of Pieces*, Deutsche Grammophon 439869: *Three Places in New England, The Unanswered Question, A Set of Pieces, Symphony No 3, Set No 1*), but without fire. Individual players like Joanna MacGregor and Bill Frisell, modernists with a feel for discord and the blues, can make an Ives sonata sound like a vital jumble of Americana; orchestras reduce his contrasts to pale patriotic soup, cowboy-film inanity. Coupling Varèse's *Amériques* with Ives' *Sym-*

phony No 4 (Decca 443172) might seem a good idea, but unfortunately Christoph von Dohnanyi and the Cleveland Orchestra reduce Varèse's futurism to Ivesish pastoral: this has none of the power and shock of Marius Constant's performance for the Erato label.

A different America emerges on John Cage's *Sixteen Dances* (RCA/Victor 0902661574), written for dancer Merce Cunningham in 1951, here performed by the Ensemble Modern under Ingo Metzmacher. Flute, trumpet, piano, violin, cello and percussion are suspended in pregnant silence. Organisation is rhythmic; unpredictable variations create ever changing shapes. Where things become denser (*e.g.*, 'Dance No 8') there is something Stravinsky-like about the static rhythms. Although the dances are named after the eight 'permanent emotions' of Hindu aesthetics, the lasting impression is of Cage's quietism. Both recording and playing are lush and beautiful, making the asceticism of the scores—the fact that we're being made to pay attention to the spaces between the sounds rather than the sounds themselves—still more poignant.

Pianist Jean-Luc Fafchamps makes a polemical point about the composers Franz Liszt/Luigi Dallapiccola/Luciano Berio with *Short Pieces from Italy* (Sub Rosa SR58). He show how Liszt's late works paved the way to Dallapiccola and Berio's fragmented modernism. His thesis is undeniable, and he plays sensitively and clearly. Like Cage, this is a modernism achieved by leaving things out rather than putting things in; the anti-romanticism of the erasing rubber.

Gavin Bryars' *Sinking of the Titanic* (Point Music 446061) is not a re-release of the classic that launched Brian Eno's Obscure series, but a new realisation. Tripled in length, recorded in glowing digital and supplemented with all kinds of narrative effects, it no longer has the desolate end-of-an-era magic of the original. In 1975, this mournful dissolution of Edwardian religious certainties into the cold waters of cut-up sounded subversive. Now it's more like a Nyman soundtrack (or car advert), glossy and vacuous, indulgent rather than critical. Bryars' Cagean/pataphysical 'subversions' just seem an excuse for recycling the coy whimsy of Imperial Britain (Edward Lear, William Walton, Viv Stanshall, etc). Horrible.

Still keeping faith with an idea of modern music as innovative and politically alert is Alvin Curran with *Crystal Psalms*, an oratorio for the victims of the Nazi pogrom of 1938, performed and broadcast simultaneously in six different nations half a century later. This wasn't just a stunt: there are moments of difficulty and non-communication that make the overall flow still more moving. Like the radio-plays (*Hörstücke*) Heiner Goebbels releases on ECM, it integrates all kinds of disparate materials with a keen ear for continuity.

However, both collage methodology and subject matter beg comparison to John Zorn's *Kristallnacht* (Eva WWCX2050), doing Curran few favours. In contrast to Zorn's state-of-the-art, hair-on-end aural shocks, Curran's deployment of national radio choirs seems ineffectual, helplessly respectable. Will establishment prayer repel Nazi attacks, or the ability to think the unthinkable? Effective anti-fascism (I would argue) requires the latter.

Interesting, too, to compare Schnittke's use of *angstvoll* violin to Zorn's: both evoke middle European facility with the instrument, but Zorn uses a player who can improvise (Mark Feldman), and records him with hallucinogenically in-focus precision. Musical forms are pushed to their limit rather than just quoted (Zorn can even make guitarist Marc Ribot play with verve!). Both politically and aesthetically, Zorn is light-years ahead of the rest; but then he should be, because, after Frank Zappa's death, he has become our finest 'classical' composer: in other words, he inculcates the emotional resources to face the horrors of the contemporary world, to situate the self *vis-à-vis* the social totality.

~1995~

John Cage
A Firenze
Materiali Sonori CAGE493 CD/Book

JOHN CAGE presents us with a paradox. If you accept the institutions of classical music (*i.e.*, composer/score/reading musician), his works constitute a fiercely intelligent interrogation of its procedures and limits: his ideas never repeat, the twists and turns are stunningly, fastidiously inventive. But Cage's influence has also been widespread outside classical music: conceptual art, performance art, post-Chicago free jazz, free improvisation, sound installations, ambient and chill-out soundtracks—all have been touched. His experiments may enliven the mausoleum of obsolete gestures that constitutes a classical concert, but can they compete with the wealth of experimental sounds available since he started to widen the parameters of musical art in the '40s? Here is ample material with which to make a judgement: a concert disc and a hundred-page booklet (part of the Materiali Sonori series; other issues include Durutti Column, The Residents & William Burroughs; Nyman, Budd & Roedelius; Frank Zappa).

The concert was given in Florence on 21 June 1992, with Cage in attendance, just a few weeks before his death. Six minutes of an interview—including some astonishingly naive assertions about nano-technology saving the world from ecological disaster—occupy track one. At the concert the main performer is pianist Giancarlo Cardini, who specialises in Cage and 'frivolous' music by the likes of Satie, Ricordi and Rinaldi. There are contributions from singer Francesca della Monica, flautist Roberto Fabbriciani and bassist Stefan Sconadibbrio (the last two noted for their *premières* of Ferneyhough, Scelsi and Nono). Sound is excellent and the musicians have a great feel for Cage: silences are pregnant, dynamics deft and attacks clean. Sconadibbrio's version of *Ryonji* (1985) vies with Irvine Arditti's *Freeman Études* for state-of-the-art dazzle, and

Cardini shines on *Two* (1987) and *Winter Music* (1957). The concert is well-programmed, with an explosive ending in the brilliant *Music for Amplified Toy Pianos* (1960).

Wire magazine's piano-guru Andy Hamilton has denounced Cage's chance-based methodology as 'meaningless,' but the utterly recognisable quality of this music speaks otherwise. In comparison to Morton Feldman's restful vacancy, for example, Cage's taste for jarring knocks and sounds-isolated-in-silence reflects his longstanding personal interest in Japanese music. Producer Giampiero Bigazzi rather overdoes the applause, but his pride at the occasion is understandable (there's a winning anecdote about persuading Cardini to admit him to the sold-out concert and their hatching the idea of the CD release together). Altogether, this disc constitutes a vindication of Cage's music.

The booklet fares less well. It is certainly lovingly produced: beautiful photos, interviews and texts in parallel Italian/English, stylish graphic scores. Bigazzi deplores the riot at a Cage concert in Milan in 1977, along with the 'last games of cultural militancy' Italian intellectuals were then playing. Fratini and Nesti salute Cage's philosophy as a corollary of the USA's 'model role in planetary development' (their enthusiasm for JFK owes more to Oliver Stone's Hollywood fantasies than to Noam Chomsky). The essays construct an ideological Cage: in accordance with the 'end of history' proposed by Yankee minimalism, Cage allows affirmation of the capitalist order whilst saving a perch from which to decry the heartless vulgarity of commercialism. For Italian intellectuals reeling from Berlusconi's machinations (not to mention the rise of Fascism and the rehabilitation of Mussolini), such a version of Cage seems like the perfect cop-out. There are also frequent (patriotic?) swipes at Serialism and Darmstadt. However, the nihilism at the heart of Cage's aesthetic makes any political usage highly unstable; his deconstruction of art music surely requires a harder look at society than Bigazzi and friends are prepared to deliver.

* * * * * * *

Leo Ornstein, George Antheil and Henry Cowell
The Bad Boys
Hat Hut hatART 6144

George Antheil
Sonatas for Violin and Piano 1923, 1948
Montaigne MO782022

AVANT-GARDES ARE DESIGNED to provoke debate: useful to look
back once controversy has cooled. Not because the mere passage of
time operates any kind of filter—a complacent notion, since it actually requires *activity* (discussion, reissues, exhibitions, broadcasts)
to establish reputations—but because, as Tharg once editorialized in
the sci-fi comic *2000AD*, those who are ignorant of history are condemned to repeat it. For example, how do those 'bad boys' of the
piano from the '20s—Leo Ornstein, George Antheil and Henry
Cowell—measure up today?

Leo Ornstein was a conservatoire-trained virtuoso who, one day
in 1913, felt compelled to compose a barbaric thrash sonata called
Danse Sauvage. He used it to cap his recitals of Chopin and Scri-
abin, inciting riots, controversy and press. The impressario Martin
H. Hanson made him a star on successive European tours. Then (as
now) the great selling point was 'crossing boundaries': classical music injected with the 'mechanical barbarism' of jazz.

In his autobiography, *Bad Boy of Music*, George Antheil tells
how he got his own big break: he read in one newspaper that Hanson was going to Europe, and in another that Ornstein had left his
management. Antheil at once went home and worked up a thunderous technique, then auditioned. Hanson gave him the job. Antheil
went down a storm in Europe too, and found an enthusiastic sup-
porter in Ezra Pound, ever to be relied on to talk up some propagan-
distic tripe about music (or politics).

However, as Peter Wilson points out in his sleeve note, the
commitment of Ornstein and Antheil to 'modernism' was superficial. Both quickly returned to the neo-classical fold. Today, even
their 'iconoclastic' pieces sound like squibs. Left out of the limelight, it was Henry Cowell who pioneered the techniques that led on
to Cage's prepared piano; his pieces have an intriguingly naive, non-

classical openness to sound that shows up the stentorian pomp of the others.

Further evidence of the triviality of Antheil's talent (and his debt to Stravinsky's *Soldier's Tale*) can be found on the *Sonatas* played by Reinbert de Leeuw. De Leeuw also performs today's 'bad boys' Louis Andriessen and Steve Reich: like Ornstein and Antheil in their day, these composers are currently considered 'ultra-modern,' but musically are just as in thrall to tradition (the true heir to the Ornstein/Antheil tradition of daft showbiz, though, has to be Andriessen's *protégé* Steve Martland, with his pumped-up muscles, 'provocative' statements designed for publicity brochures, and in-sipid academic compositions). Although musically uninspiring, these three discs constitute useful evidence of the fluff considered 'radical' in past decades: a salutary lesson for South Bank publicists operating today.

* * * * * * *

Rico with Kuubo & The Rare Riddim Crew
Rising in the East
Jove Music JOVECD3 CD

VETERAN OF successive waves of Jamaican Music—Count Ossie, Prince Buster, charting with 'King Of Kings' in 1964 as Ezz Reco & The Launchers, The Specials, Gary Crosby's Jazz Jamaica—legendary trombonist Rico Rodriguez now surfaces with a band from Japan. Recorded in Tokyo last summer, this album is released here on a tiny label hailing from Ladbroke Grove (however outer-national it's become, some things in reggae remain the same).

Bandleader Kuubo is an intriguing figure. Inspired by the '70s reggae explosion, he tracked the music to source, playing with the Trenchtown College Band in Kingston, Jamaica. It was there that he met Rico in the late '80s. His Rare Riddim Crew pride themselves on being able to play every Jamaican style, from Ska to Jungle. The danger of such an approach is of course repertory professionalism—is Rico's function here just value-added authenticity, equivalent to U2 employing B.B. King to play the Blues?

Luckily, Kuubo embraces instrumental reggae in all its quirky glory. This is evident from the chinkering piano of the opener, 'Don't Stay Out Late'. 'Soul Serenade', a 'Rasta Style' reworking of King Curtis's soul smoocher, has the horn section expertly echo

Rico's vocalised quaver with subtly discordant harmonies: tinny, '60s, wrong-but-right. 'Easy Snappin'' steals the bass line from Nina Simone's 'My Baby Saves His Loving Just for Me', but records it warm and fuzzy, giving the melody instruments a fetching edge. Kuubo is evidently a fan of Studio One production values, combining majestic treadmill rhythms with the quaint wobbliness that is Ska's calling card. 'Vin Lawrence Park' has a cracked vibes riff placed in just the right off-kilter space in the mix.

By the time you get to 'Chiang Kai Shek', with its excellent sax solo cutesy Shikai Naomi (he recalls the on-edge poignancy of Roland Alphonso, Joe Harriott and Lol Coxhill rather than the cabaret calypso-fantasies of Sonny Rollins), and 'I Know' with its pumping Roscoe Gordon-style piano, you're convinced that Kuubo has learned his craft with respect and invention. Rico, as ever, is gorgeous—his sound rich and golden, his majestic trombone lines purring like a somnolent lion.

* * * * * * *

KURT SCHWITTERS
Ursonate
Hat Art 6109 CD

KURT SCHWITTERS created some of the most beautiful art of the twentieth century, collages he called merzbau. At a distance, the colours shimmer: go closer and you see they are made of old bus tickets and litter. Now Eberhard Blum has recorded *Ursonate*, Schwitters' legendary poem of 'primal', non-referential syllables. Published in 1932, it is an ambitious forty-one-minute opus that makes Dadaist Tristan Tzara's celebrated 'Zang Tumb Tuumb' (which named a record company) look like a squib.

Ursonate obeys classical form, being in four movements, each with a 'proper' Italian name (rondo, largo, scherzo etc). This makes it even more absurd. Current interest in deep punk (situationist, lettrist, dada) has stressed the negative thrust of twentieth century modernism: Schwitters, though, was also a constructivist. *Ursonate* would be as much at home at the Bauhaus (he actually recited it there in 1924) as at the Cabaret Voltaire.

Eberhard Blum does a great job, being very dry, precise and rhythmically charged. Sets of syllables repeat, like someone reading out phonetic transcriptions from a phrase book: Blum's delivery is so po-faced and urgent the result is hilarious. Joyce's polyglot *Finnegans Wake* makes a continuous joke about how the phonemes of one language might be understood in another. Schwitters and Joyce were revolutionary modernists, composing works for a new international: what they do refuses the security of a national language or culture. Here, Victor Borge, Stan Unwin, the Goons, Lord Buckley, Ella Fitzgerald, Eek-A-Mouse and Shinehead are all relevant pointers, but the joy of Schwitters is that there is no 'humour' or 'art' to cushion the absurdity. 'Ribble Bobble Pimlico' from 1946 lets in some English words, just as his contemporary collages included pro-English (or anti-Nazi) images; his use of 'bop' is pretty hep too.

Rinnzekete bee bee nnz krr muu?
ziiuu ennze, ziiuu rinnzkrrmuu,
rakete bee bee.

Ursonate sounds like one of Tharg's *2000AD* droids making contact—half a century ahead of time.

~*1996*~

Ascension
'LP'
Shock/Fusetron

THERE'S SOMETHING ABOUT guitars. They upset people. Ascension know this, but get beyond mere rockism by a shrewd take on the history of the instrument.

In its peculiarly dialectical manner, Punk both abolished and preserved the electric guitar. Solo capability was denigrated as muso irrelevance, whilst the dial was turned up on distortion and 'tude: the sociopath aspect of the guitar rectified and roused to stalk the land.

No Wave issued an intriguing proposition: the anti-jazz of Free could be equated to the anti-rock of Punk. As is the destiny of righteous avant-gardes, the music bombed commercially, but it leaked transgressive anger into the airshafts.

Still fighting the punk crusade, and harried by a wave of heavy metal, indie bands of the '80s could only tolerate a lumpen-folkie jingle-jangle or Velvets-drone. Jazz, though, learned from No Wave how to swallow the sword of Hendrix (finally!); for a while it looked like jazz (Sharrock, Ulmer, Frisell, Decoding Society, Chadbourne, Jenkins, Universal Congress of) could outpunch rock where guitars were concerned. But jazz is a musician's music; since 1966 it has only reached out to a mass audience by lying to itself (fusion, neoclassical, ambient, triphop, Living Colour—call it what you will).

Nottingham's grubby rock scene came to the rescue: Napalm Death and the Earache roster injected back the technical slam-bang utterness Morrissey had banished from counter-rock. But who could uncurl the tight fist of Hardcore's politico-vegetarianism, carve protodelic psychoplasmic guitar-sculptures into the fetid air? Zorn? No! (Too tight-ass)...Ascension? Yes!

The (backdoor) key was provided by Derek Bailey. Away in his corner, untouched by the Punk Wars that raged for younger fry, he made the necessary technical advances for anti-spectacular, blues-sprung guitar individualism. A materialist critique of the kind of 'transcendence' achieved by devices every musician knows backwards (but played forwards to patronise the ignorant). Cancel classical harmony, strummed ho-hum, tonal 'beauty,' cosmic spells, arena cavorts, calibrated excellence: construct a guitar language out of actual guitar sounds, the plucks and duff clucks ignored by the soaring air-brush heroes.

Ascension's Stefan Jaworzyn is one of the few London guitarists to have realised Bailey's virtues, and by dint of volume, aggro and f-word 'tude, somersaulted them into a music the rock-polloi might understand. On 'A,' his twang—a mix of Zoot Horn Rollo, Vic Fleck, Craig Scanlon and '50s flying saucer—is framed in stop-start silences that are simultaneously arty (Paris existential) and laddish (Small Faces). On 'AA,' feedback sonorities are ripped back to expose his patent metal, a complex two-way playoff. Though not as pure a showcase for his unique sound as 'A,' it gets further in the end, and the closing bars (as in *rattled*) are ecstatically fertile, the moment when everyone starts smiling ('Stefan's good tonight, in-nee?').

Drummer Tony Irving is all low rumbles, bad reverb, earthquakes, thuggish thuds, with a stop-listen-start wit rare in a Mekquake-style behemoth. His contribution is more crucial than guitar-fetishists are likely to clock; exasperated, short-fuse dynamite threaded with horizontal cymbal bits.

No growth without pain; Ascension are the uncomfortable sound of improv busting into the popular arena. Granted, utter-gutter guitar rock is hardly what A&R-souls are tuned to (they're too busy searching the land for wannabee-Carnaby union-jackshit prat-pop). But when the 'Nirvana turn' is eventually made, Ascension are poised for sating mass ear-wishes. And even if they ain't, they still sounds topper, guv.

* * * * * * *

Eugene Chadbourne & Jimmy Carl Black
Pachuco Cadaver
Fire Ant
Richard Ray Farrell & Jimmy Carl Black
Cataract Jump
Fritz Records
Various
The Music of Captain Beefheart Live
Ultimate Audio Entertainment

IN JUNE 1993, Eugene Chadbourne and Jimmy Carl Black came to England and toured from Hoxton Square to Hebden Bridge. *En route*, they recorded a session for Radio 3's *Mixing It*. Guitarist and 'banjoker' Chadbourne is a product of No Wave: turned around by hearing Derek Bailey, he recorded three albums of subversively comic Free Improvisation, then teamed up with John Zorn to tour America playing deranged Country Music. Drummer Jimmy Carl Black was a founder member of the Mothers of Invention, though this is a set of Captain Beefheart covers (according to Black, 'Zappa wanted to be avant-garde, or thought he was, but Beefheart was the *real thing*').

This quote appears in a booklet Chadbourne has drawn, summarising Black's stories of life on the road. Like the music, at first glance it looks insultingly scrappy and careless (the buyer at G&S Music, the Zappa-oriented mail-order company, opined that the whole album was worthless), but actually it confirms the power of Chadbourne's aesthetic. He dissolves every extraneous consideration, every fetish dear to professionalism, in favour of the *communiqué* that matters. And arrives at spidery arabesques of great beauty.

The banjo is to the fore, and many songs become wild, strychnine-laced work-outs. 'I'm Gonna Booglarize You, Baby' is expanded with sitar, didgeridoo and bassoon: an etiolated baroque of scavenger debris. Chadbourne's version of Improv includes huckster comedy, live-album asides, lo-fi atrocities. It is the essential corrective to the pressure to elevate Free Improvisation to the art-plinth. The real test is repeated listening, and the album gets better every play. Beneath the chaos, Chadbourne and Black grasp the structure of the songs, and they never make a sound that isn't fervently felt.

Black's collaboration with guitarist and singer Richard Ray Farrell recalls the music he made with Geronimo Black in the '70s: heavy R&B/Soul. John Mayall's nephew plays sax. Loose production abets the Blues Festival feel. Bar-room blues with true grit, a glistening solidity rock bands rarely catch. You think it's hopelessly out-dated, then one night you go out drinking and hear some in the flesh: you discover that your dedication to ponce-assed limey fashions has been depriving you of good times. Anyone who can do the 'Blueberry Hill' lilt with this much dignity ('Can't Get Over Losin' You') has something Dire Straits will never learn. Farrell's guitar on 'Sweet Thing' is magisterial and urgent. Beefheart's 'Sho 'Nuff'N Yes, I Do' and Zappa's 'Road Ladies' are brought back into the hard blues genre they never really left. The R&B Revival starts here.

The Music of Captain Beefheart is played by a posse of Swedes blessed with a virtuosity that is downright scary. Slide guitarist Denny Walley had tenure in the Magic Band, but it's the chilling precision of the Morgan Agren/Rolf Hedqvist rhythm section that impresses. There have been many attempts to repeat Beefheart's 'impossible' rhythms, but these musos have got it down so cold it is ludicrous. They have even found a singer, Freddie Wadling, who can rumble and warble correctly. However, like all reproductions, you end up wondering what the point is, merely noting that it lacks the succulent miasma and brutal unmusicality of the original. It'd be amusing to see them tour, though: the Swedish Captain Beefheart (in a bill with the Tooting Blind Lemon and the Australian Doors, of course). Chadbourne's improv/lo-fi approach subsumes Beefheart's songs to his own personality. However, by approaching the music so clinically, the Swedes unpick it. If there are any composers out there working on Nancarrow-style rhythmic extrapolation, these would be the musicians to use.

* * * * * * *

Anthony Coleman
Selfhaters
Tzadik TZ7116

ANTHONY COLEMAN makes confrontational music, art-jazz primitivism begging for a political explanation. 'Hidden Language' has harsh, discordant winds and pummelling percussion. Wild, almost infantile lack of tonal control is martialled by a tight rhythmic discipline reminiscent of Noh Theatre. Like Loos or Polwechsel, the viciousness of art precision is combined with the dramatic impact of rock. 'Bim' could be a Lettriste Doo-Wop ensemble performing BYG classics by Jacques Coursil. Rabble-rousing *klezmer* clarinets are deconstructed into dirges. The Broadway standard 'I Don't Know What Love Is' becomes an occasion for long held squeals, sad dropouts, the leader's melancholic trombone.

Bass and drum sonorities associated with the propulsion of funk and rock are held back for serene art contemplation. This could almost be Canterbury rock, but there is no relief in whimsy. Duke Ellington's 'The Mooche' seems to be played on car-horns, cardboard-boxes and police whistles: a Beckett play where the clowning suddenly turns tarnished and tearful. Organ and accordion supply fairground moments arresting in their cheesiness.

'Goodbye And Good Luck' has *klezmer* clarinet and a Jewish story: vaudeville with a tragicomic edge. As usual with John Zorn's Tzadik label, the packaging is eloquent: the term 'selfhaters' is apparently part of a Jewish pride movement. Marx and Freud are reduced to specimens of cultural betrayal, and the music trembles with irony and sarcasm. Only in New York.

* * * * * * *

Joe Maneri Quartet
Dahabenzapple
Hat Art CD6188
Mat Maneri Trio
Fever Bed
Leo Lab CD022

WITH ONE eerie warble, Joe Maneri blows away the retro-blues of the neo-cons: new ways *can* be found to play the saxophone! Playing Greek weddings in New York, Maneri explored Arab-inflected metres and microtones. His late exposure (he was born in 1928) guarantees a fully-fledged style that musos fresh-out-of-Berklee cannot possibly manage.

Maneri is probably best known for *Three Men Walking* (ECM). The label's dislike of the funky side of things led them to choose the greyest music played by that band, while their publicity emphasized the fact that the saxophonist studied with a pupil of Alban Berg.

Those who attended Maneri's lecture on 'microtonal improvisation' at the South Bank last year were in for a big surprise: the man is a sharp-talking, street-sussed New York character. He could talk the balls off Carnegie Hall. For Maneri, 'microtonality' is an excuse to subvert classical repression and celebrate the vocalised rule-bending that has characterised blues and jazz from the start.

Not that Maneri plays 'comedy music'. Glancing, halting group improvisations wend themselves into reflective backwaters jazz has never found before. Joe's son Mat plays violin according to the same methodology. Cecil McBee's bass is as sturdy as you'd expect from a veteran (he's played for Yusef Lateef, Alice Coltrane, Abdullah Ibrahim), but he's utterly committed to Maneri's concept. The quartet's interaction is uncanny; they breathe together. *Fever Bed*, Mat's own record, is great too. In Ed Schuller he's found the strong, melodic bassist necessary if trio music is going to fill the air. The magical, suggestive music of the Maneris erodes the Euro-divide between spontaneous wit and deep thought.

A fat Sicilian who looks like he might sell you a barrel of olive oil brings on his hip, violin-playing son; they proceed to save jazz from the drones. It's a great story; what's more, it's true.

* * * * * * *

Katharine Norman
London
NMC D034 CD

KATHARINE NORMAN makes DAT street recordings, but wisely doesn't suppose mere technology can justify the price of a CD. She montages her sources using loops, digital tinctures and overlays. Despite such techniques, *London* is not aimed at New Age listeners (who also require a pile of lush triads before they will step on the magic carpet).

Use of environmental recording is a hotly contested topic. John Cage's Zen-like pronouncements about 'surrender to nature' and 'transcending human intention' left a poor conceptual legacy, one in which less scrupulously inventive artists have floundered. Cage's actual compositions were challenging and incongruous, almost perverse in the way each new work drew attention the material mediation of musical ideas, yet his name is now regularly cited by people who wish to give therapeutic mindwash, muzak, and mainstream pop—surely the most socially conformist sonics available—an 'avant-garde' *cachet*. Norman prefers to cite Sergei Eisenstein.

'London' begins with Norman's mother talking in her front room about doodle-bugs and the Blitz. Sonic filtres reminiscent of Laurie Anderson colour her voice, but this merely serves to emphasize the *distance* between inhabitants of East End terrace houses and artsy New Yorkers. A stroll down Walthamstow Market alerts us to the hilarious patchwork of accents that make up a cosmopolitan working class; we end up in foot tunnels beneath the Thames. The succession of recording ambiences—living room, street, reverberant tiled cylinder—stays in the mind like an abstract composition, but one made up of myriad details amusingly familiar to any Londoner ('mind the gap!'). 'Trilling Wire' has Jonathan Cooper play Braxtonish, high-pressure clarinet against a tape-collage. It demonstrates that Norman's skill at documentary montage comes from the same insistence on musical event that created the supposedly 'inaccessible' soundworld of Darmstadt modernism.

'London' recalls Walter Ruttman's pioneering blank-screen sound 'film' of 1930 Berlin, *Weekend* (now released by Metamkiné). It uses new technology to help us imagine the complex reality of the city. In her sleeve notes, Norman says that it was the Gulf War which made her think of asking her mother to talk about the Blitz. Although there are oldsters around with more pointedly political things to say (that the famous use of the tube system as underground shelters was only granted by the authorities after riots and Communist Party agitation, for example), Norman's interest in the historical and social resonance of her sonic materials has a musical tension lacking in the fatuous 'deep listening' proposed by Cage's epigones.

* * * * * * *

Iggy Pop
Naughty Little Doggie
Virgin Records VUSMC102

ON HIS last tour Iggy Pop started talking about reincarnation. Throughout the world, the militants of Materialist Esthetix trembled. Had one of their most inspirational cadre deserted? Had settled life in California washed the Ig brain with New Age gloop? 'I want to come back as a great black poodle,' he announced, 'and my mistress will wear a miniskirt, and I'll jump all over her long legs....' Phew. The title of this likewise reasserts the 'Now I Wanna Be Your Dog' Fundamentalism of the original Stooges. The Iggy sound is a modern classic. It's so alert to its function that there is no place for the ornament and veils that conventionally attract the dusts of time; so pared-down it cannot date.

Naughty Little Doggie opens with 'I Wanna Live', powered by a riff so primal you think it must be stolen, but as usual with Iggy it's new (another one for Mark E. Smith to swipe, in other words). Guitar sound is lush, each power chord bursting forth like an iridescent peacock's tail. The lyric is a militant statement of rock'n'roll attitude (compare The Ramones' 'I'm Not Afraid of Life'), though Iggy is witty enough to acknowledge twenty-seven years in the business by adding 'a little bit longer...now' to the 'I wanna live' refrain.

'Pussy Walk' is a hard swinging lust anthem, cut with the broken caterwaul Iggy debuted on *Zombie Birdhouse*. Listen to the pumping friction of bass versus lead and you're hearing an electric combo play Count Basie; it's authentic Yankee *rawk* in other words. Bliss. 'Innocent World' touches the bathroom-song unconcern Morrissey learned from Jonathan Richman, while 'Knucklehead' is New York Dolls frenzy with better bass push, plus frothing guitar-pools from Eric Schermerhorn; as usual Iggy transcends the tug between heavy metal luxuriance and hardcore Puritanism by sticking his voice in at the moment of guitar-note production. He makes his guitarists sweat, there's no escape. 'To Belong' is a swelling moment of philosophical reflection on the spiritual plight of America: 'To belong here, I'm giving up my soul....'

'Keep on Believing' has the pile-drive insistence on limited notes that connects Evan Parker's minimalism to punk (if only he knew). Like the prose of William Burroughs, there's a whiff of atrocity about such a scorching-off of the usual civilised wrapper. Sensitive people shy away, but they should grasp that what doesn't kill you makes you strong. 'Outta My Head' is a chiming hillbilly mantra-fest that recalls the Velvets and threatens to revive the execrable 'We Will Fall', the John Cale-fuelled mistake on the Stooges otherwise-classic debut. 'Shoeshine Girl' is one of Iggy's 'Cookie McBride'-style folk ballads, Ewan MacColl caught down on his luck in a Detroit rail tunnel with a bunch of pill-popping delinquents. 'Heart Is Saved' is *Soldier*-era slob rock with added heavy momentum. The closer, 'Look Away', is somewhat overblown, enervated, droning, but a pleasant enough chill-out after the muscular exertions of earlier tracks.

Rock stars used to be expected to 'progress', now they are celebrated if they simply 'survive'. With *Naughty Little Doggie*, you realise that Iggy's rock is still more directed, expressive and honest than anything the young fry have come up with all year.

* * * * * * *

Various
Moods of the Day—Morning Ragas
Decca 448675 CD
Moods of the Day—Afternoon Ragas
Decca 448676 CD
Moods of the Day—Evening Ragas
Decca 448677 CD
Moods of the Day—Night Ragas
Decca 448678 CD

DIPPING INTO its vast archive of Indian classical, Bombay PolyGram packages four CDs with nature photographs evoking the four parts of the day. They could have called the series, *New Age: It All Started Here*. Instead, the booklet (same text repeated in each) headlines a remark made by conductor Zubin Mehta to the *Indian Express*: 'India does not need an involvement with Western music since it has a beautiful legacy of its own classical music, and fusion just does not work.'

The notes explain 'some technical differences between Indian and Western classical music', indicating the intended audience: Tchaikovsky listeners. But how does it sound to *Wire*-ears buzzing with multicultural crosstalk and street invention? Excellent, actually. These are the big cheese performers: Pandits Hariprasad Chaurasia (bamboo, six-hole flute), Ram Narayan (sarangi, an instrument with 4 bowed strings and up to forty resonating ones), Brij Narayan (sarod, a twenty-five-string lute) and Shivkumar Sharma (santoor, a zither) with Anindo Chatterji and Dilshad Khan on tablas.

Experts who 'explain' Indian classical music by pointing to its sixteen-beat raags and complex scales create a similar obstacle as sleeve notes to symphonies which list scherzos and retrogrades: alienation of the non-technical listener. Actually, you *don't* have to count out these raags to sense how they structure the improvised flights. If you respond to the communicative pluck of guitars played in blues, jazz or rock, this playing speaks.

This music contains tougher stuff than the shimmer plundered by 'scene-painting' fourth-world eclectics. Areas of intimate fiddle well up like liquid pools inside the counted structures. The confidence with which the tabla player taps out the delicate filigree of sub-beats to the melodies is touching, an echo of wholeness from a smashed civilisation.

Classical Indian music's refusal to play the update game is its strength, but also its limit. Unlike jazz, this form can't eat other musics for breakfast. Still, the fresh glee of its improvising remains a reproach to the jaded seen-it-alls of postmodernism, for whom all tradition is a dusty closed book: a tonic, the, rather than a solution.

~*1997*~

Andrew Blake
*The Land Without Music: Music, Culture and Society in
    Twentieth-Century Britain*
Manchester University Press

THE TITLE refers to Germany's description of Britain during World
War I. Andrew Blake, a Professor of Cultural Studies at Winchester,
wants to contest that judgment. His discipline is regularly dissed in
these pages. Maybe it's simply academia getting too close for comfort; a quick list of *Wire* faves for a dose of theory—Benjamin,
Adorno, Barthes, Deleuze, Jameson, McClary, Plant—shows many
mentors in common. Andrew Blake's book stems from seminars
held at the University of East London. Marshall Berman's *All That
Is Solid Melts into Air* provided a basis for discussion. Again, a *Wire*
resonance: Kodwo Eshun began his review of David Toop's *Ocean
of Sound* with his coinage 'all that is solid melts into aether' (*Wire*
141).
     The provenance of this much-quoted phrase tends to be forgot-
ten. It's from *The Communist Manifesto*. As often when classic in-
sights are recycled, elements go missing. Marx was not describing a
natural, eternal property of things, but a historical event with an
agent: it is capitalist economic 'progress' that does the melting. And
in *The Communist Manifesto*, the response called for is not postmodern giddiness, but proletarian realism. The full quote runs: 'All
that is solid melts into air, all that is holy is profaned, and people are
at last compelled to face with sober senses, their real conditions of
life, and their relations with their kind.'
     Blake is no Marxist (his politics steer closer to *laissez-faire* an-
archism), but he too wants to cut through to something real. He has
sung in choirs and played saxophone (he was in Man Jumping, an
'80s jazz/minimalist outfit he admits would be 'stretching a point' to
call Canterbury Rock). This grasp of music as a material practice
enables him to puncture various myths. Herbert von Karajan's obitu-

arists regretted the 'smoothness' and 'brutality' of his conducting. Blake shows that this mysterious quality stemmed from Karajan's insistence on adequate rehearsal-time and state-of-the-art recording, both rare in London. The classical establishment's critical standards are exposed as ignorant and parochial.

An opponent of what he calls Rock Romanticism, Blake points out that Jimmy Page achieved his guitar sound by miking his amplifier twenty feet from behind (rather than by studying Aleister Crowley and taking drugs). An illuminating dissection of musical 'Englishness'—Benjamin Britten organising the Aldeburgh Festival in rural Sussex with financial backing from the BBC, Faber and Decca—echoes Eric Hobsbawn: in the hands of a technocratic ruling class, 'tradition' is a fabrication. The musical cement of 'patriotic' nostalgia—Glenn Miller and the Inkspots—reveals the same dependence on America as military victory in World War II. Here, Blake's musical investigations unite personal and political history.

However, though he defends Adorno's dialectical method (whilst contesting his judgments), Blake's sociology is closer to Chicago School market-research than to Frankfurt School Marxism. Hostile to both Punk and the New Complexity, Blake sees all assaults on the mainstream as arrogant and elitist. Here he adopts the patronising, peculiarly middle-class version of postmodernism: let's surrender 'elite' culture for 'the popular', and everything in the garden is lovely. So Susan McClary's reverence for Madonna is defended versus radical-rave theorists Simon Reynolds and Joy Press (whose partisan views are attacked as Adornian: 'if it sounds bad, it's good'). Blake concludes by commending the Classical Lite of Judith Weir and Mark-Anthony Turnage; apparently they break with the 'male elitism' of 'establishment Modernism'. As in McClary's *Feminine Endings*, what starts as brave critique lapses into apology for the South Bank/Sunday papers status-quo. Lo-fi, Free Improvisation, new compositional strategies by Braxton, Zorn, Barrett and Fell all indicate that Blake is falling for false, conformist answers to real musical and social dilemmas.

Blake's own account of the origins of Radio 2—from ENSA, which organised entertainment for the troops, to the Light Programme's *Music While You Work*—shows how easy-listening and non-serious music were deployed to serve the needs of national capital. Although a severe critic of Little-Englandism (and scoring PC-points by calling Britpop racist), the only way forward for Blake is the market. Bhangra and Ambient, for example, are vaunted for their potential contribution towards the British export drive. So Blake cannot criticise the economic basis of patriotism: the interests of said national capital. The contradictions of commerce and populism require more careful unpicking than this.

Blake's formal analysis also suffers from reluctance to pinpoint contradiction. Despite attacks on traditional musicology as 'mere description', that charge can be levelled at his graphical exposition of Colosseum's 'Valentyne Suite'. If, instead of resorting to positivist notation, Blake interpreted form as a site of conflict, he might register how commercialism tends to reduce music to an ever-same, to product-for-the-solvent rather than a life-changing experience. However, since this can only be revealed by showing up the aesthetic limitations of mainstream product—a practice Blake condemns as 'elitist' and 'Modernist'—such sober assessment of the real conditions of music never arrives.

Writing like someone who has never been poor, Blake is blind to the harsh denials hidden behind consumer choice. Instead, commercialism is celebrated because it 'enriches' the culture—by supplying a diversity niche-marketed to precisely the identities market-research sets up in the first place! It is amazing that a commentator who grounds his approach in history and a tough assessment of musical form cannot grasp the profound connection between musical innovation and revolt against market categories (the '20s and '60s seeing crucial developments in both). If Blake understood how avant-garde dissent keeps such ideas and possibilities alive, maybe he wouldn't dismiss *The Wire* as an 'anorakzine'; and maybe *Land Without Music* could explain why, although *laissez-faire* capitalism makes every cultural certainty melt into air, certain economic iniquities remain strangely insoluble.

* * * * * * *

Luther Thomas
BAGin' It
CIMP #112 CD

LAST TIME Luther Thomas was in London, he was playing classic-soul baritone behind James Chance. The king of punkjazz lounge nihilism doesn't use just any saxophone player. Luther Thomas emerged in Missouri in the late '60s, where he joined the Black Artists Group (the acronym explains the weird album title). This was St. Louis's answer to Chicago's AACM, a self-help organisation committed to musician-defined music and Free Jazz. As Joe

Bowie's Defunkt attests, BAG players have a strong feel for street-level grooves. In 1981, Luther had his own shot at No Wave funk with a band he called Dizzazz.

This is 'pure' acoustic 'jazz', but Luther's aesthetic imbues every note with soul. Much as it offends the categorical mentality, which would like acoustic music to be tasteful and timeless, Free Jazz is as much about bringing the verities of porch blues and gospel into the public sphere as it is about aspiration to high-art abstraction. The band consists of Luther on alto, Ted Daniel on trumpet, Wilber Morris on bass and Denis Charles on drums. Everyone plays with the character and weight that is specific to the Afro-American tradition: there is none of the blandness that is the curse of collegiate musicianship.

'Swimming Lake Oliver' sets up an airy groove, the horns chittering at each other, a hovering sense of expectancy created by the listening openness of bass and drums. Aylerish solemnity is leavened by Ornetteish playfulness. The way Luther breaks into Daniel's solo is at once supportive and challenging, like stumbling over a joke in a dense paragraph by Hegel. 'Tag (You're It)' is a game of pass-the-musical-idea. It works better than many contrived 'concepts' in both Improv and Classical because all four players are so buoyant in their musical current (none of the blush-making creaks of Steve Beresford's ghastly *Fish of the Week*, for example). 'Don't Tell' is finger-poppin' and folksy like a superior Don Cherry tune; 'Kool Aid' is bop-for-the-hell-of-it, bright fountains of virtuosic tension spraying up between chunks of melody. 'As If It Were Love' features plangent rhapsody from Luther's alto: a tender trio encounter unmatched in contemporary jazz.

Art is symbolic politics, mimicry of social stances and attitudes. By playing acoustic harmolodics with a dash of punk humour ('For Don C') or making sophisticated full-throttle art out of the fractured music of the socially defeated (the broken blues of 'Don't Tell'), the Luther Thomas Quartet recall the way Paul Klee and Max Ernst learned from the art of the insane. The bulletins of Political Correctness issued from the Lincoln Center by Stanley Crouch—a critical pontiff who wants Jazz to achieve the cultural authority of opera—can only see such high-tech infatuation with humble acoustic hoe-downs as perverse and degenerate. To these ears, Luther Thomas's application of cutting-edge musicianship to the pleasures of realtime spontaneity and chance is incredibly moving.

* * * * * * *

Edgard Varèse
The Complete Works
DECCA 460208 CD

IN 1924, composer Edgard Varèse (1883-1965) and his *Hyperprism* were denounced by London's *Evening News* as 'Bolshevism in music'. Seventy-three years later, the French modernist has come to occupy a key position in today's genre-wars. Notorious for his sirens, Theremins, industrial-tape interludes and cataclysms of (carefully researched) ethnic percussion, Varèse was never embraced by the musical establishment. Only a handful of composers—Iannis Xenakis, Pierre Boulez, James Dillon, Iancu Dumitrescu—show signs of having understood his futurist intent. And however much one admires these later composers, it is debatable whether they have taken Varèse's shockworld further, or simply recuperated it to statistical or orchestral schemas.

Varèse's music delivers on promises made by the Italian Futurists (whose thousand-volt rhetoric was belied by Russolo's feeble compositions). His idea of contrasting sound blocks, montaged like colours and shapes in an abstract painting, is inspirational to those for whom resort to traditional form implies acceptance of divisions of class and culture. In a debate broadcast on Resonance FM, DJ Si Begg managed to unite a panel of musical dissidents (including free improvisors, academic composers, goth-rockers, designer concept-engineers, guitarist anti-intellectuals and a lone Frankfurter) with an enthusiastic description of playing Varèse to techno fans in the early hours. Varèse holds out the prospect that 'classical' (or 'rational') organisation could be stripped of its class trappings and speak to those in love with the sheer noise of electric guitars, feedback sizzle and bass-speaker reverb.

This double CD-pack tries for a definitive Varèse. It's well played (Royal Concertgebouw Orchestra, Asko Ensemble) and conducted (Riccardo Chailly), and the recording has a spatial depth that improves on previous attempts. Hearing a new performance of a score (plus some tweaks by Varèse's collaborator Cho Wen-chung) freshens up one's concept of the music. Though most classical reviewing ('Rattle takes the third movement a little slow for my liking....') seems designed to avoid any assessment of the music itself, it is unarguable that the score *can* give music a multi-dimensionality lacking in genres (rock, dub, electronica) where the master-tape is the work of art. With Varèse, the game is worth the candle.

However, *Wire* ears are CD-oriented. Consumer barbarians that we are, we judge a disc by what it delivers rather than by what it tells us about a 'great composer'. Here, the decision to include works Varèse himself discarded (*Tuning Up, Un Grand Sommeil Noir, Dance for Burgess*) dilutes its impact. Producer Andrew Cornall refers to *Poème Électronique*—a 1958 work that signalled the future for Varèse—as 'one of his tapes of 'organised sound'' (the condescension of those quote-marks shows how Varèse still offends classical propriety). Tracks are cued too quickly, so that follow-ons impinge on the standalone majesty of the individual constructs.

Nevertheless, this is still some of the mightiest music ever made (Eric Dolphy's *Out to Lunch* was epochal because it was the sound of jazz players taking on board these ideas). In *Arcana*, a lions' roar (a greased string pulled through a resonant box) answers the brass with a timbral groan rather than a 'note', anticipating bassists like Bill Laswell and Joelle Léandre. In *Offrandes*, the initial trumpet motif etches itself into the brain like a schizo-pink zigzag in a late Kandinsky. Impressionist forces—a soprano, a harp—are freed from their oceanic miasma to become sonic symbols deployed in the full glare of reason. Pipping woodwinds recall Morse code. In *Octandre*, the harmony is less atonal than alchemical, the layered instruments generating weird synaesthetic effects, like tasting the leads of a battery and hearing metallic orange sing. *Intégrales* is all nervous tension and waiting, the epilepsis that precedes orgasmic release, Richard Strauss's pioneering effects retrieved from operatic kitsch. *Ecuatorial* is a sci-fi B-movie for the ears featuring an intoning Incan priest, diabolized church-organ, swooping Theremins and a drum apocalypse. *Density 21.5*, four minutes of solo flute, proves that it's not exaggerated volume or instrumentation that makes Varèse so transfixing, but control of proportion in time: what looks like a recipe for effete prettiness becomes as chromium hard and alien as anything here.

After Varèse, all twentieth-century classical music is disappointing. This is why—in the virtual realm of listening autonomy, if not in the dreary concert-halls of official postmodernism—his devastating music opens the door to the virtues of Doo Wop, Dub and Free Jazz. The New Bolshevism in Music starts here.

~1998~

Bassholes
Blue Roots
Revenant RNT 204

I DIDN'T WANT to like Bassholes. First, they've got a stupid name. Second, although the packaging conforms to Revenant's classy house-style, the two boys in the band (Don Howland, guitar and vocals; Rich Lillash, drums) put a girl showing her nipple on the cover. I wanted to dismiss them as careless trash-hounds, along with the PC-baiting sleeve notes (by Dick 'Blues Boy' Rosenthal) extolling the virtues of horny-macho workerism. But then I played the disc....

Rosenthal states: 'The two-man style heard here is, in some respects, a musical outgrowth of the great Columbus corncob bands of the '20s and '30s.' It's certainly recorded that way: a scabrous, paper-thin, sepia-tinged, lo-fi rumble...but, how this music *rocks*! Bassholes will appear in heavy type in the next edition of Joe Carducci's *Rock and the Pop Narcotic*. They're the Neanderthal offspring of The Fall and the Magic Band ('Nakema'), Link Wray and 'Funky Drummer' ('Light Bulb Boogie'): a significant achievement.

Revenant have released avant-garderie by Cecil Taylor and Derek Bailey, old-time bluegrass by the Stanley Brothers and a convocation of psychotic '20s gospel (*American Primitives Vol. 1*). The label has successfully isolated the strain of raw weird annoying *scratchiness* that marks great music (from Sun Records through to Shannon Jackson and Caroline Kraabel). On 'Bald-Headed Woman Blues,' Howland's guitar achieves an out-of-tune stomp as brash and brazen as Ivy Rorschach's. 'Sleepyman Blues' sounds like an out-take from an out-take of *Kill City*, an audio abortion even the bootleggers threw in the garbage. On 'Missing Linkster,' Lillash makes Thunders/Pistols chaos walk again, while 'Candyman Blues' sucks better than the New York Dolls. Maybe even *Bob Dylan* could be one of us ('Titanic Blues')! Freaky.

An aging punk wakes up on a bleak polluted morning. It dawns upon him that, all along, he's been committed to a heresy as antique as Heraclitus and Giordano Bruno and Josef Dietzgen, as ageless as the stars. I'm gonna buy a copy of *Blue Roots* for my girlfriend's brother's birthday. Yes I am. Rock'n'roll! What a thing. Phew.

* * * * * * *

Eugene Chadbourne
Jungle Cookies
Old Gold 3/4 2CD
Insect Attracter
Leo LR256 CD

JUNGLE COOKIES arrives in a plastic bag. There's a six-page magazine (a sub-heading warns 'more and more weird noise, combined in a manner to make it as incomprehensible as possible'), plus two CDs inside a page of colour photocopy folded so that the resulting size sits comfortably next to neither records, compact discs or tapes. It's an old ploy: make the product as annoying as possible, and see if there are any takers for that. The music likewise.

Chadbourne explains that his version of Jungle was inspired by Derek Bailey sitting at home playing guitar to Hackney's pirate-radio DJs. He preferred these informal domestic jams (unreleased because of fears of offending copyright) to the Avant label's official—and much praised—*guitar, drums'n'bass*. The idea of Bailey collaborating with someone without their knowing it was key. *Jungle Cookies* uses recordings made on Amsterdam's Haringpakker Steeg at all hours of the day and night, threading street documentary through Chadbourne's own sped-up drum tracks and banjo playing, plus contributions (usually unwitting) from such Amsterdam luminaries as saxophonists Luc Houtkamp and Walter Malli, banjoists Tony Trischka and Volcmar Vercerk, Chadbourne's daughters Molly and Lizzie, plus an open-air gig featuring 'rock legends' Lenny Kaye and Jimmy Carl Black. Chadbourne follows John Cage's injunction to listen to the sounds of everyday life, but insists on the present-day composer's right to edit the results. Zen self-denial is booted out the window.

The resulting chaos is introduced by Molly Chadbourne's corrosive 'meltdown' of Madonna, where packaged glamour is sabotaged by lyrics about the gunk between your toenails, and proceeds to a 15-minute epic that weaves a skipping Stockhausen LP into the juddering remains of a Sammy Davis Junior CD vandalised by a year-long burial in Eugene's backyard. Swathes of rubbish, ejactamenta, and stupidity ('speed ecstasy does not exist!' shouts a dealer) are programmed by someone with a keen ear for surprise. Chadbourne is particularly sensitive to sensations of depth created by his sound sources and achieves many a superb jump from vista to close-up. Paradoxically, it's the continual disorientation and surprise of the segues that gives *Jungle Cookies* coherence and character. Just when you're prepared to dismiss the whole monstrosity as random garbage, some intricate interaction occurs that could not have been set up other than by Chadbourne's perverse procedures. The whole two-hour thing has an easy flow that is very different from the muscular decisiveness of Zorn or the gleeful non-sequiturs of Ground Zero.

Insect Attracter consists of realtime improvisations. It nevertheless benefits from Chadbourne's insistence that, however democratic the ethos of Free Improvisation, he is going to splice and edit in order to craft a worthwhile disc. Chadbourne's rock-fan feel for 'product' saves him from the *longueurs* of conceptual-art proceduralism. Calling his music 'Insect & Western', Chadbourne associates the agitated, scratchy sound of his banjo—and Mischa Feigin's balalaika and Gino Robair's mandolin—with the fidgety movements of crickets and termites. 'Mourning of the Praying Mantis' is a haunting suite: slow modulations spiced by nervy, tentative playing, as if a bunch of Cajun string-players had discovered the Italian composer Giacinto Scelsi's experiments with timbre. 'Termite Damage' features hilarious funk-in-quotes from Chattanooga's Shaking Ray Levis: the music appears to disintegrate, but the band swing just as hard through the silences as through the outbursts. 'The Cricket in My Life' is a concerto for Carrie Shull's classical-sounding oboe, Chadbourne's hokey banjo sounding deliriously incongruous. Pat Thomas bridges the gap with piano that is alternately classically sonorous and slyly funky.

A final bluegrass breakout indicates that however wide Chadbourne casts his net (Thelonious Monk's 'Misterioso'; car-horn symphonies; the stop/start 'game' piece 'The Swat'; Alex Ward's atonal classicism), everything is refitted from an agit-pop, DIY-folk point of view. His magisterial feel for time (the trump card of any dialectician) enables his musicians to shine like they have on few previous recordings. On this showing, Chadbourne's Appalachian Marxism (what he calls his 'communist banjo') is just the medicine Improv requires.

* * * * * * *

Charlie Feathers
Get with It
Revenant 209
Jenks 'Tex' Carman
Chippeha!
Revenant 207
Various
16 Down Home Country Classics
Arhoolie CD110

CHARLIE FEATHERS is the great lost rockabilly. Like Elvis, Jerry Lee Lewis, Carl Perkins and Johnny Cash, he recorded for Sam Philips' Sun label in the mid-'50s, but his stab at the big time—'Defrost Your Heart,' released in January 1956 (Sun 231)—sold a measly 919 copies. He subsequently cut sides for Meteor, King, Kay and WalMay—in 1962 he and Bill Haley were on a label sold from Holiday Inn gift shops—but without success. Sun obsessives, though, have always had time for Charlie Feathers. In 1968, British rockabilly collector and retailer Dan Coffey took him into a studio. Now John Fahey's Revenant—the label which holds that pre-war gospel, bluegrass, lo-fi rock (The Bassholes), avant-garde jazz (Cecil Taylor) and free improvisation (Derek Bailey) all evince a similar aesthetic—have granted Charlie Feathers a de-luxe, double-disc release.

The booklet features a superfine poem-in-prose by Nick Tosches, a report by Peter Guralnick on Feathers performing at the Hilltop Lounge in Memphis, and detailed track-notes by Colin Escott (the English author responsible for classic accounts of Hank Williams and Sun Records). It's printed in red and gold on shiny art-paper. Vintage photos of Feathers and colleagues turn from black to gold under the light: spectral glimpses of the period when American culture mutated and gave birth to the global phenomenon we know today. Page numbers are printed inside minuscule reproductions of the labels on the original seven-inch singles. The care and expense of the packaging suggest Revenant want to rewrite history, redress wrongs, buck the rule that says music must sell a million before it matters.

Disc one collects together Feathers' commercial releases, disc two unissued tracks. As Feathers' thin hillbilly plaint sets up 'I've Been Deceived,' it's evident that he's blessed with the authentic rockabilly strain. Recorded at Sun for its subsidiary Flip, the double-stopped fiddle (on the break, its keening cry made the more effective by broken whistling accompaniment), weeping steel guitar and steady-tempo electric guitar have an unstoppable momentum: emotions hammered into fence-wire. 'Peepin' Eyes' is a mid-tempo barn dance: falsetto accompaniment to Feathers' voice on the chorus makes it doubly effective. As Escott points out, 'Defrost Your Heart' outdoes George Jones for pathos: Feathers' vocal inflections are amazingly nuanced, with the shocking *presentness* that arrives when singers are forging as-yet-unattested styles. 'Get with It' and 'One Hand Loose' are rockabilly dynamite, the explosion that occurs when a bunch of hicks decide they'll rock the joint as hard as any swing combo they've hear on the radio. 'Bottle to the Baby' is replete with Gene Vincent-style hiccoughs, evincing the proto-epileptic craziness that drives all true rock'n'roll. This is blackface minstrelsy that has binned the burnt cork and invited in everyone for a crazy time. Just flick that plastic comb through your hair and get real *gone* for a change: an individualism *possessed* rather than possessive. In later years, Feathers simmers down. Like Elvis at RCA, the King recordings sound stage-managed, though the vocal acrobatics on 'When You Decide' and 'When You Come Around' are still priceless. By 1959, he's trying western numbers to appease the folk fad (released under the name 'Charlie Morgan'). The country pop of 1962 is indifferent.

Disc two is patchier, footnotes to the *oeuvre*. Again, the drear influence of 'Tom Dooley' makes itself felt (on 'Talkin' About Lovin',' Feathers performs a vocal gimmick worthy of Rolf Harris). Covers of bluegrass and country hits exhibit a reined-in style. There's also a pleasing jam with Junior Kimbrough (an early 'cottonpatch blues' inspiration). Though Guralnick argues otherwise, it doesn't seem likely that Feathers could still be capable of the trembling zaniness of 1956. Like Cubism and Bebop, rockabilly was a *moment* rather than a genre.

If you're looking for the missing link between George Formby and Tiny Tim, Revenant can help; his name is Jenks 'Tex' Carman. Billed as the Dixie Cowboy, he sang songs in Cherokee and played Hawaiian guitar. His astonishing evocations of trains and battles are surely one of the many roots of Eugene Chadbourne's guitarism.

The disc is packaged and annotated with Revenant's customary finesse; out-of-time eccentricities are thereby given a strange glamour, like someone with a vast record collection who insists on playing you something impossibly rare—but also rather ghastly. A US Air Force recruitment-broadcast tells more about '50s America than Hollywood would ever let you know. Fascinating.

If Revenant have successfully launched Country Music into the stratosphere of cool, it may be time for *16 Down Home Country Classics*. Cheekily titled, this isn't a collection of vintage hits at all, but a sampler from the Arhoolie label ('at a down home price,' a sticker promises). It's still brilliant. Rose Maddox and the Strange Creek Singers glory in their fiercely non-standard vowel-sounds, while the virtuoso banjos and violins spit fire. The Armstrong Twins' 'Eight Thirty Blues' has bravura picking that plays more games with the tempo than bop allows, let alone rock. As a Maddox brother exclaims during a guitar break: 'I can't stand it, it's driving me insane!'

If the roots of rock are this fantastic, how come the flowers on offer today look so sad?

* * * * * * *

Roscoe Mitchell Trio
The Day and the Night
DIZIM 4101 CD
Lake-Workman-Cyrille
Trio 3: Live in Willisau
DIZIM 4102 CD

ROSCOE MITCHELL made his name with the Art Ensemble of Chicago, but as a player he's best heard away from the AEC's theatrical approach. In '60s Chicago, jazz discovered how to use space and silence; Roscoe keeps that tradition alive. He opens with an eight-minute outing on flute, his burgeoning sense of melody holding the pace, Gerald Cleaver's percussion touching off a sparse yet richly-varied universe of sounds. Bassist Malachi Favors tracks Roscoe's line without reducing it to metrical banality. John Cage's Zen lost-ness is brought back into breathing song. Roscoe has his own rustic sound on alto, tenor and bass sax, using a slo-mo weightiness to make his musical production something much more than a run-through. Favors and Cleaver know how to mess with the beat, arriving at things that sound casual, even careless: this frames Roscoe's expressive individualism in appropriately distressed patterns. When Coltrane played with Ornette's band on *The Avant-Garde* he had something of this querulous uncertainty; he was put down for it by the critics, but Roscoe shows there are worlds here that seamless confidence cannot broach. 'For Lester B' is a restructuralist's tenor ballad, level notes dropped in at such strange-yet-logical intervals it's like listening to a cubist painting.

Altoist Oliver Lake's music is more rhythmically driven. He springs from the St. Louis scene; its musicians have always had a stronger R&B streak than their Chicago counterparts. Lake is an authentic proponent of his horn's Louis Jordan/Bird/Dolphy lineage: tensile brilliance, coil and spring, pirouette flash. Like Reggie Workman (bass) and Andrew Cyrille (drums), Lake knows *exactly* what he's doing. When Lake squeals up high it isn't last-flabbergast expressionist exhaustion, but a deliberate panel in an architected structure, the distinction between spontaneous gesture and grand plan erased. People who can't hear into jazz procedure think the stuff all sounds the same, but once you cotton on, the splice of intuitive ensemble groove and sudden conscious twists and rhythmic proposals can be intoxicating. As here.

On 'Shell' Cyrille plays a drum solo that in terms of space, surprise, wit and cunning timbral contrast could serve as a lesson for any number of symphonic and electronic pretenders to organising sound. Workman (who's played with everyone from Coltrane to Company) is wondrously resonant, drenching everything in classy funk. On 'Wha's 9' his convoluted riff is so infectious that it should be immediately be stolen—Ian Dury-style—by some enterprising drum'n'bass producer. The large Willisau audience clapped the trio to the echo, but Dizim's arrestingly close-focus recording ensures this doesn't diminish one's involvement with the music one bit. Indeed, sounds are so deftly mapped you feel like abandoning the 'jazz' word—that jive term for discounting the most important music of this century—and calling this a Sonic Event. Far fucking out!

* * * * * * *

The Ed Palermo Big Band
Plays the Music of Frank Zappa
Astor Place TCD4005
The Muffin Men
Frankincense: The Muffin Men Play FZ
Muffin Records Productions MRP054-97/98

ED PALERMO'S sixteen-piece has been playing a Zappa set at New York's Bitter End for the last four years. The leader evinces a spiky wit in the booklet's 'relevant quotes', but musically he pursues the smarmy West Coast jazz that was always part of Zappa's armoury. No vocals. Lovingly transcribed from the records, arrangements are complex and impeccably-rehearsed. A multi-layered, lavishly marinaded, smooth-jazz dinner-on-a-tray rather than the expected burnt-weenie sandwich. Solos are taken by such as vibist Dave Samuels and saxophonist Bob Mintzer, and guitarists Mike Stern and Mike Keneally. The latter is the sole Zappa *alumnus*: since he can texturise his line with timbral twists, the little-known Keneally—in true NYC cutting-contest style—kicks the overrated ex-Miles sideman's ass into kingdom come. Keneally's reinvention of HM can compare—probably favourably—to Buckethead's.

Adhering to Zappa's greasy/hairy aspect are the Muffin Men, a septet of Scousers with silly hats and strange trousers. They've been rocking out Zappa songs to appreciative European audiences for seven years. Since the perverse complexity of Zappa's music was a deliberate retort to the lame sub-blues and mutter-about-drugs of San Francisco (and the pose-to-the-feedback-with-shades and mutter-about-drugs of New York), these Muffins also realise the need for discipline. Playing tight, all-notes-covered arrangements of 'Zoot Allures' and 'San Ber'dino' is not easy, folks!

When I saw the Muffin Men at rockers' heaven (Worcester Park Tavern in South London), they had Jimmy Carl Black (Mothers Of Invention and Magic Band drummer) on vocals, so they inclined to stompin' R&B. They've got a fantastic drummer in Paul Ryan—he can both slug out the backbeat *and* improvise—and they also improvise the instrumentation to great effect (*trombone* on 'Don't Eat The Yellow Snow'? Yo!). On record you miss Zappa's production-values, but *Frankincense* is a likeable and conscientious momento nonetheless. They play 'Jones Crusher' like they mean it (which is quite scary).

Given the choice, I'd probably plump for the Muffin Men's rockism over Ed Palermo's jazz chops, but the stylistic divergence between the two bands is a reminder that it was really the *juxtapositions* that made Zappa's music great. Juxtapose me, baby! Talking of which, will Lo-Fi (the Durannies' new art label) sign Dogbiz and release *his* astonishing 'tribute' to Zappa's *musique-concrète* segues and 'weird' moments? The United Mutations await with impatience.

* * * * * * *

Kurt Weill
Marianne Faithfull & Vienna Radio Symphony Orchestra
The Seven Deadly Sins
RCA VICTOR 74321 60119 CD
Loes Luca & William Breuker Kollektief
Kurt Weill
BVHAAST 9808 CD
Hanns Eisler
Deutsche Symphonie Opus 50
Berlin Classics 0093262BC CD

SHARPLY CRITICAL of the bourgeois division of labour, Bertolt Brecht and Kurt Weill wrote for untrained voices. Their music is travestied when interpreted by singers and musicians who adopt the colourless, uninflected style of the academy. So Marianne Faithfull is a likely contender: the sleaze of her cracked vocalese promises strong renditions. On *The Seven Deadly Sins*, she sings Anna's part an octave lower. Her accent is a somewhat nomadic, ranging from Marlene Dietrich Teutonics to round-the-old-joanna Cockney. Such stylization is abetted by a thin recording for the vocals, giving her a pre-war, end-of-telephone aura. Unfortunately the Vienna Symphony is twiddly and conscientious rather than leering and driving. The *Seven Deadly Sins* isn't rich on tunes; by the time the inevitable 'Alabama Song' bonus rolls on, you're thinking Faithfull could have been better served by Gary Windo on sax, Ray Manzarek on organ and Charlie Watts on drums. Faithfull gives much-needed focus to the proceedings, but she's too restricted by the institutional framework to unleash Weill's fire—or her own.

The Willem Breuker Kollektief combine accuracy and character with an elan that can reach the peaks of Duke or Zappa. Dutch chanteuse Loes Luca has a fluting, limpid voice. At first it seems too pure for Weill's cabaret, but its unmannered directness frees it from the yawning pitfalls of cliché. 'Les Filles de Bordeaux' pulls on memories of 'Mack The Knife', but becomes the vehicle for a superbly moving performance. Arrangements recycled from Breuker's back-catalogue confirms the Kollektief as Weill's most inspired interpreters. The silent-film pacing of Breuker's solo on 'Der Song von Mandelay' and the jazz eruption that is 'My Ship' (dig Alex Coke's bossa flute!) are both snazzy-into-sublime.

Despite being banned by Nazis, censored by so-called democratic governments (Paris 1937, London 1938), hounded by McCarthy as 'communist' and denounced in Stalinist Russia as 'atonal', Hanns Eisler's 'anti-fascist' symphony is disappointing, a turgid collation of Wagnerian stage props. Chesty baritones declaim and anxious sopranos shriek. Brecht's 'Song of the Class Enemy' sees fabulously abrupt and politically-shocking lyrics (untranslated in the booklet) reduced to churning operatic predictability. Although professedly 'twelve-tone', there's no confrontation with sound. Eisler is better remembered as the composer of the upfront, anti-integrative score of *Kuhle Wampe*, where busy brass blew all Shostakovich-style string melancholy to blazes.

~1999~

Theodor Adorno
Sound Figures
Stanford University Press (pbk)

ROUTINELY DENOUNCED by the dullards of youth, media and cultural studies as 'elitist'—a useful scapegoat for people whose own publications are riddled with insider jargon and footnoted obsequiousness to professorial privilege—Theodor Adorno is actually one of the few writers to grasp the dynamics of musical creativity. For those who believe that musical experience is a gateway to truth, but who prefer historical and scientific rigour to mystical assertion, Adorno is the perfect guide: an antidote to the enthusiastic irrationalism of Trendy Theory (music as surrender to Chaos, the primordial Other, the all-dissolving Flux etc).

For Adorno, 'sound figures'—the musical material worked on by those who make music—are a sedimentation of social content. Music is not a pre-existent set of abstract relations gradually uncovered by rational progress, but a knot in the development of human relations. To deal with it carries a responsibility: orientation *vis à vis* the whole of history. To those who wish to separate off music as a specialised—and ultimately trivial—pastime, Adorno's approach is anathema. He raises political issues, but without burying artistic distinctions under sociological oughts. He unmasks the way in which human institutions—from sonata form to the discotheque—are actually historical products, susceptible to criticism and alteration. A refugee from the Nazis, he discerned in appeals to primal myth the shabby economic interests that put Hitler in power.

Adorno's writing is difficult because it's active, not because it's boring. It bristles with slogans that sabotage positivist underwriting of what merely is, interrupt the expected, turn the glare of reason on the reader. The object of thought is never severed from the concerns of the thinker: his reflexive wit achieves a poetic simultaneity of vision which is the opposite of the tidy departments of orthodox academia. If you've ever wondered why magazines that treat 'jazz' as a distant realm of sepia-tinged excellence are so tedious, Adorno comes up with the answer: 'judgments on the internal tension and legitimacy of any artistic practice have always been made possible only by the relation to current—and advanced—production' (p. 36). That's why discussions of Miles and Coltrane in the context of electronica, free improvisation, and world music have a bite lacking in jazz-heritage tributes. The mere recital of dead fact is pointless: for Adorno, anything true is alive with innovation and controversy.

Sound Figures is a collection of essays, radio talks and lectures from the latter half of the 1950s, though you need to refer to the painstaking bibliography in Max Paddison's *Adorno's Aesthetics of Music* to find that out. This lack of dating by the editors of *Sound Figures* is criminal. Far from being someone whose ideas float in an eternal think-tank stamped 'philosophy', Adorno has determinate things to say about both music and society. *When* is crucial.

The 1950s was the period in which American capital reshaped Europe in its image. By an ideological sleight of hand, Communism—which had been an ally in World War II—was turned into a 'totalitarian' menace equivalent to Nazism. Criticism of capitalism was made taboo by association with Russian Communism. The recent Jackson Pollock exhibitions in New York and London served as a reminder of one strand of Cold War propaganda: the use of strategies derived from Dada and Surrealism (both strongly linked to the revolutionary left in the pre-war years) to underline the 'free' nature of market capitalism. Stalin incarcerated modern artists in psychiatric clinics; the CIA encouraged bankers and tycoons to buy their pictures. Rather than heralding the workers revolution, post-war Modern Art became a badge of elitism.

That is precisely what concerns Adorno in these discourses. Far from being the shrill proselytiser for high culture depicted in the average Routledge 'student guide', Adorno questions the notion that, in a society based on inequality and exploitation, liberated music can service a particular class. True, he's militantly opposed to any dumbing-down of the musical advances made by Arnold Schoenberg and the 12-tone school. He argues that retreats to tonality reek of condescension. He argues from a vision of what society might be (enlightened and self-defining), denying that it is the task of the privileged to manipulate a less enlightened mass. One suspects that it is this revolutionary purity—rather than 'elitism'—that offends a generation who dabbled with revolution in the '60s, but are now reconciled to positions of privilege inside a 'spectacle' they once promised to smash.

'The public at large is always better,' says Adorno, 'than those few who appeal to popular taste with the intention of thwarting the emergence of music worthy of human beings.' (p. 39) Anyone who has argued with record-company personnel or arts administrators will recognise Adorno's targets: careerist pragmatism, refusal to credit subjective reactions, projection of stupidity onto the public, acceptance of class division. Adorno is allergic to the hierarchical view latent in marketing statistics: society seem from the point of view of capital. Anyone committed to the productive spark point of artistic form will derive inspiration from his polemic. Those out to exploit the residue of artistic movements—biz employees, style-guide journalists, PR smoothies, cult-studs analysts—naturally find Adorno a nightmare. Despite—or because of—an almost psychotic inability to deal with any music that molested his attention as a commodity (no honourable exceptions for anyone!), Adorno's po-lemics have the *destructive character* of seismic cultural turns. If bebop or punk or free jazz needed a philosophy to express rage against recuperation and exploitation, this is it.

When Adorno described the Absurd as 'a condition that loses its justification as soon as it ceases to be provocative and instead sets itself up as a positive standard' (p. 205), he had already—in 1958—precriticised existentialist Paris, post-Cage experimentalism, Pop Art and Saatchi's Sensation. It's sad to think that the scare term 'elitism' has been sufficient to quarantine Adorno from the very people who need him most. Adorno makes the all-too-solid crust of society-as-usual rear up and quake: the waves of phony-rebellious conformism recede; the shallows seem shallower than ever. Who will make the Giant Steps?

* * * * * * *

Army of Ghosts
The Horror
Parallelism

THE DUO OF Ryan Noel (tenor saxophone) and Brain Army (drums, vibes, spoken word) emerged from a band called Aylers Angels which operated in Washington DC and Boston between 1996 and 1997, recording for the Hot Cars Warp label and gigging with Cra-nium and Cromtech. One discerns devotion to the frying power of Free Jazz, so it's no surprise to learn they've played with Maurice McIntyre and shared bills with Peter Brötzmann. Brain Army (real name Brian F. McPeck) keeps the strings on his snares loose, resulting in a rattling attack: his flailing collision of free-form and punk-funk lands him somewhere between Ascension's Tony Irving and Denardo Coleman.

With its heavy precedents (Coltrane/Ali, Shepp/Roach, Mateen/Bruno), sax/drum duets aren't to be undertaken lightly. These two have the spleen and gall to bring it off. Any hint of self-consciousness or circumspection would taint the all-important rawness. Army of Ghosts keep the flame blue and hard and pure.

The theme of the album is American imperial warfare and the overlooked suffering and anger of the common soldier. Tapes of shellfire and interviews with embittered veterans drive the point home. Now that the technical wonders of Free Jazz are regularly deployed for purely aesthetic ends, these reminders of its roots in social hurt are shocking but welcome. Army of Ghosts tackle big issues but deal with them head-on: blunt, ugly music that harks on truths and sticks in the memory.

* * * * * * *

Autism
The Comforts of Madness
Durian

ROGER TURNER is one of the fleetest, most accurate percussionists it can be your astonishment to witness, but (like saxophonist Lol Coxhill) he has a knack of avoiding sterile situations where his virtuosity is ahead of the music. He'll spread his kit all over the floor and end up—drumstick in mouth like a pirate swarming up the rigging—crackling a crisp packet, or using stage-prop sausages to belabour a mic stand. He credits himself here to 'drums, garbage,' and it's this refusal of certified value that keeps his music provocative and fizzing. Autism is a trio with Helge Hinteregger on saxes and sampler and Uchihashi Kazuhisa on guitar and electronics: an unbroken 60-minute improvisation in a smart white package issuing from Vienna.

Random tinkles, scrapes, and phuts are gradually sucked into a powerful slipstream. Tiny squeaks from Hinteregger and electronic crackles from Kazuhisa indicate that Turner has found musicians thinking to the same super-divided beat. It's funk or jazz with the resonant substance erased: all that's left is a cubist sketch of edges, pivots and angles. An extraordinary negative shape streams through the music: the sum total of everything the musicians do not play.

The rush never relents, but the absence of murk clears space for cartoon hysteria and dazzling morphs of sonic icons. Evocative sections are spiked by tiny slivers of speed. This is improv on helium: an addictive dementia.

* * * * * * *

Bashful Brother Oswald
Don't Say Aloha
Rounder 0080 CD

NONPAREIL DOBROIST Beecher Ray Kirby gained the stage name Bashful Brother Oswald in the 1930s. He was touring with Roy Acuff's Smoky Mountain Boys when a girl singer named Rachel Veacher joined the band. Wishing to avoid gossip, they claimed she was his sister: he became her blushing brother in a hokey comedy act. Today he's recognised as the Grand Old Opry's longest-running performer: since January 1999, he can boast of having played there every weekend for sixty years. In the early '40s, when Acuff and band made trips to California to star in movies for Columbia, they'd perform their whole Opry show live down the telephone for broadcast, bantering with the compère Judge Ray on stage in Nashville. Oswald learned his style from listening to the Hawaiian lap-guitarist Rudy Waikiki in Flint, Michigan, in 1929. Chuck Berry, The Shadows, John Barry, Johnny Thunders (and hence the Pistols) all owe something to the Bashful Brother's Dobro twang.

The Dobro is an acoustic guitar with metal strings and a chrome plate instead of a sounding board. Oswald plays it with a slide, producing a choked, corrosive sound, the instrumental equivalent of an aching throat. He has played countless sessions; records under his own name are rarer, so this album cut at Starday Studios in Nashville in 1998 is something of an event. The high points are the instrumentals: 'Amazing Grace', with its majestically controlled pace, and the all-too-short hillbilly hokum of 'Cripple Creek'. 'Bible in the Barn', about an old couple dying together, pushes lachrymosity into the realms of the absurd, as does 'Should I Tell My Wife I'm Dying?'. Urban sophisticates will doubtless jeer (until their sixth bottle of beer, when they'll find themselves as choked as Oswald's unerring slanted double-stops).

Oswald has brought in Onie Wheeler, who sings a sugared, diluted version of Hank Williams. His wheezing harmonica is so cowboy-stirs-his-beans, you long for an attack by bloodthirsty Iroquois. But every time the Dobro strikes up, it's great. 'It is very satisfying,' Oswald tells Bonnie Smith in the liner notes, 'to sit down and pick for an audience that you know is listening to you'. And so say all of us. Bashful Brother fans look forward to an all-instrumental album.

* * * * * * *

Carl E. Baugher
Turning Corners: The Life and Music of Leroy Jenkins
Cadence Jazz Books

BORN IN Chicago in 1932, Leroy Jenkins has never made it easy for himself. In jazz, the violin has always been considered a freak instrument. On top of that, he plays 'outside', refusing even the niches built by Ray Nance and Stuff Smith. On the other hand, people who've seen him in concert become devotees. Carl E. Baugher, garage-band rock'n'roll bassist, witnessed the Revolutionary Ensemble in the early '70s—a co-operative trio with Jenkins, bassist Sirone and drummer/pianist Jerome Cooper—and flipped: 'the most exciting live group I've ever heard.... I was virtually walking on air for days afterwards. The whole town was buzzing about 'that violinist'.' A contributor to rock zines *Goldmine* and *Crawdaddy*, Baugher's appreciation of records makes this an excellent *catalogue raisonnée* of Jenkins' *oeuvre*.

Baugher has also talked extensively to Jenkins, giving this brief, 150-page biography the special buzz of a first-time sketch (just as the best Trane book is C.O. Simpkins' raw'n'ready *Coltrane: A Biography*). Baugher is no prose stylist, and readers lacking the albums may wish to skip his blow-by-blow accounts of LPs, CDs, and unissued tapes. However, at its best, his screed recalls a Jenkins' solo: fresh, honest, bracing. It's undimmed by the half-truths and innuendoes spun by 'mature' critics with an eye on the critical *status quo*.

Leroy Jenkins emerged with Muhal Abrams, Anthony Braxton and Leo Smith as part of the AACM co-op in the mid-'60s. Although today's Chicago scene hails that tradition, it's a little like Jesse Jackson claiming the mantle of Malcolm X. Things sure don't feel the same. The AACM were black musicians who didn't see why the whole of modern music—spatial situationism, aleatoric surprise, sarcasm, noise, instant invention—shouldn't be part of the improvisor's armoury. The confrontational chill of the playing, the isolation of musical gesture, was stunning. Jenkins probed the giddy extremes of the music: you couldn't really get further from jazz, soul or disco than a violin refusing to follow the chord changes. Like Leo Smith's trumpet, Jenkins' violin tone actually teems with swing and the blues, but you're being asked to appreciate that quality unpropped by social ritual.

Jenkins' early story is fascinating: the church-hall band which played William Grant Still and Clarence Cameron White (and other African American composers with three names); hit singer Lil Green ('Romance in the Dark') as a neighbour; the outbreak of World War II; the time in Florida among lighter-skinned relatives, and the tension caused by prejudice against his dark wife. In May 1968, Jenkins played on *Three Compositions of New Jazz* by Anthony Braxton. Check the level of commitment that went into that astonishing record: 'Braxton and I were living together in a musicians' building on Drexel. Every morning we got up and listened to it before we went to work. That was our national anthem. That was our wake up music. Man, we played that thing to death before it came out. We played it a thousand times and when it came out, we played it another thousand.'

It was exposure in Europe that made Jenkins' name. Hearing that gig opportunities were good in the heady air following May '68—the Art Ensemble of Chicago were wowing audiences ('they not only had money, they had motorcycles, too!')—Jenkins and Leo Smith jumped on a ship to Paris. Braxton flew in, and the three played gigs under the name the Creative Construction Company. They were provocative and crazy (Braxton fried eggs on stage). They hit big. Braxton's composerly ambitions alienated the others, and the group broke up (this story provides a useful corrective to Braxtonolatry). Used to dealing with reluctant paymasters, they occupied the BYG label's office and escorted an employee to the bank. Back in New York, the Revolutionary Ensemble was formed, Jenkins' most conducive context as a soloist (his empathy with Sirone was amazing).

Inevitably with biographies of professional musicians, musical analysis gradually replaces picturesque detail. Baugher is eloquent about the Mixed Quintet (improvised chamber music for violin, flute, clarinets and French horn), the harmolodic outfit Sting with vocalist and twin electric guitars and, for a musician now in receipt of arts funding, the inevitable opera (though the three-page synopsis of Ann Greene's libretto—a mystical fairytale—is a taxing read).

Baugher makes astute remarks about both amplification and recording of the violin.

Books like this are the building blocks of criticism, the essential facts and opinions set down without strategy. Baugher has merged himself with Jenkins' story as indelibly as Boswell did with Johnson: a rocker discovered revolutionary black jazz and was transformed in the process (Baugher spent ten years writing for *Cadence*, America's most rigorous jazz magazine). Like the parable told in Tavernier's *Round Midnight*, the anti-racist thrust of such support is touching.

However, as a late Jenkins album like *Forty Years of Discovery 1954-1994* (CRI) spins in the CD-player, sounding like an (albeit extraordinarily vital) rendition of Janacek compositions, some questions remain: Has art been a means of buying off protest? Does recognition as a composer really compensate us for the brain-bending bedazzlement that was Leroy Jenkins as an 'anti-jazz' revolutionary? Jenkins recalls a BYG festival in 1969, a muddy field in Belgium. As he came off stage, veteran drummer Philly Joe Jones was 'laughing like mad because he'd already seen what the crowd was like, they were expecting traditional jazz or *something*.... It was like an orgy. They were throwing mud, and we were just throwing this really wild, aggressive music right back at them! Everybody got off on that, man. We got off on it and they did, too.'

Playing old records by the Revolutionary Ensemble still has that effect. What can we do to make this music alive again today?

* * * * * * *

Matt De Gennaro & Alastair Galbraith
Wire Music
Corpus Hermeticum Hermes031 CD

AMERICAN ARTIST Matt De Gennaro traces the procedures of Fluxus back to Athanasius Kircher (1602-1680) and John Tyndall (1820-1893), who researched into the sonic properties of long tensioned wires—what Pythagorians call the 'celestial monochord'. In 1998 Gennaro visited New Zealand and hooked up with Alastair Galbraith, who has played in The Dead C and Handful of Dust.

Packaged in Corpus Hermeticum's characteristic style—raw cardboard unfolds to reveal a brown-paper sleeve printed with a medieval woodcut—this CD was recorded live at Everything Inc, an arts lab in Dunedin. Conducted into the 'dungeon-like' basement by torchlight, the audience was plunged into total darkness for the eighteen-minute performance (three soundcheck additions bring the running time up to forty minutes). Gennaro and Galbraith rubbed their rosined hands over piano wires stretched across the space. On the last piece, Galbraith plays scrapy violin and uses an appropriately sore-sounding tape-loop.

This isn't the harmonically-congruent 'gorgeousness' used in many sonic installations. The ear cannot bask, but must follow the touch-sensitive drama of the playing. What at first seems threadbare and abrasive becomes fascinating. Although the idea was to place the listener inside an instrument—the basement has been turned into a giant sounding-box—the players' scrabbled immediacy recalls the far-out string techniques you might encounter with Malcolm Goldstein's violin or William Parker's bass. Though they'd probably be disgusted to hear it, these intuitive occultists have broached the giddy realm of creative improvisation. One wishes them the best of luck.

* * * * * * *

William Hooker
Mindfulness
Knitting Factory Works KFW213 CD

WILLIAM HOOKER has emerged as drummer of choice for atomic jams at the Knitting Factory. He's accompanied Sonic Youth guitar-stormers Thurston Moore and Lee Renaldo, he's played with zoot-horned harpist Zeena Parkins. He's even forced Elliott Sharp to do more than noodle. This is his best release yet, and brings on Glenn Spearman—the only living saxophonist name checked by a cantankerous Frank Kofsky before he died—and turntablist DJ Olive.

Spearman begins with a muezzin-like incantation, answered by a flurry of tribal toms. His tone is fluid, glistening and broad, with a beautiful rotund honk in the lower register. When he distorts his sound, it's a deliberate modification, like an actor signalling he's choked-up or angry. A certain theatrical quality marks all Hooker's music, but he keeps the gestures technically adroit enough—filled with nuanced expression—to avoid vacuity. DJ Olive spins records of pipping electronics, refusing the referential in-jokes of much turntablism. His arbitrary jigs and jags successfully burst the sax/drum dialogue out of wholefood Trane-tribute torpor. Hooker keeps his swellings of sonic jetsam tethered to earth with an extraordinarily physical assault on the drums.

Mindfulness is free improvisation in that it's organised around alertness to the moment, but helpings of echo bestow a rhetorical grandeur few European musicians would be keen to indulge. Like a Sun Ra trip to outer space, everything has a breathing, organic lope. Spearman whips out phrases to connect the events triggered by Hooker and Olive, his liquid Pollock-splatter a coordinating network rather than pissed provocation. His multiphonic screams—and Hooker's cymbal pile-ups—are carefully layered, textures kneaded for ear-alert reflection. DJ Olive wrecks his records to expose their abstract values.

Towards the close of 'Living Organs', Spearman cites the rhythm from 'A Love Supreme', but there's no idea of emulation, it's a structuring pulse. His falsetto and honk start up an internal dialogue, provoking some astonishingly speech-patterned scratching from Olive. On the final 'Archetypal Space', DJ Olive plays a record with a held chord. The wham-boing scratches she adds in would be rubbishing if you accepted the record's brief, but they are actually assertions of realtime action over processed spells. Hooker's beats become amazingly independent. That's the key: the ability to make many things happen at once allows him to mould his extraordinarily disparate sonic materials into a triumphant suite.

Hooker's CV goes some way to explain why *Mindfulness* is so successful. Born in 1946 in New Britain, Connecticut, he first played drums in a rock and roll band called The Flames—'Louie Louie', 'Funky Funky Broadway', 'Can't Sit Down', side one of James Brown's *Live at the Apollo*. He backed Dionne Warwick and Gary 'US' Bonds. He took a course on twentieth century composers, and wrote a paper on Alban Berg, all the while listening to the latest jazz abstraction on the Blue Note label. Moving to New York in the early '70s, his first album featured both David Murray and David Ware, the two main contenders for the post-Trane crown. However, Hooker fell out with critics Stanley Crouch and Gary Giddens, something he blames for his eclipse on the jazz scene—helped by the neo-conservatism of the Reaganite '80s.

So, with the advent of the Knitting Factory and the notion of combining what he calls 'industrial strength' rock and Free Jazz, Hooker could outflank the critics, and bring his long-nurtured concept of musical organisation to the fore. That's what *Mindfulness* allows us to hear: a musical intelligence refusing narrow definitions of jazz as wholeheartedly as it's embracing Coltrane's universalism and experiential extremes. The energy, grip and urgency of Hooker's message is palpable.

* * * * * * *

Kevin Norton
For Guy Debord (In Nine Events)
Barking Hoop BKH001 CD

TO INVOKE the name of Guy Debord—founding situationist, author of *The Society of the Spectacle*, blistering voice of the May '68 revolution—and to print a photograph of burnt-out cars and scattered cobble-stones on the streets of Paris on the cover of a CD: such ploys set a heavy agenda. Add in sleeve notes that attempt, Greil Marcus-style, to summarise the situationist critique from an American angle (fleas patronising a lion), and you're heading for trouble. Swimming against the current of this presentation, however, is Kevin Norton's music—which wins. Maybe it's because multi-reedist Anthony Braxton is aboard.

In 1969, stranded in Paris, Anthony Braxton recorded *This Time* for BYG/Actuel with Leo Smith and Leroy Jenkins. Braxton later declared the label had binned the best music, but for those who cared (*i.e.*, a few punk situationists in the late '70s), this LP was the most accurate—most direct, least theoretic—expression of May '68. In the intervening years, attempts to build on *This Time*'s sense of imploding categories have been sporadic, flawed by attempts to pin labels on movements pointing elsewhere (punkjazz, black sci-fi, noise, materialist esthetix, cyberhythm, DIY-dada). Now, Kevin Norton—percussionist of choice for Anthony Braxton for the last five years, and hence John the Baptist to revolutionary black music's Messiah-without-knowing-it—dedicates his music to Debord, thus positing Free Jazz as part of the revolutionary process. Rigorous musical thought conveyed by straight instruments cuts through ethno-twaddle and cyber-twiddle to the real issues of the epoch. No more dreams of transcendence in the virtuality booth, comrades—here's some *événement* actuality!

You scan in vain the pages of Debord's journals *Potlatch* and *Internationale Situationniste* for any reference to jazz. Apart from being scorned as primitive chic for French consumers (Jacques Fillon in *Potlatch* #21), the key cultural question-mark of this century—black American music—is notable by its absence. At a conference on the legacy of the situationists held at the Hacienda in 1996, Debord's translator Lucy Forsyth defended this omission by citing Debord's love of Free Jazz and John Coltrane. Perhaps situationist disdain for the commodity entailed keeping record-listening private. Nevertheless, Forsyth's claim rings true: Free Jazz is undoubtedly the correct musical equivalent of the lettrist extremism that Debord linked to proletarian insurgency against the rule of American capital.

In nine 'events' recorded at the Tri-Centric Festival at the Greenwich House Music School in 1998, Kevin Norton plays drums, vibes and gongs, Braxton blows sopranino, alto and contrabass clarinet, and there are bass and cello solos by Joe Fonda and Tomas Ulrich. David Bindman and Bob De Bellis play flutes and reeds. Norton's unbroken suite—lasting an appropriately hard-to-market thirty-seven minutes—lets different members of the ensemble step forward to give their version of the music under scrutiny, Muhal Richard Abrams-style.

As a composer, Norton doesn't emulate the complexities of Braxton's solos, the way he thinks ahead and plays retorts to his future line and retorts to those retorts from an imagined future, weaving brain-boggling *millefeuille* layers. Indeed, on the opener, Norton's motif on vibes is pretty much 'Jingle Bells'. When Braxton snorts contra-bass clarinet at some pipping simplicities from vibes and flutes on 'Endemic Characteristics', it's like Asger Jorn dripping paint across some trite and kitschy oil-painting—a searingly alert artist discovering vast fields-for-play in insufferable clichés, dramatising material relations the representation-bound artist only touches on unconsciously. One suspects this is what Norton wanted, and the effect is staggering.

On 'Dedalus' (the titles indicate 'events' within the suite rather than different tunes), Norton pushes bowed-string melancholia to the brink of sarcasm; Braxton's overblown sopranino echoes the metallic scrape of his cymbals (despite an intellect that number crunches harmonic possibilities like a silicon chip, Braxton responds to the specific sounds he hears, not official note values). Unlike the fluff heads who confuse art with healing alternatives, Braxton's solos mimic the sickening velocity of smart weaponry, forcing attention on anxious truths. His stance is that of the exultant champ jabbing at the structure he's boxed in. The precision and invention of his blows are scary, yet supremely logical. If he's occasionally abrupt and crude, it's the violence of the mathematical genius underlining a result with such force he breaks the chalk.

'Revolutionary Practice' is—as befits the title—a collective improvisation, David Bindman's restless-native congas submerged in a sick-grey Mahlerish pall, the sound of overcast skies gradually ripping apart to reveal the sun of truth. The players have been spiked with enough contrary impulses (*aka* 'musical ideas') to stave off repro-'60s free-jazz rhapsody. The idea of hearking a groove you don't obey becomes an image for free thought in a society whose rhythm you oppose; any other strategy (beat-conformity or no beat at all) would be self-delusion.

Norton's 'drum solo' on 'Fragment' has the drama of a composition, but without tempering the physical impact: Norton's different effects—cymbal shimmer, rattling rim shots, bass-drum pummels—suggest delegates shouting at each other in the revolutionary assembly. The concluding 'Deliberate Intention' pricks any political afflatus with a reassertion of the Norton/Braxton dialogue at the start: Norton repetitive and simple, Braxton alert and speculative. Of late, Braxton has neglected to promote his instrumental prowess, preferring to present himself as a composer. Whether or not it's conscious, the way his tone changes at the point of entering the written finale here is a withering retort to bureaucratic orders.

With *For Guy Debord*, Kevin Norton hasn't just delivered a stunningly coherent piece of advanced jazz, he's also proved that music can embody ideas and polemic: the case for social revolution as a sensual experience.

* * * * * * *

Michael Prime
Micoplazma
Digital Narcis DN004 CD

MICHAEL PRIME finds beauty in unlikely places. His photos of waste ground and rubble highlight varieties of texture, colour and shape. He mixes the roar of machines with the sounds of arctic winds, trickling water, squarking geese. It's proficient and hi-tech, and on a superficial level, impressively glossy. One of these pieces was a loop for an installation at The Tannery in 1994.

No doubt Prime adheres to some post-musical, post-humanist aesthetic (Cagean, ambient, cyber etc), but his soundtrack stirs feelings, and it is this emotional colouration that is being offered to the purchaser. The tone is familiar: grand, impersonal and ineluctable.

'Hallucination of Falling' builds to some kind of climax, and there's some movement and event on 'Entangled Particles', but everything heaves under a thick coat of portentous echo. The need to adhere to the atmospheric *diktat* of the genre (the cyber-natural sublime) smothers detail and interaction. Recording technology is fetishised as a wonder in itself, with Prime's own part in the process occluded, as if the fingerprint of the artist would be a bathetic banality. Children's voices are heard, but they're distant and non-specific, mere ciphers. We can't hear what they're saying. Prime's aesthetic is closer to Riefenstahl than to Schwitters.

In Prime's soundworld, industry and nature become equivalent, omitting their mediation by human activity. Both are glamourised, made scarily alien: you are standing by the waterfall, two million gallons an hour, the stress inside the steel walls would liquefy your body cells in an instant. As with Wagner, this musical 'flow' is really stasis: surrender to fate. Whereas DIY-dada experimentalists (from Dogbiz to Adam Bohman) foreground the personal labour involved in producing sound, Prime invokes the chill and pompous ambience of the corporate foyer. The exploitation, violence and danger of actual industrial production is screened out by awe-inducing images of hi-tech mastery.

The wreckage documented in the photos and the capitalist mode of production do bear a relation, but it's not one Prime encourages us to trace. As the cover indicates (Asger Jorn's *détournement* of conventional oil-painting botched into a Monet magic garden), Prime is a naive afloat on the treacherous waters of modern art; all he can do is go with the reactionary flow.

[N.B. This review was commissioned and then rejected (quite understandably!) by The Wire. *It is included here because the thinking I was forced to do—facing music I did not like—contributed to the critique of cyber-aesthetics that eventually led to my split with the magazine and my decision to foment the Esemplasm. OTL 25-i-2008]*

* * * * * * *

Various
Howard Riley Trio
Angle
Columbia 494433 CD
The Day Will Come
Columbia 494434 CD
Ray Russell Quartet
Dragon Hill
Columbia 494435 CD
Rites and Rituals
Columbia 494436 CD
Tony Oxley
The Baptised Traveller
Columbia 494438 CD
4 Compositions for Sextet
Columbia 494437 CD

SONY MUSIC Entertainment (UK) Ltd decide to remind us of the state of British music between 1969 and 1970. Three artists—Howard Riley, Ray Russell and Tony Oxley—are represented by releases from each of those years. The original LPs became fabulously rare and sought-after, tokens from an era when the corporates (at that time, Columbia) couldn't tell the difference between jazz, rock, austere modernist free improvisation and hippie-dippie free-form noodling—and no one could predict which one might become a new mass-selling genre.

Today, as he occasionally pops up from academia to contribute resourceful piano to improvised gigs by the likes of Eddie Prévost and George Haslam, Howard Riley seems an unlikely case for corporate sponsorship. However, in 1968 Riley had recorded duets with John McLaughlin (in a pre-Miles, pre-Mahavishnu incarnation). Riley plays modern jazz (Monk, Evans) infused with an English pastoral sensibility over a somewhat incompatible rhythm section of Barry Guy (bass) and Alan Jackson (drums). Guy wreaks some astonishing skronk effects, rattling his bow on close-miked strings, linking Siegfried Palm's performances of Xenakis to Scott La Faro's work with Ornette Coleman. On 'Angle', Guy's solo is a delirium-inducing window on freedom. However, it's a window Riley's pretty tune shuts down rather than resolves.

Two years after this recording, Riley and Guy encountered Tony Oxley's drums on a recording for Incus (*Synopsis*). Oxley had the rhythmic *nous* and audacity to shatter Riley's pastoralism into glittering shards, making for a great record: here Riley's Debussy-like nostalgia and sonorous harmonies feel like a straitjacket. 'Three Fragments' on *Angle* is a short, through-composed piece with Barbara Thompson on flute. This brief flash of modernist clarity—Webern-like pointillism—is quickly dampened by 'Gill', where an Ealing Studios/Richard Rodney Bennett folksiness suggests dubious collusion with record buyers' rural yearnings.

The cover of *The Day Will Come* shows ivory chess warriors towered over by a matriarchal fertility sculpture. 'Sphere' (Thelonious Monk's middle name) hints at Cecil Taylorism, but 'Winter' leads back to the restful minimalism of folk modes: the kind of slow, meditative, chordal langour that is termed 'jazz' at the ECM label and Berklee School. Guy's excitable skills sound in need of braver company as he punches out anti-linear heresies beneath the blanket of Riley's limited range of chordal resolutions.

Current interest in guitarist Ray Russell was piqued by 'Stained Angel Morning' on David Toop's *Guitars on Mars* collection, where he came across as a premonition of the deathmetal improv of Ascension's Stefan Jaworzyn. *Dragon Hill* opens with eerie harmonics from Ron Mathewson's bowed bass, an ensemble flourish, then a statement of the kind of nagging flattened interval that began *Kind Of Blue*. Pianist Roy Fry goes off on a Tyneresque vamp, Alan Rushton beating out a nervously irregular metre.

Ray Russell's electric guitar is the wildcard as he scribbles energetically over what is basically a hard bop arrangement. His stinging, urgent tone is out of Eric Clapton and BB King, an unusual sonority for jazz. At one point, he pushes against Fry's harmonic direction, achieving the sensation of hearing two musics at once that marks successful Free Jazz. However, Russell cannot manage a sustained harmonic argument, and it's more a jam than an improvisation as Russell essays various rock riffs. Some of the tracks feature horns; Harry Beckett's lithe trumpet is notable, though Russell's guitar sounds somewhat thin and hysterical in a big-band context.

'Can I Have My Paper-Back Back' uses a Mingusish riff and electric piano, making Russell sound like Robben Ford with Joni Mitchell's LA Express. Though he's refreshingly off-the-leash, one starts to recognise Russell's licks: there's not much of the dissatisfaction with the already-heard that drives creative improvisors. 'We

Lie Naked In White Snow' is a smoochy bossa, proto-Pat Metheny. 'Mandala' is Horace Silver glimpsed through a fog. Sessionmen floundering around in an era before they acquired the skill to sound boring hardly spells 'avant-garde'.

Rites and Rituals shows the influence of Coltrane's *Africa/ Brass*, though the resultant over-excited jazzrock more nearly resembles '70s groups like Nucleus, Centipede and Emerson, Lake & Palmer. Six minutes in, the title-track improvisation takes off and sounds good, but the return to the arrangement is stilted, recalling the crude conjuncture of ill-digested musical effects encountered in early Pink Floyd. Russell sounds winningly demented over a sub-Softs riff on 'Abyss', but bass and drums aren't equipped to respond to what he is doing. Like their contemporaries The Amazing Band, the Ray Russell Quartet certainly aspire to states of exaltation, but they haven't examined the musical materials with enough detail to shake off cliché. If form isn't grasped and reshaped, ordinary consciousness remains in charge.

With Tony Oxley's two albums, the listener is tumbled into an entirely different universe. Working in the early '60s in Sheffield with Derek Bailey and Gavin Bryars, Oxley had worked out a way of combining the out jazz of Coltrane and Bill Evans with serial alienation and Cageian chance. His sextet (Bailey on guitar, Evan Parker on sax, Kenny Wheeler on trumpet, Jeff Clyne on bass, Oxley on drums) create a writhing, living monster of sound where the 'soloist' is merely the crest of a wave of iridescent chaos. There is no beat, but the whole thing has an organic groove. There are no lapses into embarrassing known quantities, yet the music has an inexorable surge.

Baptised Traveller from 1969 is the less radical of the two, as Oxley settled his accounts with jazz. Evan Parker performs a powerful, excruciated post-Shepp tenor solo. The zigzag theme of 'Crossing' fits the rhythm perfectly, suggesting a waterfall cascading between massive rocks. Cymbal spray hangs over the tenebrous gloom. Charlie Mariano's 'Stone Garden' lives up to its Zen title, Derek Bailey's guitar providing alien lights—almost the sound of electric current itself rather than legitimate notes—to its haunting theme.

4 Compositions for Sextet is by the same group, plus the hair-raising 'reinvented trombone' of Paul Rutherford. It is a stone-cold, drop-dead, ice pick-in-the-forehead masterpiece. The fact that it has been unavailable for thirty years has distorted every account of British music. Sounds stain the musical surface and then run off into gullies and hairline cracks like slip glaze on a Japanese pot: an astonishing fusion of chance and design. The music raises the blood, as if the musicians are tracking processes within the listener's body, massaging the pancreas, fingering the kidneys. Bailey's 'experimental guitar' voicings—choked licks, stunted chords, shrill screams—always seem to lie alongside the others' contributions rather than overlay them.

Oxley's 'drum solo' on 'Amass' is a Varèsian montage of determinate timbre: punishing power and glancing metallica suggest an art-factory Industrial Symphony of molten steel and mighty hammers. The music starts to sound Beethovian in scale, like a natural force. It was too much for the marketing department at Columbia, and Oxley was dropped. He went on to RCA, then independence (helping found Bailey's Incus label), and finally obscurity and exile in Germany. But *4 Compositions for Sextet* is out again now: an artistic manifesto no one can ignore.

~*2000*~

The Peter Brötzmann Sextet/Quartet
Nipples
Unheard Music Series UMS/ALP205 CD

THE RECORD which made Peter Brötzmann's name was *Machine Gun*, released on his own label in 1968. The LP had a juddering quality that made purchasers think there was something wrong with their pick-ups: never before had such a bruising ensemble made a record. *Nipples* was cut the following year, another historic release. The title track was produced by Manfred Eicher—shortly to found ECM Records—but the band hated his mix. In liner-notes written in March 2000, Brötzmann says 'we were working hard all day long, nobody did like the way the engineer was working on the sound, and very frustrated we drove home with about 20 minutes of music we could use'. For these twenty minutes, two English musicians— Derek Bailey (guitar) and Evan Parker (tenor)—faced Brötzmann, Fred Van Hove (piano), Buschi Niebergal (bass) and Han Bennink (drums). Side two of the vinyl release was recorded without Bailey and parker at another studio six days later (engineer this time was Conny Plank).

Brötzmann started out as a painter, and his records have a distinct aesthetic, visual and aural. Just as his bellowing tenor sax reaches subtlety and soul via crude emphasis, his covers favour forthright type and polarised photos. You can understand why Eicher—shortly to become the doyen of designer euro-jazz, all middle-tone nuance—was nonplussed. From title to last note, *Nipples* finds poetry in unmediated human materials. Of course, this is far from mere boorishness, having more connections to visual art (from *Art Brut* to the *Neue Wilde*) than it does to, say, oompah brass bands or Motörhead (even if Lemmy also used an umlaut).

Nor has *Nipples* much in common with the recent Noise of Merzbow or the feedback of Lo-Fi. It can't be played at low volume as domestic colouration, the playing is too expressionist and active.

Either turn it up and experience its cascading energies and interplay, or keep it from the CD-player. With Brötzmann, the tenor sax becomes a megaphone for stuck-pig squeals. Then, by repetition and variation, he forces this unlikely source sound into music. Parker's glottal grunts and hard-edged cut-offs are the perfect foil to Brötzmann's existential romanticism. Van Hove packs in impossible zillions of piano notes. Derek Bailey is heavily electronic, playing the sound of amplification—hints of sonic danger—rather than pitches. Niebergal (who died in 1990) opens up troves of glittering timbral variegation with his bow. Bennink is a clattering goodtime delight, so quick to think of a surprising burst, his beats are always a shock, however well-founded in paradiddle lore. When the ensemble peels back to reveal the bass/drum foundation, you realise they've been building a whirlwind in rubble. Bailey adds such apt notes to Niebergal excursions, you think you're listening to a contact-mic on the bassist's left hand.

The quartet track is less extreme, with Van Hove buoying Brötzmann in a Flintstone version of McCoy Tyner with Coltrane. This is music played at such a pitch of impatience and self-criticism that every note bursts with expression, a bustle of question-marks, a hive of conflicting vectors. If it's all too much, it's because you're frightened to be alive.

* * * * * * *

Alan Clayson
Edgard Varèse
Sanctuary (pbk)

HITHERTO A commercial no-go zone, the twentieth-century classical avant-garde is now deemed sexy enough for its most extreme composer to receive popular paperback treatment (other volumes in this series cover Josephine Baker, Serge Gainsbourg and Pink Floyd). Like many of his generation, Alan Clayson first heard of Varèse via name checks on records by the Mothers of Invention, and he tops and tails his biography with discussions of Frank Zappa. The book promises much: Varèse, after all, is one of the few classical composers whose music has enough bite and shock to interest those who have experienced the joys of drums and reverberating speaker-bins. It'd be good to read about Varèse from the rock angle, where writers mix music and sociology with an aplomb lacking in classical-composer biographies, whose world-view is stiflingly middle-class.

Clayson's claim to fame is a book about the Beatles in Hamburg, *Backbeat*, now a major film. Perhaps that explains why his prose leaps over documentary niceties for *mise-en-scène* fantasy, suggesting a film treatment. This is a book about Varèse 'the man,' and drags with it all the dubious ideological clobber such a concept will rouse in a family man from Henley-on-Thames. Replete with would-be-racy phrases like 'the sock-smelling frowziness still common to young male student accommodation,' Clayson's stabs at vividness provide a stream of jokey-blokey sub-witticisms. The effect is incongruous and distracting. The main points of the story are covered (Fernand Ouellette's pioneering biography provided the skeleton for Clayson's 'research'), but they are drowned in prurient speculation. We're told about Varèse, the good-looking conductor, 'flooding the libidos of the sillier females in the orchestra'. Only silly women fancy men? It prompts the retort: 'How does Clayson *know*? Was he there?'. He wasn't.

As the book proceeds, it dawns on the reader that Clayson cannot grasp what Varèse was attempting to do, and rather resents this insult to his intelligence. Varèse wasn't a star with a mass following: so his supporters were 'snobs,' enduring his 'sound pictures of dementia' for a chance to gossip over a glass of white wine. No one with any sympathy for Zappa's take on Varèse wants piety about art music, but Clayson completely misses the point. Zappa used the pop podium to vaunt a galaxy of avant-gardists condemned as 'failures' by straight society. He connected their outcast status to his own painful experience of High School. Clayson, in contrast, is acutely embarrassed by lack of success. Anyone who persists in artistic endeavour without economic reward must be a pseud or a degenerate (or both). Wyndham Lewis's satirical boho-baiting worked because it was driven by clear-eyed recognition of aesthetic value: Clayson lacks any such principle. He remains doggedly ambivalent about Varèse's *oeuvre*, twice referring to it as 'the manufacture of funny noises'. He mocks Varèse for seeking sponsorship for audio research during the Great Depression, and thus adds his voice to the philistine chorus which condemns advanced art as a luxury, failing to see that Bell Telephone Co's unswerving loyalty to the 'value of the investor's dollar' (p. 134) (words from their letter of refusal to Varèse, who was asking for a grant for research into electronic music) was another manifestation of the vicious principle which was causing unemployment and war in the '30s.

In discussing Nazi Germany, Clayson ascends from the mildly irritating to the downright offensive: 'Under the Nazis, even Richard Strauss, that most Teutonic of then-living composers, had been oppressed by government intervention in artistic matters. Unlike Hindemith—along with Schoenberg and Bartok—he was not, however, willing to let it force him from his home or prevent his music from being heard.' (p. 132) The charge that communists and Jews who fled Nazi Germany were 'willing' exiles in comparison to those who, like Strauss, bravely soldiered on, is to denigrate the victims of one of history's most monstrous crimes. Debunking is a great game when played on the rich and powerful: when it's played on the persecuted and uprooted, it's vile.

There have been two previous biographies: Fernand Ouellette's *Edgard Varèse* (1966) and Louise Varèse's *Varèse: A Looking Glass Diary 1883-1928* (1973). Clayson says the Ouellette isn't worth buying because it's 'short on in-depth estimation of motive' (p. 9), but that's actually its strength. Varèse was uncomfortable with the idea of biography, but worked with Ouellette, amassing unpublished writings (including a sketch for his amazing sci-fi opera 'L'Astronome'), press-cuttings and other materials. After Varèse's death in 1965, Ouellette subtitled the book 'a musical biography,' but kept it free of the rib-digging bumptiousness which is Clayson's mode of 'estimating motive'. Clayson remains blithely unaware of the modernist scruple which fired Varèse and Zappa: the radically democratic demand that art be an opportunity for objective assessment of the social unconscious, not a vehicle for individual expression and celebrity. He is obtuse enough to reproduce two quotes which explain why biographical trivia—reducing Varèse to conformist concepts—diminishes the power and potential of his art: 'Facts about Varèse's life and work are difficult to obtain. He considers interest in them to be a form of necrophilia; he prefers to leave no traces'—John Cage; 'I don't think about the composer of pieces I enjoy listening to, I'm only listening to the results'—Frank Zappa.

One of the characteristics of dishonest thinking is that it projects its repressed urges on the enemy. The Nazis wanted to rule the world, so they invented a 'global Jewish conspiracy'. Clayson can only conceive music as a matter of social prestige and individual vanity, and so everything is reduced to his cynical measure. Actually, the life of Varèse is proof that careers and personal advance are *not* the only things that drive a person: but you don't need bodice-ripping yarns and sneers at the avant-garde to tell you that, you just need his music. Loud.

Christopher DeLaurenti
N30: Live at the WTO November 30 1999
Sonarmap Unnumbered CD

CHRISTOPHER DELAURENTI is a sonic artist based in Seattle. He runs a 'hardcore free-improvising electronics duo' with Alex Keller, hosts a radio programme broadcasting twentieth-century music and, along with noted guitarist and out-music activist Henry Hughes, writes for *Tentacle*, a print magazine which encourages creative music in the North West. The current issue includes a sympathetic and informed review of Roger Sutherland's *New Perspectives in Music*, showing that absolutist avant-garde rigour holds no terrors for this bunch. The truly bizarre development—now that 'avant' is a term capable of extracting subsidies from such progressive forces as Ford motor cars and the Japanese equivalent of BT—is DeLaurenti's sudden and unironic turn towards anti-capitalist politics. Maybe that's one advantage of being based in Seattle (though the City of London riot this year known as J18 didn't seem to inspire anyone at the London Musicians Collective).

Ever since the Impressionists broke out of the life class and started sketching people in modern apparel on the beach, everyday materials have been the prime swagger stick of the rebel artist. Dada film-maker Hans Richter called for artworks to be built from 'the documented fact'. In America, though, unshakeable faith in the transcendental category of 'art' led to Pop Art's 'Neo-Dada' misconstrual of Dada, replacing its politically-motivated assault on bourgeois values with the eternal opposition of art and life (a point made by Richter in his book *Dada: Art and Anti-Art*). The progressive ironization of 'reality' supplied surprise and entertainment for the final chamber of historically-arranged galleries. The vacant products of this post-Duchampian process—Cage's *4'33'*, Jasper Johns' beer can, Warhol's unedited films, Minimalism—transformed art into an intellectual endgame.

The problem is that Zen moralism is not sufficient to make everyday life under capitalism sublime. Cage's avidity for unprocessed reality—materials undominated by concepts—eventually becomes tedious and oppressive. Although the technological advances of ciné-reel, super8, video, magnetic tape and digital recording are indeed wonders in themselves, most American life/art experimentalism ends up celebrating predictable liberal values and quandaries. You come out of the gallery or film-club, and gaze at glittering nighttime city streets and think (for two minutes) 'Wow, life is so much richer than art!'

But what if the streets themselves turned into world-historical theatre? Born in 1967, DeLaurenti is himself a product of American experimentalism. His approach owes debts to Cage and Warhol. But with *N30*, he has outflanked the pointlessness of official US Avant by documenting an occasion of genuine world-historical import: the demonstration against the World Trade Organisation in Seattle on 30 November 1999. N30 showed the world that not everyone in America is content with the depredations its 'liberal' economics inflict on the world. 'The whole world is watching!' shouted the demonstrators, and they were right.

DeLaurenti edited down his four-hours of DAT tapes—made in the thick of the riot, as protestors prevented delegates from entering the meeting, and the police replied with tear-gas, pepper-spray and plastic bullets—to one 60m suite (it's preceded by two short pieces which prove DeLaurenti's skills as a street-talk documenter and orchestrator of noise). He presents discrete audio chunks, each of which makes a particular point. The far-off trombipulation of the teamsters' lorry-horns receives cheers from the turtle kids as they realize that the forces of the organised working class were—on that day—with them. There's advice and exhortation from more experienced agitators; the crack of tear-gas grenades being launched; denunciations of the police ('shame, shame, shame!'). You listen on the edge of your seat, every shout and noise significant, the raw emotion on show extraordinarily moving. Slogans ripple through the crowd like the chants during a Funkadelic show, abetted by drumming from assorted troupes. The polyrhythmic sensibility America imported with its black slaves informs both the demonstrators and your listening. This demo rocks!

Maybe all that avant experimentalism wasn't such a waste of time. Christopher DeLaurenti has documented the sound of a generation reaching towards anti-capitalist consciousness.

* * * * * * *

Julius Hemphill
Blue Boyé
Screwgun SCREWU70008 CD

BORN IN Fort Worth, Texas, in 1940, the late Julius Hemphill was a founder-member of BAG (Black Artists Group) in St. Louis. Although modelled on Chicago's AACM (Association for the Advancement of Creative Musicians), BAG people (Joe Bowie, Oliver Lake, Luther Thomas) were always a bit more streetwise, their blues and funk delivered with more conviction than that of the Art Ensemble of Chicago. Hemphill made a splash in late '70s New York, contributing spirited and earthy solos to the World Sax Quartet. This double album was recorded for his own Mbari label in 1977, aided by sax pupil Tim Berne, who now returns the compliment by reissuing the album on his own bijou imprint (*Jazzwise* called the downtown/designer packaging—origami cardboard and kinky print-faces—'infuriating'; such abuse would better be aimed at the usual jewel case).

Hemphill overtracks flute, sax and minimal percussion to create sparse, bluesy pieces. His improvisations are based on a simple pentatonic motif. Blues and swing work by rubbing against the rhythm, creating dialectical antagonism, so unaccompanied sax tends to sound a little thin. There are exceptions (Coleman Hawkins' 'Picasso' (1948); the terrifying architectonics of Anthony Braxton's *For Alto* (1968); Alan Wilkinson's outrageous *Seedy Boy* (1994)), but this isn't one. Though Hemphill's blowing is never less than poised and intimate, he is perhaps better remembered for his fabulous, extravagant contributions to freely swinging collectives.

Billy Jenkins with the Blues Collective
<sadtimes.co.uk>
Voice of the People VOCD002 CD

TALKING JAMES Carter up a storm—contrasting the saxophonist's approach to the stale procedures of jazz neo-classicism—Cecil Taylor hit the nail on the head: 'When Carter walked on stage he stunned me with *what he do*! He made one harmonic sound—*eeerrrrgh!*—and then he walked off the fucking stage! And he comes back and makes another sound. When he had to deal with that rhythm and blues shit [*i.e.*, bass'n'drum supreme team Jamaaladeen

Tacuma and Calvin Weston], it wasn't about notes. And when James did this *obbligato*, man, it wasn't just technical, it was passionate!'

Cecil could have been describing guitarist Billy Jenkins. *Listen to him explode on 'Resting on My Bed of Blues'!* His phrases smash through the iron bars laid down by Thad Kelly (bass) and Mike Pickering (drums)—*eeerrrrgh!*—with a gestural panache that has NEVER heretofore been achieved by British electric guitarists (Jeff Beck nearly got there, but only in fusion contexts which were too spacey to allow his licks to burst the seams; maybe Steve Marriott had it—for half a minute—back in 1966; and maybe Mick Ronson on a good night...). Jenkins packs the ice-pick-in-the-forehead, take-this-statement-and-hang-it-in-yer-ass, right-note-in-the-wrong-place R&B *attitude* which Zappa admired in Gatemouth Brown and Guitar Slim and Johnny 'Guitar' Watson. It's like a barbed-wire fence swearing at you. The notes jump out like they're possessed. It's astonishing.

But—born too late for the platinum escape-hatch that popped open for Hendrix and Cream—what can Jenkins *do* with this outrageous talent? His answer is to wrap his guitarism in lyrics that trash Mississippi clichés, a suburban surrealism derived from pantomime, *The Beano*, Sid James, punk, street furniture and shopping centres—any aspect of contemporary life toxic to blues cliché. Comedic bathos repels superficial listening, tests your ability to discern exceptional music. In Richard Bolton (rhythm guitar), Jenkins has a sophisticated harmonist; in Dylan Bates (violin), a player who knows that without grit the notes won't work (one day Jenkins will surely compose him a concerto of Sugarcane Harris proportions). The opening of 'Badlands'—a superb integration of dub and guitar-twang—could be an On U-Sound production: despite the jokes, the music is that inspiring, that heavy.

Billy Jenkins with the Blues Collective: a reproach to contemporary blandishments that'll be 'discovered' by arsehole advertisers half a century too late. Just like the blues....

* * * * * * *

Sonic Liberation Front
Water and Stone
Eye Dog Records EDR1003 CD

THIS BEGINS with a loop, a rumbling bass-line of *motörik* junglism. Metrically, it recalls the complex riffs favoured by Fela Kuti or Bootsy: before it repeats, it's set up an assymetrical pattern that could derive from a vocal chant. Having thus nodded to sampling technology, the loop is overlayed with realspace Cuban percussion recorded with astonishing audiophile detail: you can practically make out the prints on the fingers tapping *bata*, *conga*, and *quinto*. These guys—Nick Rivera, Chuckie Joseph, Joey Toledo and Frank 'Squirrel' Williams—make no compromise with 4/4 normalcy, making for one of the most arresting openings on a commercial album since Malcolm McLaren began *Duck Rock* with Lucumi Cult drumming back in 1983. The beats won't fit a metre that allows you to take the percussive strokes as read, yet the spaces opened-up are fiercely intended.

Into this Youruba invocation step the horns—Terry Lawson, Adam Jenkins, Kimbal Brown—playing with the *jazz-noir* simplicity and intensity of underground hero Frank Lowe. The themes are reminiscent of those Oliver Nelson wrote for *Blues And The Abstract Truth*, though again the brilliant recording keeps each instrument separate. Joseph Toledo's Lucumi vocals are the chant someone makes whose attention is fixed on the drum he's slapping. As they're answered by Howard Cooper's flexible jazz bass, you realise that drummer/leader Kevin Diehl has achieved a genuine fusion of Cuban percussion and jazz. No piano to cushion the encounter of free-jazz sonority and percussive complexity in showbiz mediocrity! All the jam bands and techno-pagan DJs who invoke the name of Sun Ra should take note: *this* has some of the Arkestra's feel for rhythm.

Latin Jazz has long had a reputation for busy banality: likewise, a long list of studio productions which fuse techno beats, ethnic percussion and jazz soloism. Stark, stripped down, but utterly coordinated, Sonic Liberation Force build up a dialogue between Yoruba and Bop from scratch, and it's an extraordinary listen. Best of all, the audio production doesn't patronise exotic timbres with electro-processed eezi-spred. Move over Bill Laswell, and tell Jon Hassell the news.

****

Various
Root & Branch 2: 'Everybody Swing'
Unknown
PUBLIC CD+book+poster+facsimiles

THE REPUBLICATION of Harry Smith's *Anthologies of American Folk* provided some essential footnotes for understanding radical American music, from Bob Dylan to Eugene Chadbourne. Could Unknown Public's *Root & Branch* collection do the same here? They present a box of materials in an A4-size folder. Inside: a twenty-three-track CD covering the period 1947 to 1963 in British and Irish folk; a wall chart of events in each year; two examples of the English Folk Dance & Song Society's 'millennial edition' of fifty-five trading cards (mine show composer Percy Grainger, and LP covers of the 1961 series *The Folk Songs Of Britain*); a booklet with track details and brief memoirs by key figures (including Billy Bragg on skiffle); a facsimile concert programme for Big Bill Broonzy at Kingsway Hall, London in 1951.

The CD works like a radio documentary. Tracks are linked by snippets from interviews: Lord Kitchener sings an impromptu calypso on disembarking from the *Empire Windrush* in 1948; guitarist Wizz Jones recalls seeing Broonzy play in a pub on Wardour Street; Ted Poole, secretary/organiser of the Swindon Folksingers Club, describes setting up one of the UK's first folk clubs in January 1960. There's trad jazz, skiffle, blues, orchestral 'Square Dance' music, ballads, and four songs by Jane Turriff, the traditional singer born in Fetterangus, Aberdeenshire in 1915. It's all rather polite.

The '50s folk scene was riven with quarrels over authenticity, politics and class. Ewan MacColl and AL Lloyd bravely attempted to connect roots folk with communist and union politics. The English Folk Dance & Song Society, based at Cecil Sharp House, was one site of contestation. When Prince Philip and Princess Elizabeth were photographed at a Square Dance at Government House in Ottawa, they inspired a national craze. The EFDSS was inundated with requests for music and information. English folk became an establishment enthusiasm, encouraged in schools and at village *fêtes*. Eventually, even the director of the EFDSS was moved to publish an article deploring the music's 'devitalisation', regretting the way the personal, 'almost animal' element in folk song had been lost.

The CD certainly features much twee ghastliness. For proof of folk's lack of demotic energy, take 'The Ring Dance' by the Haymakers Square Dance Band, a combo who had a residency on the BBC radio show *Everybody Swing*. The tune is what Bob Wills & the Texas Playboys called a 'stomp' two decades earlier. Whereas American Western Swing bands would feature a violinist or clarinet-player, a soloist syncopating a counter-rhythm to the ensemble thrust and thus driving the dancers nuts, the BBC ensemble is lifeless: patronising and staid. You can see Prince Philip and his check shirt.

Indeed, one has is hard put to locate anything here that isn't repressed and nostalgic, scared of the speed and complexity of modern life: paeans to false consciousness. Even where affecting moments emerge—the grit and chill of Margaret Barry's vocal on 'She Moved Through the Fair', for example, as she accompanied herself with guitar (and cash registers) at the Bedford Arms in 1958—the musical culture is too pinched to allow for brilliance or innovation, for *spark*. Where individualised expression survives, it's framed in a way that prevents it rattling the means of production. The ideological burden folk was asked to carry was beyond its formal density or potential for pleasure. Ewan MacColl's song about the wrongful execution of Timothy Evans in 1953 helped turn popular sentiment against the death penalty, but he still sings like it'll put hairs on his chest. His notion of the working man was Stalinist and romantic, unreal.

Despite being Chicago's slickest arranger and A&R-man, Big Bill Broonzy donned dungarees to play 'genuine blues' for the white folks (actually, his guitar licks were pure ragtime). Nevertheless, his 'Five Foot Seven' still explodes like a fire-cracker, a message from a totally different scene, where dynamism and detail can be packed into a song, where singers don't make a mark by pouring sentiment into moronically regressive form. On the last page of the booklet, there's a photo of the young Bob Dylan singing at MacColl's London club in 1962. You can't wait for rock to arrive and stomp all over this nation of bogus rural tootling.

* * * * * * *

Vienna Art Orchestra
The Minimalism of Erik Satie
Hat Hut hatOLOGY 560 CD

THE VIENNA Art Orchestra was a ridiculously brilliant big band, lavishly funded, endlessly rehearsed, peopled with striking musicians. Michael Kornhäus's studio recording—made in Vienna in 1983 and 1984—is so transparent and vivid the effect is stunning, Kandinsky-like. In 1979, the VAO issued an LP whose cover pastiched Gary Panter's cover for Frank Zappa's *Studio Tan*: the glittering clarity of that album's arrangements and recording also surface here.

VAO's leader Mathias Rüegg uses Satie's music as a pretext for his own arrangements, which are as eloquent and band-specific as those of Willem Breuker. A duet between Wolfgang Puschnig's sopranino and Wolfgang Reisinger's tarabuka on 'Reflections on Gnossienne No. 1' evokes the brittle sarcasm of Kurt Weill as it rouses bohemian rhapsody versus tight-lipped Austrian repression.

In his sleeve notes, H.K. Gruber turns intellectual somersaults attempting to place Satie in a critical relationship to Western concepts of art. However, he's prancing about on a rug that Rüegg has already magic-carpeted from the building: his arrangements excavate the sedimented social content of Satie's banalities and give his musicians genuine work to do. This chill, arch, lucid music should not be reduced to a pawn in a tedious match between art and occasion: by giving his players real problems of modulation—between significantly alluring cultural pleasures, not merely key-signatures (though these are of course related)—Rüegg creates musical moments which shrink all cultural relatives down to a single, bright-burning candle.

~2001~

Derek Bailey with Vertrek Ensemble
Departures
Volatile Records VCD002
Eugene Chadbourne with Vertrek Ensemble
Dimsum, Dodgers, and Dangerous Nights
Volatile Records VCD003

THE VERTREK Ensemble are a duo from Canada: Vadim Budman on guitars, cornet, trumpet, wooden flute, harmonica and reed cornet; Ron de Jong on percussion. For *Departures*, they flew in to London to record with Derek Bailey at Moat Studios on 13 May 1998. For '*Dimsum, Dodgers, and Dangerous Nights*,' they invited Eugene Chadbourne to their hometown of Edmonton, Alberta, to play two nights at the Yardbird Suite in March 2000. Though they look a little less fresh-faced in the snapshot with Chadbourne, it's evidently the same band, any changes more due to sensitivity to their guests than any musical turnabout.

Despite their relative youth (they're in their late twenties), Budman and de Jong are sophisticated musicians, conversant with the wide-open spaces, knockabout humour and mutual respect of Bailey and Chadbourne gigs and releases. As with French guitarist Noël Akchoté's pursuit of these two mentors of guitar materialism (what you hear is actually what's there), it's encouraging when new players have the determination to woodshed and the courage to hook up. Of course, Chadbourne was once a fresh-faced youth from Alberta himself (albeit with a background in jazz journalism and high school rock bands), when he knocked on Bailey's door in the mid-'70s. When Pete Frame gets to draw this particular family tree, he is going to trace an estimable lineage of premium string-manglers.

With Toby Robinson and his equipment on hand, *Departures* is particularly fine in the audio department. Bailey thrives on the fleet beats and timbral variety of de Jong's percussion. Anyone who's been bitten by *String Theory*, Bailey's feedback album, also recorded at Moat by Robinson (in January 2000), will want to check out these astonishingly pure and decisive wieldings of tweaked-string effects at an earlier stage. Budman plays lively, idiosyncratic, vocalised lines on trumpet, everything the formal 'jazz trumpet' of the likes of Dave Douglas tends to omit. The horn also provides welcome horizontalism: the sounds of vibrating metal-tube and guitar-string coalesce in striking ways. Whereas often employed as prettified spray-on in ambient samplitude, here the distressed moments push at natural breaking-points: both shockingly raw and beautiful at the same time. At the end, Derek suggests a cup of tea.

As one might expect, *Dimsum, Dodgers...* isn't quite such a pure experience. Noting the many bells in de Jong's equipment, Chadbourne taught the duo the chords of the jazz standard 'If I Were a Bell'. Best known to me in an instrumental version by Coltrane and Miles, Chadbourne somehow dredged up the pun-heavy lyrics ('If I were a gate I'd be swingin'...'). It makes a terrific opener. Like Bailey, Chadbourne loves to match sonority for sonority, though he always gives his licks an 'aw, shucks' twist. Budman and de Jong know how to abet a tune without locking it in, and Budman is ridiculously fluent on trumpet. De Jong is at ease with Chadbourne's cartoon aesthetic: some of his interventions are pure Spike Jones. 'I Challenge You to an Epiphone Duo' has Chadbourne and Budman loop the loop, pursuing crazy extensions with finesse. On 'Death Lives Down in That Bayou,' Chadbourne picks up his banjo and they go into the kind of exotic hoedown unheard since the Suns of Arqa transformed Prince Far I into Captain Beefheart.

Vertrek with Chadbourne recalls a '30s 'spasm' band: three extrovert sound makers keep us on the edge of our seats, scaring us and making us laugh in turns. On the last track—a moving recognition of 'Mother's Eyes' that proves that Chadbourne may be as funny as Jerry Lee Lewis, but he's also as convincing a sentimentalist—Chadbourne points out a mistake in the concert programme. Yes, his mother was a refugee from Nazi Germany, but not from the death camps: 'not too many people were refugees from the death camps...'

Seriously amusing, virtuosic, and fresh, the Vertrek Ensemble can deal with two of the heaviest artists on today's guitar. They sound like they really enjoy what they do, so we do too.

* * * * * * *

Roger Beebe, Denise Fulbrook, Ben Saunders (Editors)
*Rock Over the Edge: Transformations in Popular Music
    Culture*
Duke University Press

TWO-HUNDRED-AND-SEVENTY MILLIMETRES thick, 392 pages long,
weighing in at 609 grammes and camouflage green in colour, this
collection of essays stems from Popular Music Studies, a belea-
guered and rather guilty subdepartment of Cultural Studies. Following 'advances' made by the Birmingham Centre for Contemptible
Cultural Studies in the late '70s, baby-boomer enthusiasm for rock
and revolution was converted into youth sociology. Attention to fads
gripping the attention of current teenagers was supposed to keep the
'discipline' vital and up-to-date. Fredric Jameson's *Postmodernism*
(1991) provides the ground note for all contributors, who largely
accept his thesis that capitalist incorporation means most ideals
minted in the '60s were hopelessly tarnished by the '80s. Younger
academics seeking to prove themselves contest minor issues (Josh
Kun stresses the radicalism of Ruben Guevara's *rock en español*,
Trent Hill asks why country music gets left out, Roger Beebe notes
that Hip Hop is more realistic than mainstream MTV about death).
Unfortunately, none possess the conceptual bazooka required to
blast Popular Music Studies and its egregious presuppositions to
powder (they don't want to—they want tenure!).
    Lawrence Grossberg's 'Reflections of a Disappointed Popular
Music Scholar' laments this situation. He criticises the '60s 'rebels'
who today call for lower taxes, less government spending and restrictions on sexuality, drugs and popular music. However, his own
sociology of rock leads ineluctably to moralistic reaction and the
politics of despair. His 'assumption, one that I hope we all share' is
that 'a large part of the power of postwar popular music depends in
part on the mechanisms and systems of identification—both real and
imaginary, of all different kinds (*e.g.*, fantasy, alliance, affiliation),
and between different fractions of the population (*e.g.*, black and
white, male and female, gay and straight)—that it calls into exis-
tence and deploys'. Actually, the reverse is true: *marketing* creates
these divisions in the population, and in so doing weakens the power
of the music. All great music—from Beethoven to Hendrix—aspires
to universality, not identity. As Samuel Beckett pointed out in his
essay on *Finnegans Wake*, identity-thinking is the enemy of art, not
its ally. Bessie Smith, Tammy Wynette, and Maggie Nicols are not

'women's music'—they establish the concrete possibility of a universal humanity.

Grossberg's mapping of identifications not only implies a transcendent, supra-social, all-seeing sociologist who is somehow untrammelled by everyone else's identities, it takes marketing categories for musical ones, and confuses money-making opportunities for the few with musical and social power for the mass. Despite talk of 'deconstruction' and multiple citations from Derrida and Deleuze, Popular Music Studies blithely proceeds as if conceptual categories like 'popular' can be understood without dialectical reflection, *i.e.* examining pop in the light of its opposite—namely *un*popular music, and the avant-garde's bizarre (and usually unexamined) relation to new waves of musical commodification. As proved by the reams of drivel now being published today about the '60s, anyone who talks about the Beatles without mentioning Archie Shepp and Conlon Nancarrow—the useful minds the pop 'revolution' denied—is talking piffle. Likewise, anyone who talks about punk without mentioning reggae—Prince Buster, Doc Alimontado, Bad Brains—doesn't have an inkling of what motivated its prime movers.

The book's title promises 'transformations': what's stunning is how predictable and static are its governing concepts. Popular Music Studies remains hypnotized by Derrida's otiose critique of authenticity (so pale and overwrought in comparison to Adorno's assault on Heidegger and Jaspers in *The Jargon of Authenticity*). Essentially a religious thinker, Derrida has never forgiven post-enlightenment society for thinking it could abandon Holy Scripture as a basis for establishing truth. His philosophical motifs have become the cheapest blind for modern sophists, who think they can evade every matter of social fact by accusing their accusers of 'belief in authenticity'. In *Rock Over The Edge*, every time the 'a' word is invoked, the argument spins into scepticism and despair. The best moments arrive when writers bin the theoretical arsewipe and register how the music makes them feel, as when Trent Hill insists that Hank Williams and the Sex Pistols are somehow more 'real' than average pop.

Michael Coyle starts out making an interesting distinction between the '50s/'60s practice of hijacking hits (Dale and Grace covering Don and Dewey's 'I'm Leaving It All Up to You') and '80s/'90s rock bands borrowing the *gravitas* of long-forgotten blues and soul songs—as he says, the blanket charge of 'white rip-off' is simplistic. However, his sprinkling of Foucault and Bourdieu fails to make his exposition any brighter than similar—and much wittier—expositions by non-academics like Nick Tosches and Dave Marsh.

A muddled application of structuralist linguistics ('signifiers') and Derrida (versus 'essentializing') forces Coyle into a dilemma between the vapidity of semiotic free-play and the prison house of metaphysical absolutes. He has no inkling of the dialectical solution: Hegel's *Begriff*, which is a concept which articulates an actual process—a dynamic contradiction—in the world. Equipped with *Begriffe* like capital, musicianship, integrity, exploitation, use value—and Adorno's notion of genuine, concept-busting musical experience— Popular Music Studies might actually achieve the results Grossberg longs for.

Back in 1978, Mark P asked the London punks: 'How much longer will people wear/Nazi armbands and dye their hair?' In the same spirit (and South London accent) one wants to ask: how much longer will academics write sentences like 'the affect of postmodern music culture no longer has the same rooting in the expressive truths of modernism'? The theory examines itself in the mirror, and finds all its keywords and accessories intact. Catatonic solipsism. No wonder the book ends in a paean to the Pet Shop Boys, the one pop act which has swallowed enough postmodernist theory to decorate their hallowed dirges with its dubious opinions. Meanwhile, Eminem takes the vitality and rush and rawness of the black-music underground into the charts. Has everything 'transformed' since Elvis, or are we actually still stuck in the same morass of racism, economic exploitation, establishment moralism, imperialist wars and media lies, blackface clowns our only relief? A wider look at society—some *real* sociology—might bring Popular Music Studies out of its postmodern daydream and break it from its baby-boomer narrative.

* * * * * * *

Nadine Cohodas
Spinning Blues into Gold: Chess Records, the Label That Launched the Blues
Aurum (pbk)

When Lejzor and Fiszel, aged eleven and seven, disembarked from the steamship *Mauretania* with their mother Cyrla at Staten Island in 1928, refugees from Motele in Poland, they knew the names which their father, resident in Chicago since 1921, had picked for them: Leonard and Philip. He had already changed his own name, from

Yasef Czyz to Joseph Chess. The brothers grew up to give their assumed surname to a record label which inspired the Rolling Stones and defined rock as a form. Chess was set up to sell records to the black population of Chicago: any success in the pop charts was icing on the cake. The brothers issued gospel, sermons, stand-up comedy, doo-wop and jazz, but it was the amplified blues of Muddy Waters and Howling Wolf which gave Chess its identity. In Etta James, Sugarpie deSanto, Fontella Bass and Koko Taylor, Chess discovered strong voices which directly challenged WASP stereotypes of femininity (dig deep into the Chess aesthetic, and it's not hard to find the kaballistic sexual materialism David Bakan theorises as the progressive core of Freudian psychoanalysis). Whenever anyone thrills to the modernist primitivism of overdriven electric sound, they are responding to sounds originally unleashed by these two Jewish businessmen.

In a field riven with controversy—about commercial exploitation and racial prejudice, in particular—Nadine Cohodas's many interviews and painstaking research provide much badly-needed fact. Leonard Chess was the tough-talking front man of the label, Phil his quieter partner. They originally started in the liquor business in Chicago's "black downtown". Leonard's generous use of local expletives—particularly "motherfucker"—was legendary. He drove hard bargains and hated parting with money, yet his musicians stayed loyal. Only Chuck Berry walked out—for a three-year sojourn with Mercury Records—but even he returned to the fold. Leonard's payments to the musicians were paternalist rather than by the book: crises (hospital fees, legal bills, bail payments) were taken care of, but royalty statements were irregular. A week after Leonard's death in 1973, a man in a suit and tie appeared on Etta James's door-step, and handed her the deeds to her house. Concerned that her wild ways with liquor and drugs would ruin her, Leonard had been making the mortgage payments without telling her. The assumption was that, rather than being a money-spinner in itself, a hit record established a musician's name: they then made money with live appearances. Tough on the musician, maybe, but the arrangement certainly made for a vital musical culture.

As civil rights and Black Power burgeoned in the '60s, Chess's paternalism came under attack. One reason for selling the company in 1968 was to avoid such charges. But while Leonard Chess was alive, he kept the musicians happy. After his death in 1973—with the Chess back catalogue in the hands of GRT, All Platinum/Sugar Hill and finally Universal—musicians resented seeing their music everywhere with so little recompense. Sophisticated modern art-

ists—plotting their sales forecasts and royalties on spreadsheet software—may have rid themselves of foul-talking, deal-making wise
guys, but by taking market rationality into the grain of their production, they also render their art beige and insipid. In contrast, Chess
Records was a conduit for down-home, devil-may-care blues—
sessions were in-house and spontaneous, like at Sun—making it the
most prized label of the British Blues Boom.

Leonard had strong ideas about what would sell—he'd stamp
on the floor to indicate the tempo he was after, hold up signs saying
"more blues" to reticent bass players—but his input came from
crude enthusiasm rather than commercial calculation. Confronted
with an "artsy fartsy" advertising image for his radio station WVON
("Voice of the Negro"), Leonard took the designer (Rollin Binzer)
on a tour of South Side bars and lounges, culminating with one pa-
tron who took the poster out to a backyard, climbed on a chair and
urinated on it. Rock's ambivalence about the ways of the music
business was brilliantly caught in Nic Roeg's *Performance*, with its
disturbing cameo of Mick Jagger as a boardroom gangster: "Memo
from Turner" was a fantasy based on Leonard Chess.

As with Sam Philips at Sun Records, accusations of racism are
inappropriate. Leonard had a genuine regard for the musicians, or
they wouldn't have stuck with him. The rumour that black musicians
were not allowed to use the front door at Chess—or that Keith Rich-
ards discovered Muddy Waters in overalls, painting the walls at
Chess studios—are apocryphal, stories designed to fit stereotypes of
The Man. Chess was passionate about civil rights, donating money
to the NAACP and local black churches. Radio WVON broadcast
bitter complaints about the hosing of civil rights demonstrators in
Alabama in 1963, and helped organise a one-day school-student
boycott about class-sizes.

Cohodas's own father was a refugee who made it in America,
and the subtext of this book is that minor-league capitalism is not
necessarily cruel and exploitative. But a certain conservatism is
written into American success stories. When Martin Luther King
was shot, Binzer supplied Chess with a photograph of King standing
in front of the stars and stripes, and ran an ad in the *Chicago Trib-
une* "in tribute to the memory of a great American". Leonard Chess
did not welcome King's opposition to the war in Vietnam, and issued a comedy album by Bob Hope, a notorious hawk. His son Marshall, on the other hand, grew his hair, smoked pot and went psychedelic—and joined the anti-war movement. After the riot outside
the Democratic Convention in Chicago in the summer of 1968, Marshall and Binzer issued an album called *Peace* with a picture of

Santa Claus wounded and lying on the ground in Lincoln Park, a site where many demonstrators had been injured by police. The cover created a scandal, with many complaints, but did cause *Billboard* to wade in with an anti-war editorial.

Occasionally, the account of deals and dollars becomes monotonous, and you wonder if the biography of an immigrant who made it in shoes or hosiery might not be equally interesting. However, because pop music is such a charged area for the formation of telling symbols, it's essential to keep such actualities in focus. Certainly, the competitive world of commerce has a different set of priorities from the nothing-left-to-lose verities of the down-home blues, and it's nothing short of amazing that Leonard Chess rode the contradictions for so long. After his death, deprived of the linchpin of his personality, the label fell apart. Perhaps surprising in view of some of the anti-Chess statements made by Muddy Waters, Cohodas describes him as weeping at the graveside: "It's all over, Leonard. It's just all over. There ain't no record company. No more nothin', Leonard". It wasn't the money, Chess had insisted, it was "the game". For a brief period, expanding petty capitalism and progressive cultural politics linked forces, creating a template that has been often imitated, but never equalled.

* * * * * * *

Kahil El'Zabar/Billy Bang
Spirits Entering
Delmark DE-533 CD

PERCUSSIONIST KAHIL El'Zabar calls his groups the Ritual Trio and the Ethnic Heritage Ensemble, but there's an element of jive-ass showmanship when he moves from drumset to hand drums, thumb-piano or berimbau (or, as he does here, sings a croaky version of 'Old Time Religion'). However, if it's not going to be swamped in the solemnity of art or mysticism, jive-ass showmanship should be hailed as part and parcel of the 'heritage'. In the cover photo, with his shades and straw Panama hat, El'Zabar looks like a stoned hipster lounging about in a seedy bar—as drawn by cartoonist Ray Lowry.

However, just as music hall and clowning play a crucial role in Free Improvisation, so El'Zabar's ability to shake a rhythm from any instrument provides just the spritzer free-form jazz requires. In violinist Billy Bang, who has played avant-garde (*Outline No 12*), instrumental ethno-pop (*The Fire from Within*), white-cube art solos (*Commandment*) and consummate post-Ornette bop (*Untitled Gift*), he finds his ideal partner.

They begin with the title song, a typical pentatonic blues from Bang, full of unguarded sentiment and tinged with oriental exoticism. El'Zabar claims a special affinity with Bang, and they balance poignancy, whimsy and funk with defiant grace. On 'Song of Myself,' the tune references the major-chord tearfulness of gospel and Broadway, though an impish sense of rhythm prevents it becoming maudlin. On this straight acoustic recording, El'Zabar's various percussive gimmicks provide textural agitations which brings the music into the orbit of electronical materialism. Bang's twisting, energised lines plait together a ceaseless dialectic between linear logic and folk rhythm. Plaintive whole-tone sincerities veer off into scrabbled extensions with delightful exposed-nerve logic. The result is individual and fresh, the project of the Art Ensemble of Chicago shorn of its theatrical trappings and distilled into the notes themselves. On first listening, sound production seemed rather weedy (it would be good to hear Bang in an AUM Fidelity, in-your-face recording), but finally the spindly details add up to a spine-tingling experience: a bearskin rub-a-dub in 3D feelo-vision.

In April, Billy Bang played a Butch Morris 'Conduction' at Tonic, New York, his personality totally suppressed by Morris's dictatorial baton: El'Zabar's funky tomfoolery reassures us that Bang is still himself, his unlikely mix of sentiment and caustic still fizzing.

* * * * * * *

Tony Glover, Scott Dirks & Ward Gaines
Blues with a Feeling: The Little Walter Story
Routledge

SOME ERAS of music are so saturated with significance, each detail shines. In cases like that of rhythm'n'blues harmonica virtuoso Little Walter—born Marion Walter Jacobs in Marksville, Louisiana, the edge of Cajun country, in 1930, and dying at 209 East 54th Street in Chicago, in February 1968—it's probably best to let the facts speak for themselves. That's precisely what Glover, Dirks and Gaines do here, building a documentary narrative by presenting us with the results of extensive research. In Britain, Routledge have cornered the market in sociology and cultural studies. One expects dreary acres of postmodern theory from their imprint, but their US branch, which commissioned this book, appears to prefer the facts. Because of Little Walter's seminal influence on rock and pop, this dense, 315-page biography could actually serve as a textbook for anyone seeking to understand what recording and mass production do to folk expression, and how cultural forces like music relate to social change.

Blues musicians call the harmonica the 'harp'. It's an appropriate name: for its nagging, breathy insistence (it sounds both when you blow and when you suck in air), and for the way its wheezing chords recall church organs, and hence angelic musics. Little Walter made his name with the Muddy Waters Band in the late '40s and early '50s. His harp exploited the new powers of electric amplification just as much as Waters' slide guitar. Walter would hold harmonica and mic cupped together in his hands, sending the signal to his own amp and speaker. He'd blow hard, using the resulting hiccoughs and distortion to spike his stream of ideas. The authors here call him the Charlie Parker and Jimi Hendrix of his chosen instrument, and that is no exaggeration: Walter's ripping attack, with its sudden drop-outs and dynamic peaks, drove any vestige of rural quaintness from the harmonica. His amped-up harp sounds twisted and wonky, super-urban, like a tram's conductor-bar fizzing on the electric rail. Little Walter used every resonance and squeal from his speaker, creating a wraparound sonic which intoxicated the crowd. Glover is the author of a guide to harmonica playing which has been a bestseller for four decades. His technical dissections of Walter's solos—the differently-keyed models, the chromatic harp, the 'quiver' created by moving the instrument over the lips rather than shaking the head—are a joy.

Little Walter's importance is explained in terms familiar to jazz and improv listeners. Walter was continually inventive, resisting the temptation to rely on familiar licks. Indeed, his 'formula for success' is described as 'the *absence* of a rigid formula or pattern'. The strength of '50s R&B was that the audience recognised this quality, and so flocked to see artists like Little Walter: marketing had not yet learned to manufacture image and prey upon identity. Local harp-players would sit in, only to be outblown by the master: a version of the 'cutting contests' which enlivened swing and bore strange fruit with bebop. Walter also played guitar, and would work out his arrangements on that instrument (drummer Sam Levy said he never saw him pick up a harmonica other than on stage). The immediacy of electric amplification of breath-through-mouth shaped by lips-on-metal had a similarly explosive impact to the way the electric guitar was converting intimate finger wiggles into public bravado.

At his peak in the mid-'50s, Little Walter was a star, with heaps of dollar-bills from door-takes in the boot of his Cadillac. Like many rap stars today, his background did not prepare him for financial success, and he was involved in countless fights. He declared he liked winos and bums—'my people'. He carried a pistol, and shot himself in the leg twice. An uncompromising personality, his head was frequently cracked by police truncheons. He toured England with pick-up bands in 1964. A life of hard-touring and hard-drinking began to tell on him. Another obstacle was the folk-blues revival of the later '60s. Promoters and record men who had previously sold to ghetto audiences began chasing the white student market. Leonard Chess no longer let Walter use his mic-and-amp set-up in the studio, and he had to play acoustically behind Hound Dog Taylor on the American Folk-Blues Festival tour of Europe in 1967 (he dissed his fellow musicians as 'them damn country coons'). Little Walter's decline into drink and violence was aggravated by frustration at not being an able to dictate the terms of his art (he called the sound of his non-amplified harp, no longer loud enough to direct his musicians, 'nauseating').

Of course, the way these facts appear to speak for themselves is a tribute to the authors' musical sensitivity and political acumen. They do not stoop to the cheap novelisation which is the poor biographer's standby, instead citing contemporary *Cashbox* record reviews, gossip columns, and personal interviews. The hip lingo of yore proves to be extraordinarily evocative. All the musicians make fascinating comments (though Little Walter's sister Marguerite proves to be the most acute observer). The accounts of gigs where musical excitement caused the 'colour bar'—a chain dividing the hall—to be broken are truly inspiring. Myths about universal racial prejudice in the South also bite the dust. Guitar Red recalls: 'We'd pull up to a service station, and the man say, 'Would you like to play a party tonight?'. We'd say 'Yassuh' and he ask how much—Walter would give 'em a price. They'd have us up at the farm, in the barn. They'd have a hoedown, a big dance—and give us all that country ham and bacon to take home. We stopped at several of them, they loved the blues.' This biography doesn't give a rose-tinted view, and the narrative is often harrowing, but it's studded with the odd moments and strange tales which make actuality more exciting and hopeful than dreary generalisation: a worthy complement to the epochal music Little Walter blew on his harp.

* * * * * * *

London Improvisers Orchestra
the hearing continues...
Emanem 4203 2CD

THE LONDON Improvisers Orchestra was originally convened to tour
beneath the baton of Butch Morris in 1997. Since then, it's been
gathering regularly at the Red Rose Club on Seven Sisters Road.
Thirty-eight musicians are involved. The organisation of large numbers for improvisation isn't easy, especially if the rhythmic strategies pioneered by the masters—Ellington, Mingus, Sun Ra—are
deemed a foreign tongue and out of bounds, as is mainly the case
here. The musicians take turns to direct the ensemble, using minimal
paperwork and relying instead on gesture ('conduction') and ver-
bally-expressed concepts. Pieces are around ten minutes in length:
fourteen tracks on two seventy-minute CDs.

Freely improvised pieces begin each disk, alerting the listener
to the forces available. These musicians are skillful at staying out of
each others' way. This is not a squall or a racket, but a fine-veined,
variegated symphonic music with textures reminiscent of Webern,
Berio, and Lachenmann. Occasionally, there's a whoosh or clatter
that feels like the whole picture is fraying or quaking, a destabilisa-
tion so radical it seems to question the very idea of music. Yet the
orchestra plays on, so these effects must be desired. Some passages
betray Butch Morris's influence. During his conductions, he'll point
to certain musicians and ask them to repeat what they'd just played.
Trilling, repetitive motifs become a way for musicians to keep playing, but without the shock of inventing new lines. This generates the
melancholic, nostalgic mood which is something of a Morris trademark.

Individual direction tends to pull the music back towards traditional forms. Veryan Weston's 'Concert For Soft-Loud Key-Box' is
a nod to the piano concerto. Simon Fell's 'Morton's Mobile' uses a
chord sequence to create a semi-erased, Feldmanesque tone poem,
the 'Coronation Street' theme slowed down to ghost-town spooki-
ness. An authoritative ascending motif from Evan Parker gives the
other five saxophonists a frame to climb on in the sax sextet 'Dingos
Creep.' Alex Ward's 'How Can You Delude Youself?' introduces a
perverse, stop-start humour reminiscent of cartoons. Caroline Kraa-

136 * *HONESTY IS EXPLOSIVE!* BY BEN WATSON

bel's 'Drop the Handkerchief'—a Zorn-like 'game piece' of point and play—isolates instruments from the ensemble in quick tag exchanges.

By disc two, one is beginning to think that orchestral improvisation may work better as a generator for publicity, networking and funding than as a creative musical endeavour. The best track is Evan Parker's 'Orphy:Us,' where Orphy Robinson's overdubbed marimba provides the close-focus personality and sense of decision missing elsewhere: the way his line attempts to make sense of the aleatoric wheezing and groaning behind him is entrancing. 'Pulse Piece' by Pat Thomas has tense rhythms, but never quite bursts out of neo-classical dispersal into the Cecil Taylorish volcano it promises. 'Music for Pianos, Percussion & Harp' has effective sonorities, but then that's achieved by severely limiting the number of musicians. 'Proceeding 4,' 'Birthday Piece' and 'Prior to Freedom' all have moments of interest, but the net effect is rather tired and mournful, even dutiful. The ensemble coasts on the very fact that so many musicians are on hand: we're all here because we ought to be, rather than because we're unleashing the evil heat of our musical desires.

In her notes in the booklet, Caroline Kraabel refers to recording as 'translation,' wishing there was a term for recorded music which distinguished it from live events. She quotes Walter Benjamin from 'The Task of the Translator,' suggesting that recordings and live performances may add up to some total, ideal picture. Resort to this essay is rather strange, since in 'The Work Of Art in the Age of Mechanical Reproduction,' Benjamin directly addressed the new technologies of photography, recording and film, and laid out a programme for progressive use of new media. Since his name has been invoked, how does the CD measure up to Benjamin's strictures?

Benjamin organised his argument around an undesirable legacy from the past: 'aura,' a reverence for the uniqueness of singleton artworks. He believed mass production renders aura obsolete, although capitalist society has yet to realise all the implications. Radical artists need to strip away the aura of respect that accretes around the old ways of doing things, and emphasise the new perceptions made available by new technologies. Not in the manner of the Nazis, who used film to promote antique myths about physical perfection and social reconciliation, but in the manner of the Dadaists, who exposed the realities behind the rigmarole of 'art.' This is where this CD falls short: it is predicated on the ideal of the classical symphony, a form for which recording can only ever be a kitsch add-on. It's not the musicians' fault: the presence of Adam Bohman—manipulator of table-top gadgets and amplified toys—shows that the

LIO has no snobbery about 'real' instruments. Nevertheless, the *sound* of this CD is that of a classical recording: the space in which the instruments resound has a sacred, concert-hall quality which negates the Day-Glo, cartoon smarts of a piece like 'How Can You Delude Yorself?' Too much of the CD sounds simply like an orchestra tuning up, that grandiloquent assertion of the wonders of traditional instruments and luxury concert space.

In *Composition No. 30* (Bruce's Fingers BF27), Simon Fell showed how an orchestra of improvisers can be organised without suppressing their personalities. In Fell's release, improvisation and experiment penetrate the recording process itself. What he calls 'xenochrony'—the overlaying of musics recorded at different times—generates new rhythmic complexities unavailable even to drummers as formidable as Paul Hession and Mark Sanders. This rhythmic futurism ensures that his orchestral work never retreats into generic modernist-symphonic sound. Playing Fell's disc in your living room is not a substitute for 'being at the concert,' it's an event in its own right. On *the hearing continues*...there are *four* great drummers, yet in comparison to the pin-drop exactitude available to today's digital collagist, the mics only pick up a vague, thunderous drama. It's like having a bleary snapshot of a building when you could be looking at an architectural blueprint. The level of craft and invention which improvisers apply to their instruments needs to be applied to the recording and release format itself.

Straight recording of small groups, using a semi-distant single stereo mic, can produce astonishing CDs, especially those involving impatient souls like Derek Bailey and Roger Turner (absent here, maybe because they like to be known as 'improvis*ors*' rather than 'improvis*ers*'?). An intimate sound field foregrounds new aspects of recording technology—the silence and extended dynamic range of digital, all that virgin space for pop and click—which conventional playing hasn't yet exploited. Whole orchestras, though, blend into precisely the subservient anonymity which Free Improvisation originally mutinied against. Until the LIO thinks about mic-placement, mixing and overtracking—and invents strategies to inject personality and dialogue into that area of decision-making, perhaps adopting Sun Ra's experimental relativity—we'll be unable to hear past the aura of the concert hall to the detail of what they're actually hearing and playing.

* * * * * * *

Paul Minotto
The Prime-Time Sublime
Corporate Blob Records unnumbered CD

FOR ARTIST Paul Minotto, issuing a CD is phase two of a fine-art career. For a decade, he lived in Manhattan and painted easel pictures. These were an unlikely collision between field-painting (extending Cy Twombly's sensitivity to graffiti and derelict space) and *Mad* magazine's obsession with '50s commercial imagery, plus an upending of American lifestyle assumptions which is entirely Minotto's baby. For the last couple of years, he's been living in New Jersey and working on music with his computer, which he uses to edit and collage recorded performances of his work. Given his paintings, and the Terry Gilliam-like humour of his website (www. primetimesublime.com), one expected something cute and dismembered; the shock is that he's produced a disc whose production values outdo practically everything released by the downtown postmodernists over the last two decades. Mastered by Scott Hull— noted for his engineering work for the Talking Heads—at Classic Sound in NYC, the surface sound of this music is arrestingly detailed and precise. Play it in public and heads turn.

The title 'Holy War in Your Pants' deftly summarises the uneasy relationship between a consumer's pet desires and his/her sense of the cheapness of contemporary gratification. This uneasiness is Minotto's farcical *forte*. The opening sounds like a tribute to Michael Nyman, whose iconic soundtracks turned the classy splendour of baroque into a turbo-charged punishment machine. Minotto uses his software to make the instruments unrealistically present, but not to homogenise the total sound: each note in the complex arrangement retains its own parameters of intonation, vibrato and cut-off. Like being force fed candy-floss with your genitals wired to an orgasm-inducing vibrator, Minotto's music gives you everything you want so relentlessly and efficiently that the net effect is garish, sinister and eventually terrifying.

Minotto is not content with the postmodernism which justifies composers who recycle bygone musics with an ironic gloss. So his Nymanesque intro suddenly blossoms into a multi-coloured timbral *bouquet* only programmable by someone familiar with Olivier Messiaen: given the minimalist prequel, a surprise for the ears worthy of Varèse. Since the ascendancy of John Zorn and his downtown colleagues, promises of polystylism have become ubiquitous. Minotto's segues are so potty they reinvent the possibilities of generic misce-genation. As with the collaged elements of his canvases, unlikely sauces—a pedal-steel solo, Prokofiev's *pizzicati*, Mantovani's swooning banks of strings, vacuum cleaner groans, Nancarrowish runs, Boulezian winds—are not so much culinary additions as ex-perimental matter, causing crises in the theoretical superstructure, and transforming it. Minotto's concept of form—Alexander Calder's discovery that a small dense blob of a thingamajig can balance a large blur of another thingamajig—does not force his details into grand wall-patterns, but listens and responds to them. Minotto's mu-sic is combined and uneven, the only constant being time's ineluctable arrow. Because he recognises that under the law of value, time is money, capitalist inequity leers at you from every corner.

The cover shows the title stamped on lead-filled precipitate in the exhaust flare from the jet engine of a flying saucer carved in jelly. Aeroplane passengers debouch from a door in the sky. They descend via a fold-down stairway onto a bleak landscape whose ho-rizon is defined by an etch-a-sketched line which is actually a whip in the hand of a smiling insurance salesman. One passenger runs to-wards a black exit hole shaped like the holes in the 'Nowhere Man' sequence of *Yellow Submarine*. Meanwhile, a supermarket trolley casts a shadow on the ground. It contains...the world. This is pre-cisely the universe of Minotto's music: hackneyed triggers of 'the sublime' are used to usher you into the blind space of the artist's irresponsible playpen. Universalism is trashed as just another su-permarket option, the Infinite panned to bad infinity. The prime-time sublime: Hegel's Absolute Mind as Day-Glo bunny-rabbits adver-tised on peak-hour TV. Segued with supreme disregard for the proc-essual logic (though not sonorities) of the musics he plunders, Minotto proposes an aesthetic where his own questions as regards contemporary alienation become the ground zero of meaning. On cover and spine, Minotto's name is lacking. A blank space between brackets follows 'Prime-Time Sublime': each listener must find their own name for this art.

Prime-Time Sublime is genre transgression of such power and majestic debunkment, it prompts readjustment of the entire avant canon. The cut-ups of John Zorn sound peculiarly mechanical and formalist in contrast, glassily insensitive to the emotional resonance of the selected sonic icons. Like Don Preston when interpreting Frank Zappa's tunes, or Bill Frisell in mawkish mode, Minotto knows how to pause, to arouse that poignancy without which music cannot invade and overturn the heart. His music makes the 'radical-ism' of much recent music sound adolescent and insulated, closed to experience. However, Minotto is not lax. Every time he moves you—with a thrilling, Peter Wolf-like synth job, an expert claw-hammer banjo break (Minotto spent time in Atlanta as a working top-40 covers-band musician, and found performing 'Amazing Grace' south of the Mason-Dixon line a peculiarly emotional experience), or with a mute-trumpet evocation of 'Caravan'—you suddenly find yourself whizzed, through the magic of software-craft, to another dimension of *Prime-Time Sublime*'s strictly absurd nursery. Feeling emotional or over-excited? Go and stand in the corner!

On the closing number, 'Invocation and Fanfare of the Tahitian Garbage Fairies', a series of effects—Duane Eddy-style twang, music-box chimes, opulent samples of mooing cows, sci-fi strings, James Brown doing 'The Twist'—alternate in an apocalyptic sequence, achieving the orgasmic tension of Varèse's *Arcana*. What can such abutment of zircon-twinkle trash and true-flesh splendour truly mean? The blank, bracketted space on cover and spine awaits our answers: text, name and age to be written in loopy biro, a smiley face in each 'O', a heart trembling atop each 'I'.

* * * * * * *

Carl-Ludwig Reichert
Frank Zappa
Deutscher Tasenbuch Verlag (pbk)

MOST BRITISH music writers believe a shared language gives them privileged access to American culture, so Europeans can tell us little about rock. How wrong they are is illustrated by this gem of a book. Reichert narrates a story that has now been told in print many times, but nevertheless finds a host of intriguing facts and original points. The selection of photographs, mainly in colour, is excellent, avoiding the done-to-death images, with unexpected bonuses like shots of Zappa's antagonists John Wayne and Richard Nixon, plus a photo of Zappa's family home when he was fifteen.

DTV's 'Portrait' series places Zappa in illustrious company (the list includes Socrates, Giordano Bruno, Bach, Goethe and Freud—the only other rock stars are Hendrix and Lennon). Extra information (on topics as diverse as the Excello label, Cordwainer Smith, canine continuity and L. Shankar) is placed under a red line on each page, and there are terrific, off-the-leash 'materials for further investigation' (including a fantastic Eskimo bibliography, and a list of mid-'60s films with 'Mondo' in the title).

Reichert has used Zappa as the occasion for developing a non-academic, critical, mass-culture-sifting approach which takes Prince as seriously as Guy Debord. He is scornful of the conservatory uptake of Zappa as a cerebral jazz-rocker (only in Germany!), and emphasises his roots in Doo-Wop and gutter R&B. He is fascinating about the incident when revolutionary students disrupted a Mothers of Invention concert in Berlin in 1968, appending an unpublished photo, and cites the brilliant Helmut Salzinger, whose *Swinging Benjamin* made connections between freak rock and Critical Theory back in 1973. Reichert's words on the late-'70s commodification of rock are fierce and stirring.

There are few errors (*Ahead of Their Time* is a complete concert recording, not a 'collection of rarities'; a sub-editor must have taken the 'N' out of the song-title 'Amnerika'; on the *Cheap Thrills* sampler, Captain Beefheart joined Zappa for 'The Torture Never Stops', not 'Trouble Every Day'). My only complaint is that two paragraphs and a citation from Wilhelm Reich from one of my own essays (from Richard Kostelanetz's *Zappa Companion*) have somehow lost their quote-marks in being translated into German and become part of Reichert's own resounding conclusion (though maybe such plagiarism could be interpreted as dialectical enlightenment...).

Reichert's hip syntax and rich vocabulary present difficulties for anyone whose German is rudimentary, but it's well worth the trouble. Where else would you discover that polo-neck sweaters could generate the phrase 'das rollkragenpulloverige Getue der Existentialisten'? If Zappa were alive, he'd surely have found a place for that Teutonic compound-adjective in a cabaret number.

* * * * * * *

Daniel Sinker (Editor)
'We Owe You Nothing' Punk Planet: The Collected Interviews
Akashic Books (pbk)

WHEN CHICAGO art-student Dan Sinker launched his fanzine *Punk Planet*, it was early spring in 1994, a critical time for American punk. By signing with a major label and becoming mega-stars, Nirvana had violated punk's DIY ethic. No apologist for Kurt Cobain,

Sinker nevertheless hated the purist, exclusionist reaction of *Maximum Rock'n'Roll*, American punk's house-journal: 'many bands, including quite a few I was friends with, found themselves locked out of *Maximum*'s pages, having been deemed 'not punk.'' This book reprints twenty-five interviews which appeared in his magazine between May 1997 and August 2000.

For anyone exposed to UK media, punk evokes historic national memories: tabloid fury when Steve Jones called Bill Grundy a 'dirty fucker' on Thames TV's *Today* programme in 1976, 'God Save the Queen' stuffing the Queen's Jubilee in 1977, riots against police-protected Nazi marches. Although the Pistols and Clash had originally copped motifs from NYC punk—Johnny Thunders' wall-of-sound guitar, Richard Hell's ripped'n'torn look, the velocity of the Ramones—the 'punk' echoed back from America was another beast entirely. (In the UK, the egalitarian stance of prol punk [X-Ray Spex, ATV, Patrik Fitzgerald, Crass, The Fall] was spiked with a pinch of glam [Siouxsie, Adam Ant, Billy Idol]: American punk was straightedge [no drugs—no *lager*!], a haven from the '80s monetarist onslaught, less a dynamic contradiction than an alternative [impressions in Europe were distorted by the fact that transatlantic contacts were usually mediated by major labels].) By the end of the decade, *Maximum Rock'n'Roll* was running city-guides to 'punk clubs,' 'punk accommodation' and (horror of horrors) 'punk food.' So the 'trailblazers' in the first section are not the Stooges and the New York Dolls, but Fugazi, the Dead Kennedys, Sonic Youth, Bikini Kill and Black Flag.

With intelligence and sensitivity, *Punk Planet*'s interviewers eke out the paradoxes of middle-class youth-revolt. The discussions are practical, political and free of celebrity mystification. The big issue is the problem of communication in a system geared towards commodity production and return on capital investment: 'music' is a word for gathering people together, for cultural intervention. There's not a single reference to a key signature or the make of a guitar or amplifier. Sinker's catholic interpretation of 'punk' means including Negativland, sleeve-designers Winston Smith and Art Chantry, and a final section which opens out into post-Seattle anti-capitalism in general, including pro-choice campaigns and Ruckus (whose Greenpeace-style high-wire direct actions were voided of political significance and performed every day under the Greenwich Dome). Frank Kozick—main man of Man's Ruin distribution—voices scepticism about bleeding-heart liberals and enthusiasm for neo-liberal business deals. His views are part-and-parcel of punk contradiction and receive a fair hearing.

After President Clinton's bombing of Baghdad in December 1998, Sinker switched his cover story to the devastation of Iraq's infrastructure by US bombs and UN sanctions, conducting an eighteen-page interview with the campaigning group Voices in the Wilderness. He risked alienating his readers, but garnered a loaded and overwhelmingly positive mailbag. His dawning realisation that the US ruling class is capable of genocide-by-stealth makes for a moving read. *Punk Planet* tracked down 'the gentleman in the white shirt' who exposed Secretary of State Madeleine Albright live on CNN in Ohio by asking a question about repression in East Timor and US arms sales to Indonesia—helping spread popular opposition to a renewed Gulf War. His replies are articulate, excited, fresh. In a brilliant interview, Noam Chomsky trashes media-endorsed clichés about the 'radical '60s' by pointing out that North Vietnam was bombed for five years before anyone managed to bring off a demo that wasn't broken up by the police, whereas Gulf War protests were instantaneous, and huge. His warnings about how the establishment treats individuals who speak out versus corporate USA ('don't expect tenure') are bracing and realistic.

This book is the story of a punk who took the slogans seriously, and in so doing began to grapple with the enormity that is global capitalism. In a way, it's Sinker's *Bildungsroman*. Just as James Joyce's *Portrait of the Artist as a Young Man* ended with the author preparing to flee a suffocating Dublin for modern Europe, this ends with interviewees chafing at the limitations of punk (notably Matt Wobensmith, founder of *Outpunk* zine and inventor of 'digital queercore,' and Ted Leo from the Sin Eaters). While *Punk Planet* remains loyal to the magnificence that is the three-chord trick reverberating in a small place, it yearns to bust through commodified rad chic and the star-system to genuine knowledge (one looks forward to interviews with Cecil Taylor, Swamp Dogg, Alex Callinicos, jwcurry...). On the way, we've been introduced to some eloquent voices: after reading Jody Bleyle—who explains why opposition to commodification requires ditching competition for solidarity, and says the rock stage should be a public forum rather than a 'TV set'—you just gotta get out of the house and find some CDs by Hazel and Team Dresch. Well-read leftists won't find the news about US atrocities surprising, but anyone who thinks music should be more than a career (more than 'realising a personal vision') will find the book full of practical wisdom. Dan Sinker's neophyte politics keeps hitting nails on the head.

A final point. At a time when critics and cult-studs hacks who require a fix of *profondeur* like nothing better than to mumble on about modern man's quest for 'redemption'—a religious concept stemming from an age of serfdom and slavery, when extraction of surplus value was explained as pay-off for original sin—it's heartening to discover a book with a militant slogan down the spine, anti-guilt, pro-human and radical-subjectivist: 'We Owe You Nothing.' Say it again!

* * * * * * *

Wadada Leo Smith
Reflectativity
Tzadik 7060 CD
Golden Quartet
Tzadik 7604 CD

REFLECTATIVITY IS a remake of an album Leo Smith released on his own label in 1975. For many cushily-established panjandrums, such revision would be a recipe for disaster. Not so here. Brought up on the blues (Leland, Mississippi), from the start Smith refused to be patronised by being relegated to a style. He embraced a wide-open, modernist aesthetic, allowing his trumpet licks maximum freedom to engage in interplay with his colleagues. Ambitious goals—global musicality, event/structure dialectic, performative immediacy—meant a lifetime in academia (New Haven, Woodstock, Cal Arts) hasn't erased the plangency that is the test of an improvisor's willingness to stake everything on this note being played here and now.

Recorded with Anthony Davis (piano) and Malachi Favors (bass) in a NYC studio in January 2000, this new *Reflectativity* is so chill, pure and pared-down it will probably only reach listeners who can tolerate Free Improvisation or the works of Morton Feldman. This is a pity, because at its core (despite the light touch of Davis and Favors' beautiful tone, this is Smith's gig) is a singing, dancing, groovacious trumpet voice. Smith doesn't so much sum up the history of his instrument—Satchmo, Bubber, Hot Lips, Hubbard, Cherry—as provide an independent understanding of field holler and hokum break as critical Modern Art. Harmonic surprise and acute use of silence leaves no listener secure. *Reflectativity* dices everything you think you know about blues and jazz, then hangs the motifs out on a line. The brightness and definition dazzle.

Just to show *Reflectativity* isn't all our man can do, *Golden Quartet* adds drummer Jack DeJohnette to the trio. The band becomes something else entirely: a fleet, state-of-the-art jazz quartet. The current scene is suffering from a surfeit of blustering, Ayler-fixated saxophonists (don't try, boys, just don't try...): this is the antidote, being hair-raisingly fine in the beat department, but also speculative and crammed with ideas. DeJohnette has been involved with much fusion stodge (between jazz and rock, free and bop, improv and electro), but here he's utterly at home and sounding vibrant. *Golden Quartet* isn't as sublime as *Reflectativity*—'Harumi' is a slightly cheesy ballad—but the balance between groove thrust and internal dialogue is brilliant. Smith's silvery trumpet cuts through with unbelievable power and finesse, and everyone sounds alert. These musicians are still surprising each other: the deal is real.

* * * * * * *

Various
Virginia Roots: The 1929 Richmond Sessions
Outhouse Records 1001 2CD

FOUNDED IN 1918 as the German branch of Carl Lindström's Phonograph label, Okeh Records pioneered the issue of jazz with King Oliver's Creole Jazz Band and Louis Armstrong's Hot Five and Hot Seven. They had a strong line in other indigenous musics, and over five days in October 1929 in Richmond, Virginia, they recorded thirty groups singing ninety-three songs, of which thirty-six were released on eighteen 78-rpm records: gospel, hokum, schottishes, harmonica blues, hawaiian, rags and jazz (let no one tell you that categorical proliferation is a recent phenomenon). This reissue reconstructs that week from the shellac originals, with accompanying photographs, plus essays by different experts on each tune. Compiler Ron T. Curry includes a woodcut he's made portraying a wind-up gramophone: he calls it 'the time machine'. The whole collection breathes excitement.

As their logo, Outhouse Records use a line drawing of a farm-house jakes, making it legitimate to ask whether the intervening 74 years haven't likewise deodorised the music, making it quaint and safe. Actually, because contemporary pop and rock have been carved from these song forms, these sides have the opposite effect. Like Harry Smith's *Anthology of American Folk Music*, this collection burns across time, searing the heart with its ruggedness and idiosyncracy: if pop is going to be anything more than a trivial pursuit of celebrity and distraction, it needs to take two steps back and learn from stuff like this.

Gospel quartets are well represented, with the Sparkling Four, the Golden Crown, the Norfolk Jubilee, and the Richmond Starlight (the one cheat on the compilation, their 'Jazz Crazy Blues,' was actually recorded by Okeh in New York in December 1928, but the way it bends religious song towards secular pleasures is so fetching you forgive the compilers). Via Louis Jordan, Doo-Wop and the Coasters, quartet gospel fed directly into rock'n'roll, though it lost a good deal of complexity on the way. On the Sparkling Four tracks, the audio restoration by Airshow Mastering is amazing, bringing the four vocalists into resplendent 3D stereo. The pre-war *vibrato* sounds weird enough, but the part-singing astonishes: limited means led to concentration on note combinations which flower in artful bouquets of unexpected harmony and resolution. On 'Scandalize My Name,' the bass singer starts earlier and sings slower, using motifs which the higher-up voices take faster: the idea of time manipulation *via* sped-up and slowed-down tape is already part of the form, giving the music an instaneity lacking in musics which are patterned after the universal time of the symphonic master score. There's no beat or reverb to hide the individual voices: the four-way poise and interaction recalls the great classical string quartets.

The *gravitas* of gospel was off-set by hokum. The Bubbling Over Five's 'Get Up Off That Jazzophone' has a banjo whose plunks sound delirious next to the thinly-etched sounds of soprano sax and violin. Blues Birdhead's pipping harmonic sounds like a rusty pump, each 'break' working like a joke in a music-hall routine: novelty as the essence of musical entertainment. The Tubize Royal Hawaiian Orchestra, run by employees of the rayon-manufacturing Tubize Artificial Silk Company in Hopewell, Virginia, show how the hovering twang of the hawaiian guitar could cut through 78rpm rustle and radio static. The Raonoke Jug Band's 'Home Brew Rag' proves that cornball humour is a real entity.

Disc one all sounds great, but there are three rougher tracks on disc two (only 'Just Too Late' is unlistenably bad). This release is important in a way it's impossible to explain until you've heard Bela Lam and his Greene County Singers—followers of Aldine Kieffer's '7-shape notation system'—reveal the iron beat and wonky intonation of Blue Ridge mountain music on 'Tell It Again'. Their ancestors learnt the use of the banjo from the great trans-racial camp meetings of the 1780s and 1790s, and their rolling, ineluctable rhythms and apocalyptic imagery harks back to that time—and forward to the folk protests of the '60s. Astounding, vital sounds.

* * * * * * *

Thomas Wictor
In Cold Sweat: Interviews with Really Scary Musicians
Limelight Editions (pbk)

ALTHOUGH THE title looks daft, it turns out to be excellent premise. Thomas Wictor taped these interviews for *Bass Player* magazine, and bringing himself and his anxieties into the picture—the fan faces the wild man—makes for a dramatic and entertaining read. The interviews are unexpurgated. Details which editors prefer to glide over become part of the story. Like most consumer magazines, *Bass Player* sells a rank illusion: mass music as a meritocracy, where talent and hard work are rewarded by fame and fortune. Advertisements for instruments, hardware and teach-yourself manuals are aerated by interviews with famous names. However, few bass players in successful bands deem themselves *virtuosi* on their instrument, and the difficulties they have in explaining their exalted positions can result in hostility. Although there is sometimes *cachet* in being a guitarist in a rock band, precious little glamour trickles down to the bass player: the response to Wictor's request for an interview is frequently suspicion (rather like successful female musicians when asked about the role of women in music): 'oh, I see, you only want to talk to me because I play *bass*, but I'm an all-round musician and artist, you know'.

Thomas Wictor negotiates these issues with commendable candour. Born in Southern California, he spent three years playing bass on the Tokyo club circuit, but never got over his stage fright—'I had the stage presence of a filing cabinet'—and so turned to journalism. The bassists he interviews are Gene Simmons from Kiss, Peter Hook from New Order, Jerry Casale from Devo and Scott Thunes from the Frank Zappa band. True to form, Gene Simmons (interviewed on 28 January 1996) is the most objectionable, refusing to talk unless his face goes on the cover of the magazine, declaring that women have no affinity for lower sonorities (Wictor might have cited two women whose music make Kiss sound like the bubblegum they are—Joelle Léandre and Ana-Maria Avram—but Simmons wouldn't be impressed, because he is only interested in 'famous,' *i.e.* commercially successful, musicians). Simmons spouts bar-room banalities like they're lessons in life. However, Simmons explodes when Wictor mentions that the 'SS' in Kiss's logo resembles the lightning bolts Hitler's *Schutz Staffeln* wore on their collars. He's Jewish, born in Israel, and once rejected the album title *Gas Chamber Music* because it would be 'insensitive to what went on in World War II'. As one might guess, Simmons is more intelligent on comics than genocide, claiming that Marvel heroes got popular, not because they were Nietzschean *Übermenschen*, but 'scary, mixed-up people' like Spider-Man.

Weird to go from Kiss to New Order, but that's Americans for you—no respect for limey style wars. Peter Hook and Wictor had a brief, twenty-minute exchange during a sound check at El Rey's on Wilshire Boulevard, 12 August 1997. Hook's diffidence about fame contrasts with Simmons, both British reserve and punk principle making him modest. The man who made Giorgio Moröder's disco beats cool for a new generation shrugs off Wictor's praise, but answers him politely about his solo work.

Jerry Casale was interviewed on 18 February 1997. Devo's reputation for cynicism and stunts is explained as the rock press's inability to grasp satire by some extremely concerned minds. Casale is analytic and cute, talking about learning to fit together *Trout Mask Replica*'s parts and playing sixteenth-notes on bass. He defines Devo's amazing cover of 'Satisfaction' as a 'Jamaican sort of polka'. He's still bitter about press treatment of Devo. Despite their differences, Simmons and Hook are happy with their places in pop-music history, a satisfaction which makes them seem rather uncritical and complacent: Casale, in contrast, wants to re-form Devo and show Nine Inch Nails, Prodigy and the Chemical Brothers how the modern equipment they're using could be used.

Half of Thomas Wictor's book is devoted to Scott Thunes, transcription of a marathon interview that took place at Thunes' home on 7 October 1996. It takes Thunes much effort, but he finally manages to explain to Wictor that despite being the toast of rock bass players—Zappa's music gave *virtuosi* a chance to shine that is rare outside jazz—he's today much happier out of the industry, jamming occasionally with friends. Originally a fan of Bartók, Stravinsky and the Second Viennese School, he played jazz on bass until he heard Devo's 'Mongoloid' and 'gave it up immediately, lost all my friends'. Zappa was always looking for literate musicians with rock attitude; Thunes' break came when, after a tough audition, Zappa asked him to play with Lisa Popeil, the extraordinary soprano and pianist. Thunes was Zappa's bass anchor throughout the '80s, up until Zappa's last tour in 1988, and then played bass for Zappa's son Dweezil. His turn against Dweezil's metal—he complains that their original '*anti*-rock' became straight—is fascinatingly described, as is his subsequent involvement with the punk band Fear: 'complicated, hard-edged, fast music that people can actually dance and pogo and freak out to, instead of this analytical hard rock stuff, which only goes to the front of the stage and then stops, energy-wise'.

Thunes' devotion to Zappa *père* is 100%. There are some tantalising technical discussions of little-understood compositions like 'Mo 'n Herb's Vacation' and of stacked-fifths in Zappa's guitar solos, but these are eclipsed by the explosive, painful conflicts of the 1988 tour. Thunes was straw boss and the band mutinied. What emerges is the kind of larger-than-life, integrity-driven, musically-literate character required to play Zappa's genre-defying music: 'if you want to look at me and what I deserve, I don't deserve anything because I'm a fucking asshole. But I'd rather be a fucking asshole who can express himself whenever I want to'. It's not easy to get a sense of the people behind a music as glassy, complex and deliberate as '80s Zappa: Thomas Wictor's courage in facing this 'scary' bassist was rewarded with a revelatory interview. As if taking the Acid Temple Mothers and their celebration of musical ignorance to task, Thunes says no musician should play a note without knowing what it's doing to the harmonic environment. Right on, Scott!

* * * * * * *

John Zorn (editor)
Arcana: Musicians on Music
Granary Books/Hips Road 2000

THIS COLLECTION begins with a polemical preface by John Zorn, stating that over two decades of musical activity he and his colleagues haven't found a single writer able 'to intelligently analyze exactly what it is that we have been doing'. So here's a book by the musicians and composers themselves, 378 dense pages of explanation. Calling the book *Arcana* is a bold claim: besides being the title of the most cataclysmic eighteen minutes of music ever to terrify a concert audience (Edgard Varèse's masterpiece of that name was premièred in New York in 1927), 'arcana' are the 'great secrets of nature' which alchemists seek to discover. With a slick black cover sporting a pyramid/circle 'mystery' motif, plus words of praise from composers Meredith Monk and Steve Reich on the back—and contributors who are a roll call of the heroes of the 'downtown' New York scene—this volume promises great things.

In a period of proliferating musical margins, we are certainly in need of clarity (perhaps even a *manifesto*!). Today, all the possibilities and freedoms pursued by avant-garde composers and improvisors in the '50s and '60s—simultaneous musics, electronic experimentation, cut-up and denaturalisation, existential confrontations with noise, limitless source materials—suddenly seem to be on the menu for non-academic musicians and mass audiences. However, though the scene is awash with options, it's also extremely confusing. Listeners who've woken up to the fact that there's more to music than pop idiocy or sterile classicism are badly in need of a route map. Who are our real friends, and who is just recycling some exotic junk from the past or puffing some colleague's new CD? Maybe this book could help.

The cover and flyleaf read 'edited by John Zorn'. However, having solicited the manuscripts, the editorial task was too much for the busy composer. Poet Lyn Hejinian and Travis Ortiz were brought in to exercise their literary skills. In his preface, Zorn concedes that the writing is 'on the raw side', but given the 'incredible lack of insightful critical writing' about 'the best and most important work of the past two decades', the collection was 'necessary'. Adopting the mantle of the righteous avant-gardist berating the philistinism of the rest of society, Zorn derides terms like 'rock, jazz, punk, dada and beat'. They are all just sales tags, designed to commodify, package and sell an artist's 'complex personal vision'. Such categorization isn't about understanding: 'it's about money'.

Zorn has located a real grievance, one that has exercised some of the best minds of the twentieth century: capitalism seems to offer limitless freedom in the pursuit of artistic ends—exploding religious and sexual taboos, proposing a free trade in images and sounds—yet by rationalising the pursuit of customers, commerce actually narrows down what it makes available, emptying it of its original message. This process (what the situationists called 'recuperation') has been the target of successive waves of avant-gardes as they wrestle with the monster that is capitalist society.

However, though he has released many a 'tribute' to individual products of the European avant-garde, Zorn doesn't seem to have an inkling of what actually motivated Dada or Surrealism. It simply isn't the case that these were terms thrust on innocent artists by patronising and mercenary journalists. Dada and Surrealism were terms coined by the artists themselves to *control* their output and reception, rallying calls that connected their artistic endeavours to the revolutionary social movements of their time. In fact, it was precisely competitive individualism (the ideology of the artist's 'complex personal vision') that was under assault: no less than free improvisors today, Dadaists and surrealists were suspicious of a society that received their art like so many competing brands on an open market. They wanted to explain their artistic innovations as a necessary response to social issues (war, poverty, boredom, exploitation), resisting the bourgeoisie's habit of seeing everything in bourgeois terms ('you're only in it for the money'). The downtown crew do not seem to have found their spokesperson—their Hans Richter or André Breton or Clement Greenberg—but maybe this reflects more on their basic motivations than on the failure of the critics. Could *Arcana* actually just be a promotional device for a set of artists who should really have no more pull on your attention than anyone else pushed at you by the entertainment industry? (Skepticism! Surely a must for any scene worth its 'avant' credentials...).

If the only thing that distinguishes the artist from craven commercialism is his or her 'personal vision', then how is one to distinguish between integrity and careerism? Also, how come the commercial sphere has produced such undeniably great music: Bessie Smith, James Brown, Jimi Hendrix, Funkadelic, Beenie Man, Evil Dick? One useful indicator is politics. Having started off his career with a commendable commitment to anti-racism ('FUCK RACISM' was a memorable sign-off to an early sleeve note), Zorn currently throws his political energies into promoting what he calls 'Jewish culture'. Given US foreign policy in the Middle East, and Israel's continuing mistreatment of displaced Palestinians, playing gigs in Jerusalem with a band called Masada (named after a Zionist myth enthusiastically promoted by militarist elements in Israel) hardly connects to the radical anti-militarism of movements like Dada. Before he starts posing as the sole voice of truth in a mercenary world, Zorn should examine the ideological effects of broadcasting his own 'personal vision'. Strident defences of the integrity of 'art' are empty claims to virtue, ploys of service to any operator.

Because they are musics invented by an oppressed race, blues and jazz and reggae carry an inbuilt critique of power. Of course it's nuanced and complex (the current debate between the Lincoln Center's classicising view of jazz and the Free Jazz and Hip-Hop posses is essentially a debate between a middle-class ideology of upwardly-mobile accommodation and the revolutionary/proletarian legacy of Coltrane and Malcolm X), but black music—even if played by Johnny Otis or Red Hot Chilli Peppers—automatically connects to social issues. By proposing a concept of 'Great Jewish Music' (one far less evident in the actual notes than the tradition of black music), Zorn snapped an essential link in the chain between progressive music and progressive social aims (as a conscientious bebop saxophonist, Zorn has more credentials than most in this game).

The ideology of 'pure art' espoused by the contributors to *Arcana*—heavily dependent on John Cage's cracker barrel pronouncements, and no doubt encouraged by his eventual mega-success—has no such immediate social resonance. Not that black music is the only resource for anti-capitalist artistic endeavour: there is also a whole series of European avant-gardes to draw upon (Dada, Bauhaus, Surrealism, Futurism, the Situationists, Punk, Neoism, DIY Esemplasm...). In fact, at least two of the movements Zorn disses as mere sales tags—Dada and Punk—were precisely invented as insults to those who believe that, in an unfair and exploitative society, art *in itself* can confer redemption and transcendence. True avant-gardes proceed from rigorous assessments of both art and society, tear away the veils of self-satisfied illusion that pamper the complacent bourgeoisie. Can *Arcana* measure up to that test?

Some musicians were content to contribute unpretentious notes on what they do, totally different in tone from the angry denunciations of Zorn's preface. Bill Frisell provides some *études* to stretch any guitarist's fingers, and Mark Dresser provides an imaginative guide to achieving harmonics on the upright bass. Marc Ribot's socio-psychological study of electric guitarists and their amplifiers is hilarious; Peter Garland writes sensitively about seeing a mixed-race band of teenagers play reggae at an Australian labor-day celebration; Frances-Marie Uitti writes fascinatingly about her two-bow cello music; George Lewis makes a persuasive case for the relevance of contesting musical academia; Stephen Drury makes a pertinent attack on the smug'n'cynical cultural relativism people derive from Pierre Bourdieu's sociology; John Schott writes a pioneering study of John Coltrane, finding technical evidence to compare his music to that of a revolutionary musician from a previous epoch, namely Beethoven (Schott's comparison finds independent confirmation in Theodor Adorno's observation that Beethoven's music is all about development rather than clever tunes: as with 'Trane, Beethoven is all about *process*, 'how' not 'what'). However, none of these essays would be out of place in an issue of *Contemporary Music Review*, *Musical Times*, *The Wire* or *Signal to Noise*: they hardly constitute revelatory 'arcana'. The only writer here whose words match the apocalyptic, provocative quality of the best downtown compositions (Zorn may be a lousy theorist, but for omnidirectional deployment of musics from myriad genres, he's still the best thing in

American composition since Frank Zappa) is Mike Patton. However, far from explicating the downtown aesthetic, Patton curses it to hell in a breadbasket: 'the most intense and convincing music achieves a sexual level of expression, but what we normally feel is frigidity and limpness....' (a perfect description of the Kronos/ROVA/Douglas 'art' end of things in this critic's opinion).

All the above make pleasant enough reading, but they hardly constitute the assault on commercial misrepresentation promised in Zorn's preface. In the absence of the will and intellect to frame an explicit aesthetic (and there are essays on the Internet which examine Zorn's miscegenations and begin to do that, albeit under the useless flag 'postmodernism'), the main thrust of *Arcana* falls to anyone with the *chutzpah* to develop a world view—or at least to write at length. By default, those two contributors are Scott Johnson and David Rosenboom.

Scott Johnson makes the mistake ('The Counterpoint of Species') of attempting to base his social theory on evolutionary science. Karl Marx hailed Charles Darwin's theory of evolution as a breakthrough: he wanted to approach history and economics with the same fearless, dogma-defying objectivity Darwin applied to biology. However, this does not mean you can simply apply Darwin's theory of evolution to society. The reactionary implications of this confusion of modes (historical time is such a blip compared to evolutionary time, it hardly registers) are famous. 'Social Darwinism' is one way of describing Nazi eugenics. So it is shocking to read the following words in a book put together by someone who once bannered "FUCK RACISM" on his sleeve: artistic proclivities, according to Johnson, are a side effect of our 'abilities for symbol-making and symbol-understanding which allow us to do more practical things, like remembering how much stuff we have, or expressing contempt for Frog People while among our fellow Fish People' (p. 41). Johnson's phrases are playful, but they reveal incredibly reactionary assumptions: possessiveness and xenophobia as fundamentals of human nature. As usual, the American liberal ascribes to all humanity the particular characteristics of his own class (*i.e.*, private property and racism/nationalism). Not quite what you hope to find in a book celebrating composers and musicians whose work—at its best—seeks to explode the confines of class and race.

Having enjoyed a collaboration between David Rosenboom and Anthony Braxton, I was prepared to read his paper 'Propositional Music' sympathetically. It is not some off-the-cuff pronouncement: first written at Zorn's request in 1993, a revised version was published in *Leonardo* by MIT in 1997. This is Rosenboom's third attempt to get it right. Marshall McLuhan and John Cage are the un-acknowledged legislators of Rosenboom's new-age moralism: 'Our best chance for survival is to become part of the agency of change and accept our own transmutation into the forms which will eventually inherit our developed characteristics.' (p. 211) If Edgard Varèse had thought like this, he would be Kurt Weill—or Andrew Lloyd Webber—rather than the revolutionary sonic architect we all admire. As with Scott Johnson, the insidious effect of applying evolutionary science to social issues takes its toll. The conscious, thinking minds of other human beings remain unaddressed. Instead, the analyst takes a godlike attitude, surveying humanity as an ant heap (and like Johnson, p. 30, Rosenboom has to wrestle with the fact of the non-inheritance of acquired characteristics by DNA; since the 'inheritance of acquired characteristics' is *precisely* how society and music develop, both find themselves constrained rather than helped by their 'evolutionary' metaphor).

Although Rosenboom says some liberal-sounding things about the need for 'partnership' rather than 'hierarchy' (p. 215), there is nothing here that would be out of place in a speech by Bill Clinton. The mismatch between evolutionary theory and actual human history becomes so grotesque that he can only heal the split by appealing to mysticism: 'a fundamental change of state in earthly society may occur and a GLOBAL ORGANIC CONSCIOUSNESS may emerge' (p. 217). This is McLuhanesque mysticism of the most nebulous kind, neatly evading any kind of actuality (note the 'may'). Actually, the last time a truly 'global organic consciousness' occurred was in May 1968, when students and workers seized the centre of Paris and sent Mao Tse-Tung a telegram saying they had no belief in communist state-capitalism either; Rosenboom's daydreams, on the other hand, are pure ideology, the perfect excuse for the apolitical yuppie to consider that their highly-paid work for IBM or Microsoft is in fact saving the world. Rosenboom makes mention of 'ego transformation' and 'non-possessiveness', but the terms are so vague they could come from a corporate directive explaining the need for downsizing (*ie* you're fired, but don't complain because you've got to learn to 'accept your own transmutation'). Instead of Zorn's starting concept of art as a protest against the reductive bottom-line of capitalist economics, art becomes the 'research & development' wing of hi-tech capitalism: 'Myths based on continuous transformation and change are needed to help humanity become comfortable with its necessary evolution towards partnership-based societies.' (p. 227) Whereas progressive political figures—from John Dewey to Leon Trotsky—see emancipation in terms of ditching idealist myth for materialist truth, Rosenboom prefers to recycle the postmodernist blandishments he's learned at college. This is the 'socialism' of the Microsoft billionaire boss-circle, rather than that of the Zapatistas. What has happened to the avant-garde as an independent force, non-academic and principled, critical of the status-quo? It's certainly not here.

'The greatest single threat to human survival presently known,' Rosenboom announces, 'is that the population of minimally sentient human beings will increase beyond the capacity of the Earth's environment to sustain life' (p. 229) Thus an individual from the richest nation in the world—which has reached that pinnacle by plundering and bombing across the world—informs us that the greatest threat to humanity is the 'population', *i.e.*, humanity itself! This was the reactionary thesis developed by Thomas Malthus (1766-1834), one challenged by Marx in terms of economic theory and disproved by the actual development of the world economy in the 1860s. Rosenboom's concluding line is: 'Time will tell the story and nature will act to choose appropriate outcomes'. This breathes the blithe acceptance of unfair social realities that characterises the outlook of the privileged. It also implies that history isn't made by people, but is some kind of 'natural' process: in contrast, every progressive idea of emancipation—from Plato to the early Christians under the Roman Empire, from Charlemagne to the Renaissance, from the French to the Russian Revolution—has made the concept of *consciousness* central.

Rosenboom's idea of music's relationship to society is of some kind of cybernetic training course ('Coming societies will require transformative skill on many levels, akin to that required for intelligent musical improvisation'). This kind of smooth accommodation is *not* the impulse that inspired the improvisations of Hendrix and Coltrane—which were closer in spirit to the moral and political antagonism of the recent protests against the WTO in Seattle. In debating the direction of modern music, these distinctions matter: in his desire to broadcast the sophomoric outpourings of his musical friends and colleagues, Zorn betrays the very culture he's trying to encourage.

John Zorn will doubtless accuse this reviewer of desiring *Arcana* to conform to some left/revolutionary 'agenda', another obstacle in the way of these artists realizing their 'personal vision'. However, to return to the intent expressed in his preface, to publish a collection of conventional NYC artspeak (ideas to be gleaned from any of the many books by and about John Cage and Marshall McLuhan, or, failing that, from *Wired* magazine) is NOT to register a protest against the way commodification blocks artistic communication. In actual fact, *Arcana* serves to extend a tradition of 'art' ideology that has deflected successive generations of idealistic Americans from taking a sober look at themselves and the place they—and their nation—occupy in the world. Peddling redemption to the privileged under the name of 'art' has never looked pretty—and here it's doubly unattractive, because it's half-assed. Anyone wanting to understand the tensions and contradictions of music under capitalism would do much better to read Frank Kofsky on John Coltrane, or Charles Shaar Murray on John Lee Hooker (or, in a rather seedier version appropriate to the post-punk era, *I Hate the Man Who Runs This Bar* by Zorn's erstwhile collaborator Eugene Chadbourne, inexplicably absent here).

~2002~

John Wilkes Booze
Five Pillars of Soul Vol. 1 Melvin Van Peebles
AFFIRMATION JWB-2 CD
Five Pillars of Soul Vol. 2 Tania Hearst
AFFIRMATION JWB-4 CD
Whisky and Pills
FAMILY VINEYARD FV15 7'

COMBINING THE name of a presidential assassin with a word for liquor must constitute some kind of attack on Middle America. John Wilkes Booze also call themselves 'Southern Indiana's premier R&B band,' a claim it is hard for a non-resident to substantiate, but their emphatic drums, bass and guitar have a declarative monumentality that makes their music forceful and attractive. Their organist has all his garage-soul licks down. The recording isn't slick, but if bass and drums sound boxy, they're in different boxes, and so the composite sound is three-dimensional and satisfying. *Nuggets*-inspired punk acts often lean towards tinniness, but here a solid beat achieves heaviness without the sonic pile-up resorted to by lesser musicians. The singer's falsetto and panic-struck spoken-word is just the right spritzer, invoking such worthy constituents as 'The Blimp' from *Trout Mask Replica*, early Devo and Culturcide.

The short, three-song tribute to novelist, film-maker and soul-man Melvin Van Peebles starts funky, but rapidly tips towards caterwauling expressionism. 'Tania' was the name adopted by millionaire's daughter Patty Hearst in 1974 when, kidnapped by the Symbionese Liberation Army, she switched sides and began wielding a sub-machine gun on bank raids. Again, this short suite—just five songs—has its unapologetic music embroidered with cultural and political meanings: both packages include printed inserts which explain JWB's reasons for calling Peebles and Hearst two of their five 'pillars of soul.' Coupled with tasty screen-printed covers, one's impression is of a band intent on improvising a revolutionary culture out of the media flotsam and jetsam of post-'60s North America. All it needs is a yodel, and the unvarnished unison country of 'Meanwhile, At The Hideout' would be perfect. We await the next three pillars with impatience.

'Whisky and Pills'—coupled with 'Marc Bolan Makes Me Want to Fuck'—is the seven-inch single. It shows that the info-rich extras cannot deter JWB from their musical mission, which is live and direct and twangy. JWB are musically righteous, politically aware and undogmatic. They sound like what Bloomington, Indiana, needs right now—but then again, a non-resident can only guess.

* * * * * * *

Mike Osborne
Outback
FMR Legacy DC07-031994 CD

THIS ALBUM, recorded by Peter Eden for his independent Turtle label in 1970, is one of the few masterpieces of British jazz, up there with Joe Harriott's *Abstract* and Tony Oxley's *Baptised Traveller*. It was re-released by FMR in 1994 and quickly sold out its 500 copies, so this reprint has been long awaited. At the time, the misspelling of Osborne's name on the cover (Osbourne) was criticised, but the mistake was made on the original sleeve, and is as much part of the album's aura as John Eaves's colour-field cover abstraction, the handwritten personnel details, and the stunning immediacy of the stereo recording (the chattering impact of a hi-hat always seems to get lost in today's 'sophisticated' mixes).

Due to drug and mental problems, Osborne has been off the scene since the late '70s, and everyone misses the undefended lyricism and plangency of his alto saxophone. Ornette and Ayler were the approved permits for this kind of freedom, though Osborne himself name-checked the undersung Jackie McLean. Osborne's method of interrupting his own flights, a kind of wrenching sincerity which makes tears prick at the back of the eyes, was entirely his own invention, and flowed into the tradition of *echt* British alto (Xero Slingsby, Alan Wilkinson). On this date, trumpeter Harry Beckett was in fine form, his last-post motifs spliced with hardbop argument and Barbadian sweetness. Both horn men sounded at their best because of the mighty South African rhythm section: Chris McGregor (piano), Harry Miller (bass) and Louis Moholo (drums). Everything they play is drenched in the blues—McGregor's fragmented, chinking piano sometimes sounds like blues guitar—while remaining true to the heavy, hearty vibe which was the contribution these exiles made to British jazz. Is this jazz 'outside' or 'inside'? When everything's flowing this forcefully and the outflights are so uncontrived, the distinction seems academic. Notes revolve around a hidden centre with imperturbable logic: even when it's roaring, the music is peaceful at the core. Future Music Records starts a Legacy subsidiary: fans of great music will have to live with the contradiction.

II. ARTICLES,
INTERVIEWS AND EVENTS

Lawrence D. 'Butch' Morris *(1997)*

WHEN BUTCH Morris returned home from the insanity of the Vietnamese War—a non-medic, he'd spent his time sewing up the wounded, only exposed to enemy fire when collecting flowers for a colonel's desk—he found 'Black' Arthur Blythe and Bobby Bradford playing Free Jazz in his mother's garage. His bass-playing brother Wilber had invited them over for a blow. The music, Butch says, was shattering. It penetrated his soul. 'What they were playing was really the Black Revolution,' he told Greg Tate. Ruthless, melodic, free. It's surely this radicalism, this art-political intransigence, that enabled Morris to come up with *conduction*—his patent process of realising ensemble music in real time. With conduction, the composer abdicates the 'score' for gestural improvisation. It declares to the classical establishment that the time has come to create symphonies in the naked instant.

Sealed-off today in near-impenetrable 'heritage' aspic, it is hard to imagine how *audacious* the jazz of King Oliver and Louis Armstrong must have sounded at the time. Yes, great counterpoint *can* be improvised! Jazz questioned the need for the ponderous paperwork that had accreted around European music, the banks of violins arrayed like desks in an office, paranoid accountancy for the smallest note. Taking the jazz heresy to the heart of the dragon, Morris's conduction suggests that all the paraphernalia of classical music—from the massive orchestrations of the romantics to the dense serial charts of Darmstadt, from graphic scores to John Cage's wilful experiments—is superfluous, the clutter of an antiquated mode of musical production.

Like politicians cowering behind their spin-doctors and image-consultants—or poets who hide behind the printed page—maybe the pre-planning of composers is simply the subterfuge of those without the moral and social righteousness to stand up and make statements in real time, to risk true communication—in the flesh, spontaneously, without props. Morris lifts the magic baton and the music speaks for real? It's an idea.

How is conduction done? A few days rehearsal familiarises Morris with what the musicians can do. At the same time, they learn his vocabulary of gestures—sustain, repeat, drop out, come in, louder, softer, higher, lower. During a performance, all playing is funnelled through Morris: he stands on the podium with a baton and moulds the ensemble sound like clay. All must keep their eye on him: if you miss a cue, you're in trouble.

Morris's method does not just leapfrog the hallowed institution of a written score: it offends the egalitarian, collective ethos of Free Improvisation too. Famously, Derek Bailey packed up his guitar and left during the first five minutes of his conduction rehearsal. Morris once had what he calls a 'mutiny'. Four musicians walked out because they felt he was being authoritarian: 'I must admit that I ask for a lot of discipline. When you've got only two days rehearsal, all the information comes at you like a ball of fire. If I say I need your attention 100% of the time, I mean 100% of the time. If a musician misses a cue, I'm gonna get upset.'

Morris's signals allow him to arrange as the music proceeds. Musicians are brought in and out both individually and in groups. Morris doesn't like ragged edges. He indicates what musicians are to do, and then brings them in on one down stroke. He can point to a guitarist and a koto player and initiate a rugged cross-cultural dialogue; indicate the string players and suddenly drown a caterwauling saxophone in sweetness. The ensemble are asked to memorize certain passages by associating what they are doing with a number (indicated with fingers). This allows Morris to plunge the ensemble back into a reprise:

> 'I know who's bullshitting and *they* know who's bullshitting! The conductor is in a great position. I'm looking into the musicians' faces, and the audience is looking into their faces, but the audience can't see *me*. Know what I mean? Everybody can tell when you're bullshitting, because it shows on your face. It's kind of a crude way to look at it, but it's true. And it's all right if you're trying, if you're really looking for, say, "memory one"—but if you're not looking, I can tell!' Keyboardist Pat Thomas—on tour with Morris's 'London Skyscraper' conduction this month—said after Morris's press conference,

'The thing is, he's a musician. We're not going to be able to get away with anything. He knows all the tricks!'

One of the concerns of orchestration—one that comes as a surprise to listeners who only know music through albums and PAs—is controlling the spatial aspect of sound. Messiaen and Boulez devised serial procedures to allow 'events' to ripple through the orchestra. Xenakis used Chaos Theory to calculate effects which sweep the auditorium. Morris controls such events by using the intelligence of the musicians: instead of merely counting rests and obeying orders, they have to listen and respond creatively.

'In a large ensemble, the tabla player way in the back and the violin player over there—they will not be able to hear each other. But *I* can hear them very well. So if I want to start an idea and make it move across the room to the tabla player, I have to create a path. I have to find a way of getting that information to him. I tell this person to play what the violinist is playing, then tell another person to play it and so on. Finally, I can tell the tabla player to play it. Then I can take everybody out, and just have these two people playing this idea, the violinist who originated it— and the tabla player's interpretation.'

Although he has performed a conduction with straight musicians—the Orchestra Toscana—Morris generally uses improvisors. Indeed, he declares that conduction is predicated upon the rise of a global generation trained in Jazz and Free Improvisation. He has performed conductions with David Murray's jazz big band, with the New York avant-garde, with European improvisors, with Turkish and Japanese musicians playing ethnic instruments. He has invented special signs to ask sampler-players to 'trap' and 'release' sounds. He envisages transcultural encounters between all these forces: 'Conduction was conceived,' he says, 'to help merge the many musicians and musics of the world into one creation, one time'. Conduction represents a coming-of-age for Free Improvisation, an acknowledgment that orchestral musicians need no longer simply be dumb terminals for the composer's software; intelligence has migrated down the net, towards the performer.

As a boy, Morris learned piano, composition, trombone, trumpet, French horn, bass and flute. In Los Angeles in the '60s, Morris played with Charles Moffett—Ornette's late, great drummer. Indeed, he credits the idea of conduction to Moffett, and acknowledges its use by Sun Ra and Frank Zappa. Moving to New York, he became a founder member of David Murray's explosive Octet. However, despite such involvements—and free-improvised encounters with the likes of Billy Bang, John Zorn, and J. A. Deane—he has always thought as an *arranger*. An early job had been copying big band charts, and he was intrigued by Gil Evans' subtle adjustments when he'd toured in his orchestra.

> 'The ensemble has always been more important to me than the soloist. Matter of fact, I never felt that I was a soloist, no matter how many bands I played trumpet or cornet in. I'm not Clifford Brown, I'm not Wynton Marsalis, I'm not any of the people in the trumpet lineage. To be a soloist you need to be a competitor, there's all the verbiage in the soloist's lingo that says, I'm gonna kick his ass. That doesn't interest me. Gil told me once, I love the way you come in! He wasn't talking about the content of my solo, he was talking about how I entered after someone else had played. After Steve Lacy plays, I go, Shit—Steve Lacy played everything! Or Lew Soloff—he plays and he just *kills* the trumpet, right. And the Gil looks at me and he says, Play. He's thinking, musically, what's going to tie all this stuff up? He knows there's no way in hell I'm going to compete with Lew Soloff, but he knows I'm going to throw a new edge on the music. And that's the way I think. Create levels, create depth, create angles.'

In his conductions, Morris gives open brief to what the musicians want to give him to mould—though he does have two pet hates. One is by-rote 'jazz', when players follow his gestures with 'a bunch of sixty-fourths'—he parodies a bop lead line—the other is the idea that a 'repeat' requires the uninflected trills of minimalism. At one blow, Morris attacks two of contemporary music's most tedious clichés.

'Often, especially in the West, when I say "repeat" and give the downbeat, people's first response is to play something that could be twentieth-century minimalism. They pick two or three notes and go "beedle-beedle-beedle". As soon as they set that up and they see it works, everytime I say "repeat" they do it again. And again. And again. Night after night. There are so many *other* things that can be thought of as a "repeat"! Beethoven was a great repeater. "Ba-*dee*"—then something melodic, a space, another melodic phrase, and *then* back. It can be eight bars, sixteen bars, whatever. If I get something too compressed, I have to take it apart immediately. "Beedle-beedle-beedle"—I'm bored already!'

Butch Morris's first conduction was released in 1986, an album named *Current Trends In Racism In Modern America (A Work In Progress)*. It was a stunning debut, sounding different from anything happening at the time. Simultaneously nervous and dreamy, its only precedent was (the original) *Sinking Of The Titanic* by Gavin Bryars: sumptuous sonic surrealism, a confrontational sense of occasion. It used downtown heroes like Frank Lowe, John Zorn, Zeena Parkins and Thurman Barker, but sounded totally different from the expected Knitting Factory blow-out. Its cool, agitated drift underlined the mordant wit of the title. By focusing the ensemble on himself, Morris creates what he calls 'one organ of total comprehension'. The surreal, fantasy-landscape imagery supplied by poet Allan Graubard for the booklet on Morris's ten-CD set, *Testament*, is appropriate. Morris mentions that audiences often feel they've entered a 'waking dreamstate'.

'I've got tons of letters and notes people hand me after concerts, where people talk about things they saw, visions, where they felt they were in a landscape and up in this area there was this little patch of sky, and right here a brick wall.'

However, Morris is wary of entering into any speculation about sound and mental images.

'I don't have a legitimate interest in that. I have a legitimate interest in trying to understand the psychology of the musicians, I learn something new every time. When I get on stage, it's how the musicians respond to my instructions—to sustain, to repeat—that give me the impetus to move that information around the room, to create something. So I start dealing with the sound and build it. There's this constant discussion—I try things out until I have a really solid idea.'

Morris is wise to concentrate on the situation on hand rather than seeking programmatic effects. Since triggering visual memories relies on already-established mental associations, such an agenda invariably rescinds to musical cliché.

'I'm trying to stress silence, to get musicians to take their time. You can always stop and think. Always. One of my gestures is called expand/ deconstruct—the tendency for most musicians is to fill every empty space with sound, rather than take more time and this is what I insist on now. I want everyone to hear what everyone *else* is doing.'

Much of the music on *Testament* is distinctly impressionist. Someone whose brain had been softened by reading Gilles Deleuze—or dropping acid—would probably find it borderless and rhizomatic. Certainly, without the brittle logic of either free improvisation or the score, conductions tend to be sonic immersions rather than white-knuckle rides. Sometimes they are so pretty they suggest ballet music. Would Morris consider a conduction of, say, drummers?

'Sure. I'm going to next year. I'm open to anything. Conduction works with all instruments—if the instrumentalists can figure out how to apply the gesture to their instruments. The most difficult experiences have been with electronic-instrument builders who don't know how to cut off their sound. Or they can't control pitch—the difference between high and low. I'm interested in clean edges—beginning and ending. I'm very interested in that—that you understand you're out, or that everybody's out. Everybody's in! Anything can happen within there.'

Who is the composer of this music? Property rights crystallize once art forms have settled down; one of the hazards of new artistic procedures like conduction is that they beg questions about copyright and authorship.

> 'It's a collective. I share authorship with everybody for all this stuff. Under the circumstances, you have to register it under names—unfortunately BMI/ASCAP aren't as advanced as GEMA in Germany for instance. Hopefully, by the end of this year royalties for *Testament* will go out to everyone who's on there. I'm not looking for sole authorship. Everybody gets their share of the royalty. Then I can go on about my business and do what I do. And that's exactly what stopped me playing cornet. I didn't want what they call an "option".'

Does he miss playing trumpet? I mention that Derek Bailey said Morris was a great cornet-player in his days of 'ad-hoc' encounters.

> 'I pick it up almost every day when I'm at home—five minutes, half an hour, sometimes I get caught up in something and it's two hours. Cassandra Wilson called me up and said, I know you're not playing, but *please* play on my record! She left a little track on her record open for me for *six months*! She called me and said, Butch—come on! My horn wasn't in New York, it was in Berlin. I called Graham Haynes up, and I said, can I borrow your horn? I went into the studio, they let me practice for half an hour, I said let me hear the track, I played and she said, That's great, get out! If somebody's interested I may do it.'

Butch Morris has put himself in a fascinating position. There are many free-improvisors who will decry his hubris, just as many composers will pooh-pooh the idea that some guy waving a stick around can achieve music as valid as their dots. His management of his press conference indicated the kind of fierceness and decisiveness that can easily make enemies. He finished off every topic by asking 'next question?' and responded to saxophonist Alex Ward's request for enlightenment as to his distinction between 'arbitrariness' and 'the random' by saying 'that's for you to find out!'.

However, politeness and scene-collusion are rarely spurs to intense creativity. Those who appreciate the tight discipline that undergirds the supposed 'anarchy' of leaders like Sun Ra and Frank Zappa will appreciate that *someone* has chosen to—quite literally—'seize the baton'. Morris's conduction raises social and political issues unknown in the tight, safe world of projects like Marsalis's *Blood on the Fields* or Mark-Anthony Turnage's crass jazz-classical 'fusions'. If you organise orchestras like an Andrew Lloyd Webber, your music will sound like his. What music 'sounds like' is a result of human activity and organisation. Every aggregation of musicians—whether rock band or symphony orchestra—is really a psychodrama, an arena for testing social relations.

> 'You have to know, psychologically, when to answer someone's question and when not. You have to make people think about their decisions. Even when they're away from the bandstand. If you don't, they'll bring to the bandstand everything that they've relied on for years, and that's not what I want, I want their historical information, I want their theoretical information, I want their sociological information, but I want them to go beyond—I want them to expand their musical personality all the time, all the time.'

And sometimes, Morris breaks his own rules and lets a musician dictate their own terms. Take the case of altoist Arthur Blythe. Although he's made commercial decisions that have dimmed his reputation—showcasing his virtuosity in 'jazz' settings rather than letting his musical fire scorch the path it should—Arthur Blythe is still a monster alto sax-player, a giant in a pygmy world. When Blythe took part in a conduction in 1989 (*Conduction #15*), Morris made it a concerto.

> 'Well, what do you do with Arthur Blythe? You let him *go*! That's what he's there for. I know Arthur from the '60s—when he was *all* fire—all fire and passion, kill, go for the throat. I knew, if I could put him in the same situation I could get the same kind of fire. At the end of the concert he told me, Had we gone on a bit longer you would have had it!'

Watching Roni Size & Reprazent cook up a drum'n'bass storm live on TV recently was oddly like listening to a conduction: the same sensation of real-time risk, the wilful drive to expose expression in the instant. There are stacks of 'virtual' music-producers seeking to achieve the multi-cultural dialogue Butch Morris is after; however, his commitment to music as ritual and occasion is allowing him to coax forth evocations undreamt of in the land of the sound-byte. On the English tour, Orphy Robinson—himself part of a "Current Trends" event in 1987, alongside Courtney Pine and Steve Williamson—will be brought under the same roof as a host of free-improvisors and hi-tech classical players. The '80s English jazz 'revolution' ran aground on the treacherous reefs of marketable imagery and the star-system: maybe Butch Morris's conduction will heal some rifts, open up new ones, tear the roof off the sucker—and give Orphy's demonic vibes some much-needed space.

And the best of it is: nothing can be predicted until Morris's baton signals 'play' and the alchemy starts.

* * * * * * *

Ornette Coleman Plays *Naked Lunch*
UK: Belfast Festival at Waterfront Hall *(1999)*

BACK IN 1992, David Cronenberg filmed the unfilmable and committed William Burroughs' *Naked Lunch* to celluloid. His best idea was asking Ornette Coleman onboard, playing sax to music written by his regular soundtrack composer Howard Shore. The mood of Cronenberg's films—seedy, visceral, dark, a poetry of anxiety and disgust—owes much to Shore's distinctive scoring, which combines rich orchestration with minor-key melancholy and tonal disintegration, a wrecked Wagner. Burroughs was thrilled that Ornette was involved, and dropped by to witness the sessions. Scribbling his tender, open, key-ambiguous lines over the symphonic backing, Ornette was superb. The CD (issued by Milan America/BMG) is a fantastic addition to Ornette's *oeuvre*, proof that his harmolodic concept can embrace and *détourné* Hollywood strings.

Belfast is currently in danger of being left stranded by Dublin's IT boom. Dubliners buy their second homes there (cynics say Irish unity is going to arrive via the cheque book, not the armalite). In the '90s, Glasgow refurbished its image by massive spending on the arts: hence the Belfast Festival (sponsors include the Northern Ireland Tourist Board, the National Lottery Fund, Guinness, BT, Toyota and Ulster Bank). Ornette Coleman was picked as the Festival's 'artist in residence'. On the Tuesday before, he and his trio (son Denardo on drums and bassist Charnett Moffett) performed with traditional Irish musicians (flutes, pipes, fiddle, and bodhran). Staging *Naked Lunch*—with projected film, trio improvisation, sound-mixing and a full orchestra—manages to combine expense, *avant caché* and spectacle. London journalists were flown in and wined and dined: forget the bombs and shootings, wake your readers up to the delights of this newly hip northern city.

Into this weird conjuncture of music and politics steps Ornette Coleman, with his own weird global solution: 'harmolodics'. Ornette's panculturalism refuses the strident triumphalism of, say, Mahavishnu or Minimalism, and instead comes over cracked, wistful and scarily alien. What was the word on the street about the harmolodics-meets-traditional gig? The owner of Dr Robert, the second-hand record-shop on Church Lane, said Ornette's collaboration with the Irish musicians hadn't quite worked, it was a good try, but the three American musicians together were 'terrific' (as often, the international tentacles of alt.culture outflank politicians' concepts of indigenous virtue). It was nice to have Ornette play in Belfast, he continued, but it wasn't going to do any good—for his part, he's selling up shop and moving to Portugal.

Naked Lunch was performed at the Waterfront Hall, a vast circular auditorium opened in 1998, imposing itself hub-like on the central streets. The film was projected widescreen, with Ornette picked out by a spotlight when improvising. The film's dialogue was played at full volume, with subtitles added whenever the music threatened to drown the words. At seventy years old, Ornette Coleman's alto saxophone is still transfixing, nowness and plea in every note. Hearing Denardo's delirious drums next to symphony players was like seeing a Pop Art duck obliterate a varnished canvas, and Moffett's bass was heated and gorgeous. The contrast of Ornette's piping sax with Shore's rich, realtime strings and woodwinds promised a really special dialectic.

However, the film's narrative quickly took over, making the music almost irrelevant. Though much of the script is pure Burroughs, Cronenberg tidies-up *Naked Lunch*'s radical non-linearity. He makes Burroughs' drug-fuelled sojourn in Algiers—'Interzone'—a descent to hell redeemed by transformation into a best-seller, and consequent fame and fortune. This underestimates the tenacity of Burroughs' exploration of the psychodynamics of capitalism and the limits of language: right at the end, his *My Education: A Book of Dreams* was refusing 'literature' and instead interrogating the status of memory, fantasy and authority. As if scared by the radical implications of cut-up and harmolodics, the film imposes conventional values, with Burroughs, Kerouac and Ginsberg in the unlikely roles of all-American wannabes.

A braver presentation would have mixed the film reels and played the dialogue backwards, thus allowing the music to complement Cronenberg's beautifully gauche imagery on equal terms. It's a truism that Hollywood flirts with radicalism and then disposes of it: when the music is this profoundly and eloquently destablising, and a film pops up in the concert hall to tame it, the recuperation becomes particularly graphic. Particularly disappointing was the way Ornette's scalding sax lines were cast as horror effects, when actually they are shouts of joy and freedom. The audience left exhilarated, though mostly with Burroughs' wisecracks and obscenities. But then who except a freak would talk about a *soundtrack* after a film?

After spending a night at the Posthouse Premier (with the Philip-K.-Dick-like shock of being greeted inside the room by my own name emblazoned on a TV-screen), this freak took a morning stroll about the city. The downpour of the previous night had given way to sunshine and wind. Every street seems to end in a glimpse of vast green mountains (Belfast may be a city, but, like Irish rock music, it's drenched in countryside airs and waters). I wandered up to St George's Market, a busy site of stalls I'd spotted from the bus on the way in. What I found was a fair organised by the Northern Irish Voluntary Trust: aromatherapy for victims of sectarian trauma, sweets, soft toys and baby woolies from the Women's Institute, children's holidays at Glebe House organised by the Harmony Community Trust, a profusion of comforts for a painful situation. Belfast Trades Council had a stall: their *Council News* for November 2000 reported that North Belfast 'now has the highest concentration of poverty and deprivation in Northern Ireland', and called for a 'post-modern and multi-cultural trade unionism to transcend sectarian devides'. I purchased their excellent anti-sectarian pamphlet, *The United Irishmen & the Men of No Property: Belfast's Sans Culottes* by John Gray. On the way back to the hotel, I saw what the Trades Council socialists are up against: a hundred Apprentice Boys— Protestant Unionists, mainly over 50—laying poppy wreaths at Belfast's Cenotaph, with Ulster police brandishing automatic weapons posted at strategic street corners. Not everyone holds to the Trades Council's solution to Belfast's problems.

In *Tone Dialling* (1995), Ornette Coleman wrote: 'Have you ever taken a trip to another country where you didn't know any of its citizens, and all you needed was a passport and a credit card?

That simple gesture of confidence is what learning and growing is all about.' Such a statement could only be made by an American, and a wealthy one at that. Ornette's harmolodics are certainly a premonition of what a non-chauvinist, anti-hierarchical culture could be. Without such visions, politics easily becomes unfelt, moralistic and drab. However, while certain inequalities persist (ones exacerbated by the logic of profit driving many of the Festival's sponsors), Ornette's vision is not going to be much more than a desperate, if heartbreaking, cry—and one that movie-watchers seem well-equipped to ignore.

* * * * * * *

Ornette Coleman Interview *(2001)*

ORNETTE COLEMAN: a legend, a contrary enigma, a sparkling source of musical modernity and controversy. The man who brought Texas hoe-downs and schoolyard chants to the sophisticated jazz clubs of Manhattan. The man who abandoned key changes just when 'playing the changes' had become the definition of virtuosity. The man who was hailed as the most inventive alto saxophonist since Charlie Parker, then took up intuitive violin and can't-play trumpet (Miles Davis said he sounded 'terrible'); who in 1966 brought in his twelve-year-old son to play drums for a Blue Note album; who electrified his band in 1977, just as the Fusion fad was sputtering to a close. But legends grow old, and past achievements can look like a burden. At age seventy, you wonder if Ornette mightn't be a stranded behemoth; with Coltrane and Cage and Sun Ra all gone, you wonder if he feels out of time.

Some are all too willing to dismiss him. Deploying insider terminology like 'the Atlantics' (the run of albums Ornette Coleman recorded in the '60s for Nesuhi Ertegun's Atlantic label) and awarding them five-star accolades, jazz connoisseurs consign Ornette Coleman to the past, implying his contribution is over, his moment gone. Has Ornette got anything left to say? Or is his influence now so pervasive, his achievement so monumental, that he can now lay back, survey the scene with a satisfied smile, and coast?

It's true his impact has been enormous. Coltrane, Rollins, Dolphy, and Ayler all owe him a debt. A series of younger saxophonists—from John Zorn and Tim Berne down to newcomers like Marco Eneidi—have adopted the wayward lines, bent notes, skipping rhythms and evasive harmony that are his trademark. However,

Ornette wasn't simply providing a novel style for gifted interpreters. He's a composer and leader and teacher with a total concept, one he's still struggling to realise. And like all genuine concepts, it isn't just musical: it's a proposal about social relations, a challenge to assumptions about value, skill and status. Because he's still at odds with reigning ideology, Ornette cannot be relegated to the '60s. The battle isn't over yet.

In order to raise interest in two gigs he's playing in London in March, I've been flown to New York for a meeting in his manager's office. Like his low-key entries on stage—despite the flamboyant build-ups given him by excited promoters—Ornette slopes in as if he'd rather not fully occupy the de-luxe space he's in. He slides onto a chair by the side of the large conference table and smiles shyly, the cuffs of his elegant dogtooth jacket arrayed on the table edge. He answers every question conscientiously, though it's when the issues turn to musical construction and his theory of harmolodics that the passion starts to burn. Still, from the very start, you realise he's utterly unaware of any division between music and everyday life, that split which makes professionalised music—and its professionalised criticism—so boring and oppressive. Unbelievably, the interview ends with Ornette giving me a lesson in how to select the right notes for self-expression on violin (he's already bought a trombone for his manager): 'Don't say you can't play! Say you haven't....' Notoriously generous with his funds, he's been known to give homeless bums his keys, his bed and the contents of his fridge. For weeks on end. Like those other true leaders Bessie Smith, Tammy Wynette and Sun Ra, music lessons from Ornette are lessons in life. And like those three, he cooks for his musicians:

> 'When someone comes by my house, I accept them, they say they want to come up to learn, I say okay. James Blood Ulmer lived with me. In fact, [in the early '80s] I had all the Prime Time band staying with me, I was momma, papa, everything! They were staying with me. I'd get up and feed them.'

The only British sax veteran who breathes an equivalent openness is Lol Coxhill, the soprano saxophonist who once busked his own concert queue. For freshness and variety of linear invention, Coxhill is also the only British musician to rival Ornette. The difference in status between the two (Coleman is world famous, while Coxhill remains a precarious cult) speaks volumes about the class-bound state of cultural power in Britain, and of the beneficial effect the US black struggle had on the status—if not the financial position—of its musical spokesmen (one reason Ornette plays so rarely these days is the astronomical fees he charges; although he's open to musicians, his demands to promoters can be almost self-defeatingly ambitious). Considered in tandem, Ornette and Lol demonstrate the intimate connection between spontaneous musicality and defiance of music-biz careerism, showing how inimical to artistic invention are the isolation and paranoia 'enjoyed' by the rich and successful. Capitalist economics demand specialisation and competition, neither of which suit these players' homespun philosophy of sharing and cooperation.

In an unlikely move for a 'jazz icon', Ornette begins the interview by name-checking Bob Wills, master of yee-ha, improvised fiddle and Western Swing.

> 'I've always felt that music is something that anyone can do, and those that have devoted themselves to doing it do not wish to be discriminated against because of whatever style or idea they're playing. But, because of cultural differences and all kinds of things, everyone usually relate what they're doing via the *style* of employment. I never thought like that. I was always interested in integrating whatever was going on. I was born in Texas, and there was what was called hillbilly music then, country music, Bob Wills & the Playboys. We used to jam together. They used to play really good bebop while they were playing country and western music in Midland Texas. I grew up having a musical experience with different people, though I started out in rhythm and blues to get a job. When I heard bebop, I thought 'Oh, this music is going to free me from all sins!' [*laughs*] But it didn't do that. I really thought that was the music that *every* instrumental person was going to adopt and challenge what they could do with it. There were musicians I admired in my home town. One guy I liked better than I liked Charlie Parker was Ben Martin. Another guy was named Red Connors, and he was playing like Coltrane at that time. All these guys were just improvising. I was more or less playing what I'm playing now. I was always getting fired, with a guy asking me to play what he thought was 'straight'. I thought what I was playing *was*

straight, just instrumental ideas, but he meant keeping close to the melody. That's what I liked about bebop, because it took melodies and turned them into improvised adventures. I don't think my idea about adapting bebop has gotten any further into instrumental music from where I am now, but I do believe I've made some progress in my own growth, in improvising instrumental music.'

Ever since the initial splash and scandal of his New York debut on 17 November 1959, aged twenty-nine—he wore a white suit and blew a white plastic alto and divided the critics into two warring camps—Ornette Coleman has been one the biggest names in jazz, but the record business still finds him a difficult proposition. Nothing has been heard from him since a flurry of activity five years ago, when he formed a corporate subsidiary named Harmolodic. Evidently well-financed, the label came complete with its own website, e-mail and fan club. The label's slogan was 'equal accession to the information expression (one way one result is fiction)'. The flagship album was *Tone Dialling*, where Coleman's electrified octet slid from gangsta beats to a Bach prelude to dotty collective electronica in a manner that was fluid and freaky and sly and indelibly Ornetteish. The label also provided a niche for Ornette's acoustic quartet with his son Denardo on drums, Charnett Moffet on bass and Geri Allen on piano. To demonstrate the unlocked-in and improvised character of the playing, their album was released in two versions (*Sound Museum: Three Women* came out simultaneously with *Sound Museum: Hidden Man*; doubling-up is an Ornette theme, with double quartets (*Free Jazz*) and twinned electric guitars (*Dancing In Your Head*): in 1987, saxophonist Jan Kopinski found him in a Nottingham restaurant, eating *two* dinners...). The Harmolodic label also issued *Colors*, a duet recorded at the Leipzig Opera House with the German pianist Joachim Kühn, whose lapsed modernism produced the bizarre image of Ornette as the flame of hurt sincerity inside a Koons-style palace of kitsch. Encouragingly, this last release showed that the label would document one-off ('ad hoc') free improvisations too. The cover sported one of Ornette's distinctive abstracts. Unfortunately, Harmolodic's owner, Polygram, was bought up, reconfigured as Universal Music, and everything went awry. As Ornette puts it:

'We started out on the right track, but the record company got sold that we were with. Everybody's allowed to get big but the poor. That's a pretty good quote, right?'

Back in 1991, David Cronenberg had asked Ornette to collaborate with his regular composer Howard Shore for the soundtrack of *Naked Lunch*, his movie of William Burroughs' famous novel. The choice was inspired. Early in the '70s, critic Robert Palmer had told Ornette about the Joujouka Musicians of Morocco, and he'd flown out to hear and record with them (a selection appeared in 1977 on the 'punk jazz' manifesto *Dancing in Your Head*). Ornette had therefore witnessed at first hand a resource used by Burroughs and painter Brion Gysin to access what they were believed was precultural, anthropological experience, as direct and unmediated as sex or drugs. When Ornette Coleman explained his enthusiasm to biographer John Litweiler, he complained that in his life he'd heard lots of music which 'just sounded like music': in contrast, the Joujouka musicians didn't use a musical language or a particular key, it was like a gospel congregation in a sanctified church, an emotional immersion. If the tempered key system was traditional perspective, rendering a detached, objectified image of reality, this was Cubism: art that juddered you into a physical reaction.

For both Cronenberg and Ornette, the *Naked Lunch* project was a Trojan's Horse through Hollywood's realist portals. The newfound fame of Burroughs—orchestrated by his assistant James Grauerholz—allowed them to indulge moods, transitions and concepts hitherto unexploited by the mainstream (*Naked Lunch*'s relentless anti-capital-punishment gallows humour and anal erotics would never have made it past the censor, so the script made do with mythologizing Burroughs' life). Ornette included his own trio music (Denardo on drums, Barre Philips on bass) and a subtle and significant meditation on Thelonious Monk ('Misterioso'). He danced his alto lines over Shore's drifting string melancholia in ways that made the heart turn.

Apart from the Joujouka experience, what other connection did Ornette have to Burroughs? As soon as Ornette hit New York, he was an underground celebrity, *fêted* by the ultra-hip, and he quickly got to know Allen Ginsberg and his circle of poets and writers. In June 1965, Ornette and his trio (David Izenzon on bass and Charles Moffett on drums), plus Pharoah Sanders on tenor and an 11-piece orchestra, spent three days in a New York studio recording the soundtrack to *Chappaqua*, a film by Conrad Rooks in which William Burroughs played Opium Jones. The music was astounding, but Rooks thought it was too distracting, and employed Ravi Shankar to play sitar instead (it was released by Columbia as *Chappaqua Suite*). Ornette recalls a happier encounter with Burroughs, this time in person:

> 'In 1980, a group of people built a culture centre in my home town called The Caravan Of Dreams. They were very familiar with William Burroughs. He came there and participated with me when I was playing there. He read his poems. We got to know each other very well. I also knew him when he was living in London. He was I guess a very fluent person, at least in his words.'

Burroughs dropped in on the *Naked Lunch* recording sessions, pleased that the soundtrack had found such an apt interpreter. United in revolt against conservative America's hypocritical concepts of sense and decency, Ornette, Cronenberg and Shore created filmic poetry that glowed with satirical energies. Riding the thin line between cult and box-office, the film was moderately successful. With film/music events increasingly employed to give an ailing music scene an injection of glamour, *Naked Lunch* became an ideal vehicle for exposing Ornette's music. The project was staged in Belfast in November last year (it reaches the London Barbican on 26 March, with a trio performance on the preceding Friday). I told Ornette I was a little disappointed to find that so much emphasis was placed on the film's narrative, with subtitles replacing any dialogue drowned by the music: a deluxe showing of the film, sure, but not quite the *musical* immersion I had hoped for. Apparently, a less logocentric version was done in Japan:

> 'We went to Japan in the '90s and played that music and the people in Japan took the original *Naked Lunch* and made their own *Naked Lunch*. It was in a room of 700 speakers in the Panasonic Building and it was *really Naked Lunch*!'

I thought maybe you should mix up the reels, run some of them backwards, actually *do* the 'cut-up' the film talks about....

> 'That's just what they did!'

Seeking to nail the essence of the harmolodic approach—defined by Ornette in the *Naked Lunch* sleeve note as 'all parts are equal'—I asked Ornette about his musicians. Although appreciative of their efforts, he evidently feels disappointed that once they escape his clutches, they seem to revert to more conventional musics, abandoning his quest for a flexible process that can include all modes of expression under the sun with all their force and singularity. Although loath to badmouth anyone, it's obvious that for him the search for an open-ended music without hierarchy or closure is a moral imperative—adopting a 'style' is seen as backsliding. Ornette believes his son Denardo is a genius of the drums.

> 'When Denardo was playing with Prime Time—I'm not saying this because we are related—I would have seven people playing all at the same time, Denardo would cover them, cover the melody and still be playing himself. I haven't seen anyone analyse the concept of the drums doing that. He writes really beautiful music and he plays fantastic, but because I'm his father I don't think he gets that much attention for the way he's playing. I know he's frustrated, but he doesn't say it.'

Ornette is mildly indignant that drummer Shannon Jackson is so lauded for his playing on *Dancing in Your Head*, pointing out that he helped him play the drum patterns on the record. Nor does he warm to Shannon's observation that the new, electrified music on that record was really the unconstrained, back-to-Africa R&B played for kicks at weddings or picnics in Texas by black musicians. The way Ornette talks about his musicians is no way as rebarbative as the insults that flew between Captain Beefheart and his Magic Band when they split up, but the problematics are uncannily similar:

> 'The conditions that musicians are in...sometimes they figure out, well the leader is good, but we're playing the music that makes them be a leader, but it wasn't true.'

I mention that this sounds just like the Captain. Ornette remembers Don Vliet and his young wife Jan visiting him in New York in the early '70s: 'We used to see each other lots, they were very nice' (according to Beefheart, the wind instrument described as a 'first-time musette' on *Mirror Man*, recorded in 1967, was given him by Ornette, indicating that Ornette's 'anyone can play' philosophy was influencing him early on). Beefheart once referred to Ornette as a friend and fellow 'painter', and there are many parallels between them as artists. In their paintings, both deny 'skill' and illusion, yet their marks writhe with life. Both reject received technique, believing that animals and small children have a grace and directness that is suppressed by formal education. Accessing this state of primal innocence in adults requires intensive 'deprogramming', a discipline the musicians tend to forget once they lose contact with their teachers. If one conceives Beefheart as harmolodic rock, it's small wonder that freak rock bands such as The Contortions and Kenny Process Team understand Ornette's music better than college-educated jazzers.

I mention I'd been listening to *Tone Dialling*. It occurred to me that people usually describe harmolodics in harmonic terms— Ornette's famous refusal to 'play the changes'—but he actually uses a subdivided rhythmic approach to attain equivalence. Like the best rock and funk, the intricate ensemble patternings are reminiscent of the weave achieved by African polyrhythms. Does Ornette make all the instruments equal by conceiving them as contributions to a drum circle? In answer, I receive a quick lesson in harmolodic fundamentals.

'Everyone has the freedom to express rhythm and time equally. Since the rhythm is more adapted to a broken consistency of time, it just sounds like rhythm, but rhythm is a time and rhythm is without a time. So when you play something slow and then play it fast, it becomes rhythm, just because of the speed accelerating. Harmolodics means the harmony, the melody, the modulation, the time, and what's called the 'movements' of compositions. Singular compositions are more like the one we use to express language. When someone writes a song, they're writing music to fit a grammar. The grammar of songs is not as free as the grammar of sounds. A sound is free of grammar. When I found that out, I decided that I would try and become more clear how to write and play that kind of relationship to tempered music, to non-tempered music, to melody, to harmony and to poetry. In fact, three years ago a lady in France came to me and asked me to play live with Allen Ginsberg and Gregory Corso—to play with them while they were reciting their poetry. We did that, it was on cable TV in Europe. I haven't seen it in America. The reason why I'm telling you about that is because when you speak of everyone on *Tone Dialling* sounding so 'rhythmical,' it's because when people talk, you talk in rhythm, especially if you talk fast it sounds like rhythm. Sound and rhythm is free of grammar, which is why it's so equal to everyone. I have written this theory book based upon everything I'm speaking about, the only reason I haven't put it out is that I've been too busy performing it.'

Harmolodics allows the musical virtues associated with different genres to cohabit, letting them breathe and interact, rather than reducing them to inert stylistic ciphers. It's similar in intent to the collective equality proposed by the late John Stevens for his Spontaneous Music Ensemble, but it has a dancing propulsion that British free improvisors never seem able to get to without inviting complete disaster. The so-funky-it-hurts warped-disco bass of Jamaaladeen Tacuma (then still calling himself Rudy McDaniel) sounds great alongside the rattling, R&B guitars of Charles Ellerbee and Bern Nix on *Dancing In Your Head*, for example. The music is taut, directed, in-yer-face, polemical. Bypassing both the vapid laxity of Ambient and the thick-textured anonymity of Noise, there's enough space for all the musicians to be themselves.

'That's true. I'm also doing that in what is called 'classical' music. All music can do that. There's no music confined to any rule where that someone has to make a lesser contribution than another one because of how the melody goes or how the rhythm goes. I think what you're describing is...jazz is a music that allows a person to become *an individual soloist in any environment*. The word itself doesn't mean that there is only one way to do that. There are other ways to play. When you say 'jazz' you really mean someone is going to do something that they are interested in expressing without having to feel inhibited by the environment. Anyone can do that. You don't even have to call it music….'

(Ornette adds he doesn't like the cheap connotations of the word 'jazz', it sounds like a scam, something cynical or casual, compared to the dignity of being called a 'classical' or even 'blues' musician:

however, sometimes—as above—he is prepared to use the word positively).

I remark that at the performance of *Naked Lunch* in Belfast, Ornette and Denardo and Charnett each seemed to have an orchestra at their fingertips, whereas the whole of the Belfast Symphony seemed to add up to just one instrument.

> 'I think so too. I felt the same way. What you're describing is what I am really dedicated to advancing, to become more fulfilled in doing that with other people. I'm really interested in doing that with any musical signal, I'm not worried about the style, just the idea of how that person hears and expresses what he does on an instrument. I know music will allow *any* person to participate in it once they find out what their tone relationship is to the other tones. If you use that for a starter, usually you come up with something that's very interesting.'

The conversation turns to the problems of communication in a society where music is seen as entertainment, as a distraction.

> 'It seems that the performing society, which is entertainment, doesn't have any goals, it just has presence. When you go out at night to enjoy yourself, when you find something that you enjoy, you are not aware of the goal they're trying to reach. You just find them there.'

The pressure to commercialise is illustrated by an anecdote about Charlie Parker.

> 'When I first heard Charlie Parker in LA, I didn't have no money, no contacts and didn't know anyone in LA. I had been there for a while. I heard that he was going to play in the Tiffany Club on Normandie. I went out there to hear him. They didn't want me in there. I had my hair long and I couldn't buy nothing, so they asked me to leave. Charlie Parker came out and started talking to me. He'd heard that I played the sax. I didn't even have a horn at that time. I said I really like those left-hand songs you're writing, but he didn't play any of his songs, he just played pop

songs. I wasn't so interested in that, I was interested in hearing him play the music he had written representing what he had done with modern music. I tried to talk to him about music, but he probably thought I was out of my mind or something.

'Pleasure is not a current that you just stick in the wall. Pleasure is something that comes directly from you without being bound by the results of someone else's behaviour. You can tell the difference from feeling something natural, and when you feel something that you've been made to know how it works to give you the feeling of 'how it works'. You know that. People who can't read and write know that even better. They haven't had that signal taken out of their brain and replaced with just 'thinking'.'

Ornette refuses to see music as a specialty. Deciding what music to play is part of deciding how to live. He recalls his first gig experiences.

'I told my mother one day, I said, Mother, I don't want to play what I'm playing now because I think I'm making people kill themselves. I was playing some Rhythm'n'Blues. The Texas Ranger would come in—there was a gambling table, the guys were gambling money, their salaries, and losing, then they'd go home and beat up their wife and that. The Ranger would come in and grab a girl and start dancing with her, so she wouldn't go to jail, so I say, I'm playing music to protect this, and this is not want I want to do, I feel bad doing this. You know what my mother told me? 'What's the matter with you, you want people to pay you for your soul?' I said, Wait, what is she talking about? She made me realise one thing—that what you think you're doing and what you think you don't want to do, you think you're different than those other people, but you found that out through something that you can't do. She didn't say that, but that's the conclusion I came to. Do you know what? To this very day, I am sitting here in that same state of mind. Whatever the quality in life, I know there is something that I don't want to do and I know there is something I can't do and there's something I can do, but all of those things are as clear as me looking outside and I can't do nothing about it.'

Are you saying there's a difference between achieving your art and financial rewards? They sometimes run together, and people can think they're the same, but...

'They're not related! Not at all.'

The conversation waxes philosophical (Ornette is making me wonder if certain formulations I think of as Captain Beefheart's aren't really derived from him, a Woody Guthrie to Beefheart's Bob Dylan).

'God has given every creature an intelligence about how to survive in the form he's in. When you see animals, you can't believe human beings could be so dumb. The first thing an animal seems to do is to rid himself of anything that doesn't allow him to be.'

Ornette tells me about his background, how his childhood experiences in Fort Worth have shaped his attitude.

'The house was $30 a month rent, by the railway tracks. A three-room house. I had relatives who were better off than my mother. Her sister was very well-off. We wasn't. But the reason that I'm saying that is that I never saw my mother worry about a job or nothing. The reason I'm saying that is that she had made peace with her condition, her race and her survival, and to her that meant doing without having any relationship to your relatives, don't work for anybody, and live without as much as you can, without needs. She had that down. I didn't know what it was all about, I couldn't talk to my mother and ask her, Why are you like this? But she really instilled some stuff in me about doing without. I've learned how to do without, so it doesn't bother me. If someone takes something from me...in New York I've moved about 61 times, only because of music. Sometimes I could pay, sometimes I couldn't. I like chemistry, I used to be researching chemistry, now I'm an idiot at it, but I used to use my mind in a different way. I went to study it, but the kids were putting me down because I was so raggedy and they talked to me like I wasn't good enough to be there with them. When I was taking geometry, I told the teacher she had made a mistake, and she took me in the back and beat me to death. I couldn't tell my mom, she was scared. From then on, I really felt bad about telling someone I knew something. When I told her that she'd made a mistake in front of the class, I thought that was what I was supposed to do, but I wasn't supposed to do that. So, when I wanted to study chemistry I found out that all matter changes, changes into something. And therefore I started trying to realise that if you struck a match and it burns, it turns into something else. So I thought, That's what chemistry is. I met Buckminster Fuller in 1954. In 1983 he was giving a lecture in Aix-en-Provence, he came in one morning and said, Ladies and Gentlemen, if anyone in this place believes there's something called up and down, they are living in the dark ages. That's what he said. So I said, Oh man, I understand that! I'm going to write a piece about that.'

On learning that his interviewer cannot play music, but once had violin lessons, Ornette borrows a pen and writes down the notes which summarise the harmolodic approach.

'I think you might have three of these notes and three of these notes, everything is a chromatic, everything starts going up there and starts coming down here. So these are three changes—C Major seventh, E-flat Minor seventh, D, F, A-flat and A—and you can play the violin, and nobody in music can play an idea unless they use one of these notes if they're playing a tempered scale. And since there's twelve of them in the form of chords, if you took the same scales you have now and call this whatever you want to call it, and now play them in this sequence, put anything wherever you want to and realise that you're coming in this sequence, you won't say you can't play no more.'

The chart Ornette drew is identical to that printed in John Lit-weiler's essential biography, *The Harmolodic Life* (Quartet, 1992, page 132). Ornette also recommends the 'harmolodic guitar clef' printed in the booklet inside *Tales of Captain Black* (Artist's House, 1979) by James Blood Ulmer.

> 'Blood is the only person at that time that was studying with me that came out with something of his own. On *Captain Black*, it has his guitar harmolodic chart. If guitarists studied that chart they would all come out with something that is unbelievable. I never thought of myself as a leader. I was always trying to find someone who could share what I was doing so I could do it better. That's my concept of a leader.'

The previous Friday, Ornette had attended a concert at Miller Theater, Columbia University, where violinist Curt Macomber performed a piece by Ornette named 'Trinity' (originally written as a suite for Malcolm Goldstein, it was named after Fort Worth's river).

> 'He came in and said, I want to know about this piece. I said, Curt, as you read this piece, that's the fifth, regardless of what sound you're going to, right now it's in the position of the fifth, the third, and the seventh. If you take the fifth, third, and seventh of the tonic of any chord you still come up with a major seventh. That's the structure of music. He said, What do you mean? I said, Okay, think fifth and then go to the note you think, and when you get to that note, think of what note that is in relationship to the idea. When he does that, it just lit up, it was no more 'a style,' it was him playing what I wrote as if he was hearing it for himself for the first time, as if he was improvising.'

Do you think you should include this advice in the score?

> 'I think I'm going to start doing that. It is possible to improvise something that you read, besides just how you feel emotionally. You know how a singer sings? On *Tone Dialling*, the piece I did of Bach? It's like that, it's totally like that.'

Because his ideas cut right across the rules, trained musicians often raise their eyebrows when Ornette talks theory. Harmolodics has been called 'incomprehensible' and 'phony'. Nevertheless, for any listener with open ears, harmolodics is an unmistakable entity. It's obvious when Ornette's sidemen abandon it for something closer to convention (think of Charlie Haden or Bern Nix). It's obvious when his sidemen extend and deepen it (Blood Ulmer's Music Revelation Ensemble with David Murray), or when a bunch of musicians grasp its implifications (think of Nottingham's wonderful, undersung Pinski Zoo, or LA's Universal Congress Of). This writer is not equipped to defend Ornette's advice in the court of musicology, but if the music works and connects, how can the theory be either 'incomprehensible' or 'phony'? Perhaps it's simply that Ornette's harmolodics cannot be played by drones who follow academic rules and put nothing of themselves into the music. Perhaps that's the point.

> 'When you said you 'couldn't play,' what you were describing is repeating an idea that you heard someone play, but that idea didn't come from notes, it came from an idea. So when you think the idea comes from the notes, that makes you withdraw, because the idea cannot be repeated the way that person had it...it's like me telling you a lie'.

As an attempt to defend the very essence of what makes music worth hearing—the sting of unguardedness, the spike of expression, the rush of conviction—harmolodics may be the ultimate music lesson. As attempts to characterise what is vital in modern music (and to explain why traditional manoeuvres sound so false and sterile), both Twelve Tone and Free Improvisation have their uses, but it cannot be denied that they have also served as excuses for much aridity and inconsequence. Maybe harmolodics is the pedagogy which won't turn the musician sour and the listener off?

John Coltrane thought so. Though not often talked about in the giddy heights of Tranolotray, for six months in the mid-'60s, just before he died, John Coltrane took lessons from Ornette. The arrival of the altoist from Fort Worth had turned avant-garde New York on its ear. Charles Mingus said Ornette couldn't play a C scale, yet sounded so fresh and real on his instrument he made everyone else (including Mingus) sound 'terrible'. Sonny Rollins—the other contender, besides Coltrane, for 'top saxophonist' in '50s New York—responded by going into retirement. He was heard practising in the solitude of the pedestrian walkway of the Williamsburg Bridge, high above East River. When Rollins emerged he cut his masterpiece, *Our Man in Jazz*, playing free jazz in the company of trumpeter Don Cherry and drummer Billy Higgins, both from Ornette's current band. Coltrane, too, cut a record with Cherry (and Edward Black-well, Ornette's long-term drummer), a set of Ornette tunes named *The Avant-garde*. Often dismissed by listeners craving the full-on muezzin power of late Coltrane, it's actually an extraordinary re-cord—diffident, experimental, humble, but with a spontaneity and actuality that are riveting. I asked Ornette what he thought of it.

'I thought they had a good rapport with each other. When you make a record you know you're making an imprint that's going to be repeated. It's different from how they played in person. The thing that they didn't do, they didn't get caught behind a melody. They used the melody as a force to play on, which was good. Cherry was really advancing. Cherry could play all sorts of melodies and put solos that fit them. Don Cherry was very rare. Before he died Coltrane sent me a letter and a cheque and told me, 'I've found it, and thank you'. Him and Eric Dolphy used to come by when I was at the Five Spot and sit in with us. I think I went and sat in with him one night, a restaurant called The Blue Note, but not the famous one, this was on Hudson Street. Eric was more like a 'first-chair' [*i.e.*, classical] musician be-fore he got to New York. After he got to New York, he got freer.'

Towards the end of our conversation, George Regis, Ornette's manager, enters the room. True to form, Ornette is still encouraging him to play the trombone he abandoned years ago. He tells him he has a 'really beautiful sound' on the instrument he's given him (Re-gis blushes and waves the praise away). We are gazing over the New York rooftops between Crosby and Lafayette from Regis's tenth-floor office on Spring Street. Elated now and on his feet, Ornette becomes more emphatic, like someone finishing a solo and recap-ping the tune.

'Every musician doesn't want to be bound by re-peating, about limiting themselves to make someone else sound better. I don't think any musician like the idea of that, but every musician *does* that. I had a guy who told me once, "Ornette, here's some money—you don't play tonight". Being the 'leader' means people come to hear you, but for me I think people are coming to hear *music*. I get out the violin and play it. I think the expression of something has meaning to everybody, not just to yourself. I don't tell that guy, don't play like this, don't play like that. You play the way you believe it's going to sound, if you sound better than me or whatever, do that. The only thing I realise that I've spent time doing is—finding out how to stay away from someone else's idea. If you learn how to do that, learn how to share without doing that, you won't have a problem, but you have to have knowledge of your relationship to what you're doing and what kind of music is involved. I tell Denardo and Charnett, "When you play, do not resolve your idea". You don't have to resolve. The reason we resolve music is because there's a method of composing—chromatic notes, they go a certain way—but *sound* doesn't have that. Because what is a melody? A melody is a repetitious form of construction that has an end and a beginning in relationship to logic—sociologic—basic. But ideas, inspiration? There's no person in the world that can tell you, "Don't do that".'

* * * * * * *

When Worlds Collide
UK: Liverpool Institute for Performing Arts
25 February 2001

THE LEGACY of The Beatles still ripples in Merseyside, creating intriguing interference patterns in the culture. This concert, held at the Paul McCartney Auditorium in the performing institute he founded, brought together Ensemble 10:10, musicians from the Liverpool Philharmonic who specialise in Schoenberg, Stravinsky, Kagel and a contemporary repertoire, and the Muffin Men, a bunch of unruly scousers who have spent the last decade bringing the songs of Frank Zappa to every scummy rock dive in Europe (over 400 gigs: twenty-five tours in eight countries). No stranger himself to jibes at the class-bound state of British culture, McCartney named his own orchestral concert at the Albert Hall 'Working Classical.' 'When World Collide' was the title for this particular convocation of opposites.

Over at the Liverpool Tate Gallery, the designer of the cover of *Sgt. Pepper*, pop-artist Peter Blake, is currently curating an exhibition called *About Collage*. Interestingly enough, as shown by a life-size cut-out of Max Miller originally made for the crowd scene on *Sgt. Pepper*, his cover was not actually a collage, but an integral photograph of an elaborate installation. It was Frank Zappa's cover-artist, Cal Schenkel, who stooped to using scissors and paste in his famous *Sgt. Pepper* parody (which fronted the accusatory, Kafkaesque *We're Only in It for the Money*). McCartney must feel haunted by the late freakrock Dadaist. On this night, not only was his auditorium hosting a rock/classical collaboration with a Zappa-rich programme, but LIPA students were staging scenes from *Thing-Fish*, Zappa's preposterous, seriously-warped 'Broadway musical' (a free show was performed both before and after the main concert).

A sober-looking Muffin Men—white t-shirts, dark trousers—took the stage to play a set of Zappa instrumentals: 'Chunga's Revenge,' 'Son of Mr. Green Genes,' 'Peaches En Regalia,' 'Blessed Relief', and 'Marque-son's Chicken.' 'We play this music because we *like* it,' announced bassist/leader Roddy Gilliard, an evident dig at the classical 'robots.' The Muffins played loud, and Carl Bowry didn't hold back on guitar, treating us to a flamboyant display of chops: Zappa's guitar style through a personal prism. 'Marque-son's Chicken,' from the 1984 album *Them or Us*, proved that, far from deteriorating after the break-up of the original Mothers of Invention, Zappa's tune-smithery accumulated in power and complexity. Martin Smith's trumpet sounded especially piquant on 'Blessed Relief,' the calm track at the end of 1972's *The Grand Wazoo*. Without the froth of the vocals, it became clear that Gilliard's decisive bass playing is the foundation of the group's robust psychedelic sound.

Then Ensemble 10:10 came on to play a classical programme: Stravinsky, Varèse, and Zappa's 'Alien Orifice' arranged by Philip Cashian. In a solo recital, clarinetist Nicholas Cox only prevented some restlessness from certain elements in the crowd by really exerting himself on the final piece. When classical players throw themselves into the music and genuinely inhabit it, people listen. Rachel Lyons turned 'Density 21.5' into sinuous romanticism, while 'Octandre' disobeyed Varèse's injunctions to play barbarically loud, bringing the music back towards Debussy's impressionism. As a composer, Cashian has been 'inspired' by *The Perfect Stranger* (an album of Zappa pieces conducted by Pierre Boulez). However, his arrangement here lacked the *timbral* stink to evoke the unsettlingly-physical lure indicated by Zappa's title.

Vibist Ian Gardiner is best known as leader of the classico-prankster ensemble George W. Welch. In the second half, his arrangements brought the two 'worlds' together. The Muffin Men emerged in their habitual groovy attire, while the 10:10 musicians donned comedy hats and wigs. Gardiner's arrangement of the introduction to 'Little House I Used to Live In' from *Burnt Weenie Sandwich* was a delight, the different wind instruments showing how rooted in Stravinsky and Varèse are Zappa's motifs, even in a score originally intended for interpretation by piano. The transition from classical filigree to rock blow-out provided a fascinating moment as the Muffins reproduced by ear a much-loved—and untranscribable—passage from an album. This reference to a public-domain sound-object made their subsequent improvisations sound particularly idiosyncratic and free. Asserting the collage-Dadaist's right to any barmy connection, the Muffins stuck the *Dr Who* signature-tune in the middle of 'Sleeping in a Jar.' A climactic Bowry solo received heckles, whistles and applause, as if the audience were deliberately recalling the atmosphere of Zappa's late albums. 'Holiday in Berlin' was given an authentic Tyrolean lilt by LIPA student Meike Holzmann's arrangement, while Muffinman Andy Frizell's 'drunken saxophonist' outburst received spontaneous applause. 'King Kong'—introduced by a quote from *Le Sacré de Printemps*—was a blaster: the Muffin Men had suddenly sprouted a bigband horn section. At the end, the packed hall gave the musicians a five-minute standing ovation, forcing conductor Clark Rundell to perform a section of the medley again. No stranger to extreme music (Rundell conducted one of the orchestras involved in Simon H. Fell's *Compilation III*), he looked genuinely bemused to be performing a genuine 'encore'.

Not everyone in the audience was ecstatic. Avantist DIY-Esemplasm popsters—f-ing and blinding Mark E. Smith-style and sporting Pokémon wristwatches—denounced the Muffins for diffuse, Dead-head rhythms. According to composer/flautist Marie-Angélique Beuler, the hardcore modernism of 'Density 21.5' had been betrayed by a romantic interpretation. Cosmonauts Hail Satan's bass-player complained that resort to the intelligent, jazz-rock side of Zappa had 'blandized' any authentic class conflict. He had a point. While it was great to see Andrea Martin, 10:10's double-bass player, digging Bowry's post-metal excess, we never found out what classical decorum would have made of 'Stevie's Spanking,' 'Why Does It Hurt When I Pee?' or 'Broken Hearts Are for Assholes.' The 10:10's genteel rendition of Varèse—correct in letter rather than spirit—gave little hint that it was listening to *Ionisation* cranked up on his domestic hi-fi that provided Zappa with his first non-R&B musical jolts, thus paving the way to a life's *oeuvre* of mighty mis-cegenations. Future programmers take note....

Another dimension to Zappa was provided by a rare staging of *Thing-Fish*. Of course, the students have all the technical skills at their disposal here. Radio vocal-mics spared us any operatic bawl-ing. Sound-mix, lighting and costumes were all excellent, and sym-pathetic to *Thing-Fish*'s potato-headed anti-aesthetic. Though staged almost entirely by Norwegian and German students (in the mid-'80s, Zappa's 'Bobby Brown' was a top-ten-radio hit in those countries—given its obscenity, inconceivable in Anglophone countries), the nibbly giblets of Zappa's porcine satire were lovingly handled. The chorus of Mammie Nuns raised their 'nakkin's' and pissed over the audience as required, Daniel Knapp's Thing-Fish was scary and wise ('I got yo' language hangin',' boy!').

The yuppie-couple Harry'n'Rhonda (Chris Thompson and Siri Steinmo) were toe-curlingly perfect, and Chris Rogers applied his five-years experience singing in German rock bands to create an Evil Prince/'theatrical criticizer' no one present will ever forget. *Thing-Fish: the Musical* has long been deemed one of Zappa's 'im-possible' projects. It now looks like a scrofulous carnival-*in-utero* that could operate on popular notions of the possible (and the politi-cally-correctical) for decades to come. Welcome to the concept of 'theater piss,' peoples....

* * * * * * *

Madness & Music (2001)

> *N.B. This piece was savagely hacked around by Chris Bohn at* The Wire, *making it start with a story about Moby Grape, a band I've never listened to, so many thanks to W. C. Bamberger for allowing it to run in its original form. My recent involvement with Mad Pride meant that this subject was particularly close to my heart.*

EXAGGERATED ATTENTION to music has long been deemed a species of madness, as if any activity that cannot isn't based on words must be insane. When satirist Billy Jenkins named his London-based arkestra of moonlighting jazzers The Voice of God Collective, he coined the slogan 'Music Is the Religion,' expertly skewering the peculiar mix of certainty and proselytizing zeal that characterises all us music obsessives. We believe our favourite music is crucial, important, *true*. Such certainty challenges the pluralism and tolerance of polite discourse. It asserts unmediated response and inner conviction over logic. René Descartes got it wrong: the location of the modern, secular, enlightened soul is not the pineal gland, it's *music*.

Mad Pride is a new civil-rights movement which promises to do what Gay Pride did for gays, but this time for those suffering from the stigma of mental 'illness' (past or present). Given the affinity of music for unreason, it's unsurprising that it has a lively musical wing. Mad Pride benefits have been performed by Alternative TV, Ceramic Hobs, Hysteria Ward, the Astronauts, Fish Brothers and Alabama 3 (whose 'straight out of rehab' country trance proved so commercially successful, the band is now too contractually-bound to appear). The end of September sees the release of a twenty-track compilation, *Nutters with Attitude*, on Mad Pride Records. In Berlin, under the banner of the *Irren Offensive*, radical psychiatrists and rebel patients hold public trials. Anti-psych intellectuals steeped in the works of Michel Foucault denounce crimes committed by the state's thought police. In Hackney, they release a punk album.

To be fair, Mad Pride has also issued eloquent and barbed leaflets denouncing corporate drug-profiteering and New Labour's authoritarian legislation on 'sectioning' (psychiatric confinement). It has organised protests and pickets which have included parliament and Archway Road's 'suicide bridge,' and published an anthology of tales by mental-health patients. This volume of strident transgression was praised by novelist Iain Sinclair ('fizzing with bad energies'), named *Guardian* paperback of the week, and has now gone into a second edition. *Southwark Mind News*, a newsletter edited by one of Mad Pride's leading lights, has become essential reading for many—both mad and sane—who previously avoided mental-health professionals and their political wrangles like the plague.

Inspired by punk's disdain for official values, Mad Pride breaks with the cap-in-hand cosiness which characterises government-approved mental-patient organisations. Instead, according to its manifesto, it 'celebrates madness in all its forms as a means to all-out social revolution'. Though no one cites André Breton, Mad Pride is a street version of Surrealism. The curious ping-pong between the Parisian avant-garde and British pop has been possible because, heads abuzz with images and theory, surrealists and situationists ignored music: Mad Pride are a 'pong' to follow the 'ping' which Malcolm McLaren, Jamie Reid and the Sex Pistols inflicted on the ultra-*recherché* Situationists.

But how 'mental' is Mad Pride music? The most affecting track on the CD is 'Communication Failure' by Alternative TV, where Mark P's trembling voice—its blunt honesty, as ever, hovering on the edge of a 'mad' rejection of social status—lays out some edgy and discomforting truths. Liverpool's Ceramic Hobs play sets of Stooges covers in costumes appropriate to the Antennae Jimmy Semens fan club; their track was 'written by silent partners, underwritten by a giraffe' and 'produced in a slimy cave by J. E. Marquano'. Amongst some keening folk, tepid techno and incongrous country, the punk rock makes most sense. Its reversal of values, the heretical notion that the outcasts of society are its prophets and judges, is central to Mad Pride's stance. With punk, Mad Pride taps a vital vein of subaltern protest.

One contributor to the Mad Pride volume, Jim MacDougall, made an *impromptu* performance during an Alternative TV gig at Union Chapel last year. He has the ability to make an audience sweat, give what's happening a taste of actuality. His band Aural Guerilla recorded a 2CD set 'out of virtue and boredom, rather than expecting huge sums of money and status in the music world'. They disbanded in 1999 ('the vocalist simply became impossible to work with'). On the CD, MacDougall's *récitativ* is so attuned to the chugging, low-key punk rhythms, it's as if they were invented for the cadences of his voice. Burroughs-style, you're lulled into his stories, then brought up short by how violent and disgusting they are. Is it him, or the way he's been treated? Is he what the tabloids call an 'evil influence'? The listener wriggles on MacDougall's artful hook with a sense of outrage and disbelief, staring at the singer's Polaroid of his own scrawny feet on the cover, printed in sperm-tinted yellows. Now hawking a solo CD, MacDougall declares that he is disappointed with the 'opportunists' at Mad Pride and is looking for 'something else'.

An alliance between Mad Pride and punk is logical. It supports Stewart Home's thesis that punk's proletarian critique of the spectacle isn't finished, merely suppressed by today's media yuppies. However, Mad Pride's rockist populism is more than a little musically restrictive. If its 'celebration of madness' were genuinely pitched against the capitalist star system, would it only favour genres already promoted by big business? When popsters Madness named themselves after a Prince Buster song, they added to a long tradition of madness defined by carnival and the nuttiness of the weekend music-hall. The only 'attitude' to be derived from Suggs—now a TV personality—is escape-valve entertainment, a confirmation of capitalism's work/leisure split. The phrase 'mad for it,' used to death in youth-aimed TV adverts, derives from Manchester's Hacienda scene of the '80s. The drug-fuelled hedonism of 'Madchester' lacked the aesthetic or political suss to resist such commercial uses. What would a Mad Pride outfit sound like that genuinely didn't care about the charts, that allowed its madness to warp the *form* of the music? Maybe it'd sound avant-garde...

Avant-garde music is universally acknowledged to have been launched by Arnold Schoenberg's *Pierrot Lunaire*. It was quite explicitly mad. Composed in 1912, it's a sequence of texts sung-spoken by a moon-touched loon. Schoenberg's compositional devices—demented music-box chimes, unravelled melodic lines, vacant repetitions, clashing *tutti*, sped-up hysteria, puckish vocalese—have become *clichés* of musical dementia (performances of the score can still be shattering, especially if interpreters refuse smooth academic correctness and realise its sonic shocks). If improvisations involving abstract singers such as Phil Minton, Vanessa Mackness or Shelley Hirsch 'sound like *Pierrot Lunaire*,' it's not because they're pastiching Schoenberg. His attention to historical necessity—the gradual accumulation of chromaticism in symphonic music, the increasingly deritualised, 'one-off' nature of compositions themselves—meant opening the door to affective sonority, timbral specificity and clashing juxtaposition: a violent subversion of tempered, sonata-form logic.

The innovations of *Pierrot Lunaire* were later formalised as 'Twelve Tone,' Schoenberg's score-based rationale for superseding classical tonality. However, *Pierrot Lunaire*'s 'free atonality' can be reduced to no schema except an expressionist belief that madness—a complete dislocation from tradition, an immediate confrontation with the musical materials—packs a charge lacking in obedience to tradition. This development had parallels in the visual arts. An art-history graduate named Hans Prinzhorn was appointed by the Heidelberg Psychiatry Clinic in 1919 to create a collection of the art of the insane. Paul Klee and Max Ernst were both impressed by his published catalogue. Many of the motifs of Modern Art derive from their respectful attention to insane modes of expression. The Nazi accusation that both Twelve Tone and Modern Art were 'degenerate' derived from these connections. Before they rounded up the trade-unionists, socialists and Jews, the Nazis executed the inhabitants of mental homes because they were 'economically expend-able'. Meanwhile, the 'Jewish Bolshevik' modernism which found new meanings in the art of the insane was banned.

Olivier Messiaen was a Roman Catholic and no revolutionary, yet he expanded modern music by a traditional resource of the in-sane: he listened to the birds. The realisation that nature is a living terrain of intention and communication implies that human society is not different in kind. Consciousness is simply what happens when one species of animals begins to develop socially and so requires language. This insight can be devastating to Kantian common sense, which erects a metaphysical barrier between humanity and 'non-signifying' natural forms. Flowers have been depicted for centuries. By transcribing bird songs, themselves as unique and varied as flow-ers, Messiaen risked an openness to natural beauty which bordered on madness (try finding a park, lying down and listening to the birds: you'll weep that anything can be so beautiful, and yet so far apart from how our everyday lives are currently organised). Yet Messiaen, close to madness as he was, also applied the anti-repetitive principles of Twelve Tone to rhythm, and so invented Se-rialism, a procedure which has been denounced as 'hyper-rational,' 'cerebral' and 'merely theoretical'. How to explain this paradox?

The theorists Michel Foucault and Gilles Deleuze set up a stark chasm between rationality and madness. Their dualism cannot map Messiaen's practice. The point is that, like any effective scientist or artist, Messiaen pursued Freud's programme of 'where Id was, Ego shall be': a dialectical investigation of the hitherto unknown. He opened his ears to the birds, but by transcribing them and inserting their songs into his music, he brought them into the realm of musical understanding and collective event. Likewise, his experiments with serialising rhythm generated bizarre new beauties. Sonic events spin out from his maths like surreal coral wreaths. The lesson Boulez and Stockhausen derived from Messiaen was that mind and matter are not forever sundered, the intellect and emotion forever opposed. A rational grasp of the structure of music can body forth new emotions and experiences. These feelings are so vivid they become criticisms of a society locked in the grey repetitions of social ritual.

Karl Marx argued that human labour is not something external to nature, a divine essence like Plato's soul. Following Darwin, he called it a natural force. Serialism discovered that natural beauty could be found in the workings of maths and logic. It subsequently proved the case that musics which did not take on board the innova-tions of Twelve Tone and Serialism were incapable of absorbing new material, whether derived from other cultures or new technologies like recording, amplification and sampling. When Coltrane proposed an ecumenical world music, he needed atonality and serialised rhythm. Like Prinzhorn's 'art of the insane,' the madness of Schoenberg and Messiaen was found to be just the dialectical turn required for a genuine (rational?) approach to exotic materials such as the Balinese Gamelan or spoken-word on tape.

In this connection, Graeme Revell—an Australian psychiatric nurse who founded the Berlin-based industrial group SPK, named after a mental-patient protest group which turned to terrorism in the late '60s—issued an interesting, if flawed, experiment in 1986. He attempted to realise the 'insane scores' of Adolf Wölfi, a psychiatric patient whose work was lionised by the '20s avant-garde in Vienna (Walter Morgenthaler and Hermine Ferndriger-Marti's *Ein Geisteskrankler als Künstler* appeared in 1921). By using newly-available sound software, Revell turned Wölfi's ideas into music, reducing his madness to exotic raw material (he did the same with bush recordings of insects). As reproduced in the glossy booklet, Wölfi's collages and scores (one includes a Campbell's soup tin, three decades before Warhol) look fascinating, but Revell's interpretations are too smooth and controlled to sound like anything but post-Eno Ambient. Was Revell 'exploiting' Wölfi's legacy? In New York, a Mad Pride delegation picketed a showing of the Prinzorn collection as an 'exploitation' of schizophrenia (lacking America's brash brand of identity politics, London Mad Pride would be more likely to organise a visit). Should we wax indignant too? Moral outrage is a blunt instrument in aesthetics. Revell's sleeve notes evince a corny notion of artistic transcendence, but they're full of respect. Certainly, one should point out that Revell was wrong to use pretty harmonies: Wölfi's work wasn't 'beautiful,' it was wrecked and hurt and strange. Religious fragments in Wölfi's collage-scores gave Revell an excuse to indulge modish Holy Minimalist effects, manoeuvres which sound gratingly commercial today.

Italian music-theorist Marco Maurizi defines the dialectic of Modern Art as 'mediation criticised by immediacy'. He is using Hegelian terms to describe the joy unleashed in a musical performance when 'something happens,' when a poetic situation lifts people out of repetition and ritual. 'Mediation' describes traditional ways of organising sound, the equipment and skills of musicians and sound technicians. By 'immediacy,' Maurizi means recognition of the absolute specificity of any social occasion (something denied by classical ideology, which freezes certain works, often themselves revolutionary in intent, and presents them as timeless Platonic 'forms'). When Freud developed psychoanalysis, he did not apply generalisations or wield statistics, thus reducing his patients to objects. He examined specific 'case histories': the insistent 'immediacy' of modern music requires similar treatment.

Experiences of madness are as varied as the individuals themselves, so in order to explain how madness and music might self-illumine in ways that go beyond Mad Pride's agit-prop punk, I shall have to stoop to confessional mode. I went mad in 1983. The most striking aspect of my delusions was an apocalyptical sense of significance: everything and everyone around me related to my most urgent libidinal and political impulses. There was no waiting, no concept of 'yesterday' or 'tomorrow,' no debt to the past: Stockhausen's 'Moment Time'. There was no passive reception of ideology, no hierarchy of media power: everything was dialogue. TV was not simply a broadcasting device, it also passed on signals from your living room. The newscaster wasn't at Broadcasting House, he was the old bore with a blue suit and grey *toupé* four doors down the street, pontificating about world events from his sofa. At the height of my mania I was sectioned for two weeks. As often in such cases, the worst experience was the year of depression that followed. Since my recovery, I've found that Free Improvisation is the only musical form which regularly reminds me of my 'mad' insistence on immediacy, for an event in which everything has significance, and no person or shiny doorknob or shout in the street is excluded from the total composition. In this respect, it's significant that the two individuals who span the worlds of Mad Pride and Free Improvisation are Mark P and improvising saxophonist Lol Coxhill, both of whom are noted for heightened sensitivity to venue-specific situations.

Hugh Metcalfe, who runs the Klinker Club in Islington, believes that Free Improvisation can work as a useful therapy for mental patients, and treasures his experience of playing music both inside and outside psychiatric institutions. However, although the band he runs with poet Bob Cobbing, Birdyak, is far 'madder' than anything in Mad Pride's roster, it results from a worked-out critique of the alienation and passivity instilled by commercial media. Metcalfe's notorious and hilarious references to body noise might be deemed Artaudesque, but seaside-postcard humour debunks any recycled 'art' glamour. After speaking these words into a microphone outside the Vortex, where he'd been showing films and playing guitar with pianist Veryan Weston, he felt the need to howl a Cobbing-esque sound poem into the chill night air:

> 'Many a time after gigs I've had people say,
> "Keep on the medication", but of course I'm totally

straight. What's called "madness"—I don't use the word—can be heightened sensitivity to people's reactions. I was a day patient at the Whittington Psychiatric Hospital. I had a breakdown after my son was born in 1986. Anyone can end up in psychiatric hospital. Very good psychiatrist, Dr Dalton, who was very much into therapy and not giving you medication. Drugs are a quick way out for over-worked doctors, talking is better. I'm now back to music, running a club and being extremely busy. I met brilliant people in there. Also distressing—seven friends committed suicide, some inside, others were musicians and teachers who were living "outside", supposedly. I ran a music therapy course with the staff nurse, and we had fantastic sessions in the common room, fifteen people improvising, basically. Music's an easier way to communicate than talking. People who can't have relationships but love music come to the Klinker, make friends. It's like an extended family.'

Involved in his own campaign against psychic alienation, Metcalfe is suspicious of the sensationalistic and populist thrust of Mad Pride: 'they should lobby doctors who prescribe drugs, and suggest alternative treatments—their choice of music is patronising'. True enough, two marquees of *ee-ay-addio* punk units in relentless succession at the Mad Pride Festival in Clissold Park in the summer of 2000 did make me long for some genuinely mad Free Improvisation to interrupt the ritual. However, Mad Pride gigs are special. It's hard to play the rock game of celebrity wild man or sonic terrorist in front of an audience of self-confessed nutters. There's an atmosphere of non-hierarchical fun and civility I've not experienced in many lowdown rock venues since the early '80s. Nevertheless, though the impact of punk boneshakers like Underdog and Los Paralyticos is undeniably therapeutic, the collective thrill of thrash is more like relief from the threat of madness than an artistic crystallization of its de-alienating highs.

Of course, claiming that a dialectic between enlightenment and unreason structures both Serialism [if you've cut the Messiaen paragraphs, replace this word by Atonality] and Free Improvisation is not the only way of relating madness to music. Since Elvis Presley brought the spasmodic, arsenic-rimming, rattlesnake-clutching madness of rockabilly to the mass market, pop music has been riddled with sensationalist lunacy and psychic casualty. There is also the issue of albums recorded by the mad themselves. The advent of the Argentinean group Reynols (see *Wire* #197)—fronted by Miguel Tomasin, who has Down's syndrome and is given to nonsensical oracular pronouncements—is merely the most recent example. After a listen to an album made me equate Reynols with Psychic TV (terrific publicity, shame about the music), it occurred to me that it's both patronising and blinkered to accept 'certifiable' madness as a fixed category. Indeed, if there's one lesson to be learned from Mad Pride, it is that the mad are not some exotic type, but unfortunates who are completely involved with psychic forces that should be thoroughly familiar to so-called 'sane' minds. Art plays with such forces or becomes a sterile exercise.

Records by the certifiably insane provoke heated debate in which claims of 'empowerment' are countered by accusations of 'exploitation'. In other words, a subset of the debate that surrounds all pop music, where (at its best) singers and musicians without access to social status or capital are invited to flaunt themselves in public to make someone else a buck. Can one really distinguish between the naive 'madness' of the juvenile rapper, promised the world and then put in an impossible situation regarding drugs, money and guns—and who winds up with a bullet in his head—and the 'proven' madness of Syd Barrett, Alexander Spence or Daniel Johnston? The pop industry devours naivety and wrecks lives: what's to distinguish between 'certified' madness and the mind-bending notion that the potty amateurism of Jonathan Richman's deathless 'Road Runner' could make its singer a star?

A useful rule-of-thumb might be the singer's ability to face the world rationally, but in a world where 'economic rationality' entails starvation, privatisation and weapon fairs—what's rationality? As Veryan Weston puts it, recalling the time anyone linked politics and madness in Britain: 'Who's mad? Someone who walks around with a dustbin on their head, or Lyndon B. Johnson dropping bombs on Hanoi? Star Wars is madder than anything. R.D. Laing's ideas were good stuff, but they were suppressed by behaviouralism and Tavistock Institute reward/punishment theory in the '80s. The Klinker has got it right. It will remain pure and fertile in its madness, it can't be co-opted like rock'.

When Captain Trip Records issued *Gyaatees* in 1997—an album recorded at Koganji Temple by Sei-sou, 'intellectually handicapped' Japanese priests—their intentions might have been either 'empowering' or 'exploitative'. Under capitalism, all production is inevitably a mixture of both, since commodities have both use values and surplus-extracting exchange values. However, the Sei-sou's music appears to develop and flow freely, implying some kind of collective freedom and awareness lacking in the one Reynols album I've heard, which sounded like nothing so much as an annoying racket designed to keep a political opponent awake (do Reynols fans really love the records, is owning an LP all about one-upmanship *avant-garderie*?). San Francisco's Volvox are fronted by a singer named Ant-Honey who suffers from brain-damage, but the musical technique of the band is advanced and reckless enough to regress to his vocal actuality with conviction. Likewise, the Sei-sou's naive use of rock'n'roll rhythms could teach the London Improvisers Orchestra a lesson or two about unoppressive pulse. Madness can supply essential material for wide-eared improvisors, but on its own it's no guarantee of musical relevance.

In 1999, Sundazed re-released an album named *Oar*, originally made in 1969 by Alexander Spence. Moby Grape's most talented member had just spent six months in the psychiatric ward of Bellevue Hospital after drugs and black magic had transformed him into a pajama-clad mad-axeman. It's easy to understand its renewed relevance: Spence's winsome folk rock is recorded with a directness that suits the late-'90s fad for unplugged and lo-fi campfire confessionals, an American Nick Drake. Like Charlie Parker's wrecked West Coast sides, or those recorded by the end-of-the-line Billie Holiday, there's ample room for sentimental projection in Spence's pauses and imperfections. However, such 'actuality' is by no means the exclusive province of the certifiably insane, as any listener to the Sun, Chess, Goldband or Incus back-catalogues knows: maybe in a streamlined pop world, 'madness' is just a name for expressive grit.

In his review of *Oar* in *Rolling Stone* on 20 September 1969, Greil Marcus waxed lyrical. He knew it wouldn't sell, but told readers to buy it before it disappeared forever. Intriguingly, Marcus describes the album's winning lack of polish by saying 'sometimes his playing is about as good as Wild Man Fischer's'. This refers to a notorious album released the same year, in which all the issues of empowerment and exploitation were stacked up in multiple layers of provocative irony: a premier Frank Zappa production, released in the same clutch as his own *Uncle Meat* and Captain Beefheart's *Trout Mask Replica*. Wild Man Fischer had been committed to mental institutions several times, and this was his bid for stardom, a double-album in a gatefold sleeve. Today, despite pressure from the Wild Man Fischer Fan Club, the Frank Zappa Estate won't license a re-release, calling it 'a poor example of his production skills'. Actually, it's exemplary: suddenly not only Frank Zappa's own music, but also the relationship of madness to music—and to workaday 'normality'—start to loom clear.

The critics at *Rolling Stone* hated Zappa (Lester Bangs liked *Hot Rats*, but that was it). They craved golden minstrels singing songs from the Harry Smith anthology, not some Dadaist anticipating the generic miscegenations which exploded in the '90s. Dave Marsh called *An Evening With Wild Man Fischer* 'a particularly vicious example of Zappa's penchant for sadistic social commentary. The results are brutal, not funny except to the emotionally immature and the socially callous, and would constitute a deleted embarrassment in recorded history if the record industry had any shame.'

Marsh's ideology of 'talent'—a commodity Fischer appeared to lack in abundance, since his tunes are the kind of 'non-songs' made up by five-year-olds, or adults regressing to infants in their bathrooms—blinded him to Zappa's intent, his Prinzhorn-like curiosity about the revealing aspects of 'mad' expression, its implied critique of the limits of official culture. We hear a street recording of Wild Man Fischer selling songs for a dime in front of the Whisky A Go Go and the Hamburger Hamlet on Sunset Strip. Zappa had Art Tripp overdub percussion, turning the chaos of shouted exchanges, laughter and traffic noise into a dada suite. Tripp's needle-sharp rattles, bell chimes and marimba plops add a sinister, broken-clock dimension, recalling the accompaniment of *Pierrot Lunaire*. Atonal pointillism is used to open a window on the unconscious, questioning the assumption that the listener is above the drives, pain and fantasies of poor Larry Fischer. When he says he has voices in his head 'fighting each other, it's like a disease!,' the commotion writhes in our skulls too (when Hugh Metcalfe shows home movies accompanied by his guitar dementia, he brings in Veryan Weston, whose fluid atonal improvisations perform a similar function). Kim Fowley and Rodney Bingenheimer improvised an extraordinary prediction about the coming commercialism of 'Wild Man' shtick ('there's Wild Man Rodriguez with boogaloo drums on his records').

At Fischer's request, the sleeve carried a diagram, showing the relative status of stars in contemporary pop. It's pretty astute for a madman. At the bottom we find Zappa, Chubby Checker and Fabian—and Wild Man Fischer 'before he met Frank Zappa'. In the middle there is Johnny Cash, and Fischer 'after he met Frank Zappa'. At the top are the Beatles saying 'hello down there' to the Stones, 'Elvis,' Cream, Mozart, Hendrix, Tiny Tim and the Mothers. Whizzing to the very top, up above the Beatles—'after you hear this album'—is Wild Man Fischer.

The fantasy is really not so far fetched. By dint of the repeated broadcast and media accolades granted those who generate profits for powerful interests, pop is replete with musically-restricted dimbos who have somehow been transmogrified into untouchable stars. The human need for silly ditties—previously supplied by family sing-songs and playground chants—is turned over to a voracious commercial machine, replacing people's everyday creativity by the illusion that only bought product can hit that spot. If you list the issues dealt with by Fischer—freak commercialism, autumn, social conflict, desire, Hollywood morbidity—they are more realistic and varied than most pop albums. When Zappa arranges a 'fancy version' behind his yelping voice, the strange combination of consummate arrangent and amateur vocals has the charm of the Monkees. When Fischer tells us that he was put in an insane asylum for singing at work, he introduces a social dimension which abstract confrontations of madness and normality never examine. Why work to earn money to buy albums by people who are just like yourself? Only those repelled by the dada project of an art by non-specialists will dismiss Wild Man Fischer's extraordinary record (since critics make their living providing consumer guides to the junk 'we' are not talented enough to create, they'll be the first to stamp out such outrages). Those who turn on to Wild Man Fischer, on the other hand, make a friend for life.

Larry Fischer went on to make two LPs for Rhino Records. While lacking the dada consciousness of Zappa's production, his energy and charm endure. 'Don't Be a Singer' was a heartbreaking attack on his treatment by the music industry. Nevertheless, unlike the fifty-seven varieties of nihilist formalisms thrown up by the official US avant-garde, *An Evening with Wild Man Fischer* is a truly inexhaustible document. 'Madness' is at last dismantled as a category: facile assumptions about mental illness and 'normality' are challenged by stark criticism of the hurt inflicted on the psyche by the star system, and of the alienation and unfreedom of regular wage labour.

The Klinker Club and Mad Pride offer contrasting ways of utilising music to challenge psychic oppression. If they are not exclusive alternatives, it's because—despite the different philosophies of those involved—they face an identical cruelty, the same social system. Lol Coxhill and Mark P's redefinition of music as situation—a singleton, collective event—is one way of bridging that gap. Another possible bridge would require theoretical input. By understanding what we're up against—the commodification and alienation of musical experience under capitalism—Mad Pride might see the point of musical freedom, while improvisors might find ways of making their rejection of commercial duplicity more graphic, public and politically blatant. As Guy Debord pointed out when defending his 'logocentric' theorizing versus the mystical tendencies of other Lettrists, it's only when we fail to understand the enemy that splits appear in our camp.

* * * * * * *

Iain Sinclair's M25 London Orbital
Barbican, London *(2002)*

THE RISE and rise of Hackney-based writer Iain Sinclair has not previously been associated with music. Sinclair's imagination is aggressively visual: his accounts of urban squalor and pavement detritus read like a brilliant art critic's reviews of post-conceptual installations. No less than with the Vorticist writer and painter Wyndham Lewis, the idea of Sinclair responding to music is grotesque: musical experience is too feminine, dialectical and intangible for his cinematic, paranoically-objective prose. So how come this Barbican event was a joint venture with Paul Smith of the Blast First label? Had Sinclair discovered a musical bone in his body? We went to find out.

Sinclair's latest publication is named *London Orbital*. It contains chatty accounts of walking round the M25, London's orbital motorway. Such easy accessibility irritates those who preferred Sinclair as an underground, self-published poet (which he was for three decades), but he nevertheless remains a product of the '60s. His street-person disdain for those in power still sizzles, while his anti-Blairite satire raises gurgles of joy. The '60s counter-culture relied on music as motivator and event, its biggest bazooka versus a repressive establishment. So despite a tin ear, it's logical that Sinclair should call on Smith: music remains the main line to authentic populism.

Throughout the evening, three giant screens showed Chris Petit's silent in-car footage of M25 traffic. Blobs of rainwater shivering on back windows caught in resplendent digital detail, yellow headlights diffused in dawn mist, a deodorising amulet swinging against a side-window, an occasional hand on a steering wheel, lorry drivers looking grumpy at being cam-corded and overtaking. Memories of childhood boredom on car-trips. Flashes of restful nature: green meadows, oak trees, cows. In order to advertise *London Or-*

bital, Foyles Books on Charing Cross Road burnt a large hole in the centre of a fold-out map of London and suspended it in their window. The event at the Barbican had a similar charge: Sinclair was asking us to cast our imaginations to the periphery of the metropolis, making this high-prestige EC2 venue appear vacant, not-there, burned-out. We were trapped inside a modern Stonehenge, being asked to imagine a wheeling cosmos that consisted of nothing but three-lane traffic.

A printed programme established the conceit of the evening: we were to travel the M25 widdershins, different performers appearing at stops on the way, the road laid-out like a game-board. Smiling broadly, and pausing politely to allow laughs and applause to subside, Sinclair is a genial host, completely at ease. The affection readers feel for an author capable of sentences like, 'The grey sprawl of South London subtopia bleeds into Croydon: nothing is fixed, journeys overlap. Speed chilled with puff.' is palpable. There were friendly heckles, *impromptu* jokes, collective laughter; an overall vote of 'well done'. Those who've been seared by the nastier aspects of Sinclair's writing might be surprised at the warmth on display (if so, they've never attended a signing by a horror-fiction author).

Sinclair read a geographically-appropriate section from the book, and then one of his crew would give us a five-minute 'turn': the kind of entertainment friends might improvise during a country-house weekend. Ken Campbell performed a Max Miller-ish routine about 'gastromancy' (the exorcism of spirits *via* farts) which had everyone laughing uncontrollably. Bill Griffiths—one of Sinclair's favourite poets, and a superb one—read an uncharacteristically limp piece about shooting rabbits, and performed some Bartók piano compositions, the Barbican's sound system making their Steinway sound as wonky as a pub piano (a welcome twist). Griffiths knows his Bartók, and the unassuming way he played was poignant, the high point of part one. Given Sinclair's disinterest in today's (or yesterday's) music scene, one suspects the next act was Smith's suggestion. Scanner delivered a mediocre collection of software clichés, his samples heavy with pre-processed echo and tired drum'n'bass beats. The way Scanner 'acts' his button-pushing has a Victorian aura: this is how star conductors and magic-lantern-men 'spellbound' their nineteenth-century audiences. Maybe this performance tickled Sinclair's taste for gothic.

The presence of a drum kit hinted that punk-band-from-North-London Wire would actually play, but they trooped in to recreate a tune on laptops. Even the vocals were pre-recorded. Spindly, balding guys in black pay tribute to the 'cyber' fetish of five years ago:

more push-button self-consciousness and techno-mystification, virtual ambience as a security blanket. Novelist J. G. Ballard was billed to engage in a discussion about motorway service-stations and retail-parks ('I've seen the future and it's boring'), but he was off sick and replaced by a photo cut-out. Sinclair's attempts to pose as a prognosticator of the times flounder on the superficial politics of his Vorticist eyeballism. Bruce Gilbert added random computer effects, but things were now falling a little flat. As a drunk and vociferous Julian Cope fan complained in the interval, there hadn't been any performers with *fire*.

In part two, Jim Cauty woke things up with a terrifying five minutes of customised thrash. Unlike Scanner and Gilbert, he used the Barbican's sound system for something relevant, playing hard-shoulder recordings of passing cars and trucks at frightening volume and in ear-twisting stereo. The band came onstage in fluorescent safety-jackets to flashing orange emergency lights. A tape of the 'Alleluia Chorus' was combined with the aforementioned drumset being pounded by an actual drummer (not a Roland synthpad in sight), death-metal power-chords from the guitars and a speed-techno irritation track—all to forge an anthem to Gimpo, the KLF roadie. This eruption of rock power brought half the audience to their feet (the Cope fan raised both arms). In part one, Bill Drummond's contribution had been a disappointing chunk of wannabe-Sinclair prose. Drummond's endless Pete-Townshend-style interviews can obscure the fact that it's Cauty's Keith-Moon-style ruthlessness which made *Chill Out* and *White Room* abiding classics. Poet Aaron Williamson did a performance involving a silver-sprayed plastic chair. This included that 'mime moment' where the artist stares at an object he's brought on stage and scratches his head; considering how brain-bendingly boring such 'performance art' tends to be, Sinclair's five-minute rule was most welcome (though the crowd loved Williamson). Sculptor Brian Catling appeared in a tux and recited a poem about mortality in Bela Lugosi's accent, reaching inside his shirt to extract his own heart and kidneys, which he then ate with relish, grease running down his chin, his chewing close-miked to disgusting and hilarious effect.

Sinclair's circus of fools wasn't as dense and vertiginous as his two written masterpieces (*Downriver*, *Radon Daughters*), but it certainly made conventional meet-the-author events seem threadbare and individualistic. This, he seemed to be saying, is what popular culture could be: not TV gawp, but in-person cabaret—surrealist, unprofessional and inclusive.

* * * * * * *

Music, Violence, Truth *(2001)*

N.B. It was this piece of writing which eventually led to a parting of the ways with The Wire. *I suggested something on 9/11 to Rob Young. He said he'd read it, but didn't like what I wrote and didn't print it. I put it on our website ww.militatesthetix.co.uk. Andy Wilson found it there, liked it and got my permission to print it up as a 1,000-edition pamphlet. Young was furious at the implication of 'censorship' denying he'd commissioned it. I think he was embarrassed at being reminded of his words on Afghanistan—not a fashionable point of view in 2003 when everyone and their dog was marching against the attack on Iraq (he claimed US action had created 'a happier Afghanistan...music and song are returning to that devastated land' in his editorial,* The Wire, *December 2001). This has proved to be one of my most popular pieces of writing. I think it said things that needed to be said, and a forum where I couldn't say things like this stopped feeling like a forum....*

AFTER THE devastation in Manhattan, what can radical music mean? Einstürzende Neubauten—whose name translates, prophetically, Collapsing New Buildings—earned their avant-garde stripes in Britain by applying pneumatic drills to a stress-bearing beam at the Institute of Contemporary Arts. After 11 September 2001, such transgressions surely pale into insignificance. Indeed, any comparison might seem offensive. Musically, telethon America responded to the tragedy by drawing on the sombre *substratum* of hymn-singing which unites country, soul and reggae. Music designed for church—unmediated, communal, local and introspective—inevitably sounded kitsch delivered by top-selling stars for international broadcast, but in such a context 'audio terrorism' does appear distinctly silly. Should the noisy end of the avant-garde shut up, and confess its misdemeanours were all a ruse?

The avant-garde registered its own peculiar response to the disaster. Rushing in where angels fear to tread, Karlheinz Stockhausen voiced what some may have felt, but none dared say. For him, the crashing planes and collapsing towers felt like art: 'What happened there is: now you must re-adjust your brain. The greatest work of art imaginable for the whole cosmos. Minds achieving in a single act what we in music can only dream of, people rehearsing like mad for ten years, preparing fanatically for a concert, and then dying. You have people who are that focused on a performance and then 5,000 people who are dispatched to the afterlife, in a single moment. I couldn't match it. Against that, we—as composers—are nothing.' Surely the guy is crazy? In Stockhausen's defence, he did go on to admit it was a crime, because part of the 'audience' were 'not consenting'. This demur didn't soften Gyorgy Ligeti's retort: 'Stockhausen should be locked up in a psychiatric hospital'.

A comment by one TV reporter—that the image of the planes crashing into the towers 'repeated in the memory like a nightmare loop'—was strange. You didn't need to repeat the images in your head, TV did nothing else for days on end. As usual, the mass media materially create the psychic conditions they moralise. But what should artists do when reality outdoes them? Stay quiet? Admit anti-art destructivism was just a tease? Confess that these tumultuous, apocalyptical events we call 'radical' were really just conjury with lutes and viols, a luxury product ornamented with *frissons* of phony danger?

Such evasions smack of the brittle repression of married couples who put away their teenage albums, and call their yen for music a 'passing phase'. For us, giving up on extreme music can't be the answer. Quite the opposite: it's by paying *closer* attention to the internal structure of radical music—'violence' and all—that its historical and social meaning might be decoded. Stockhausen's equation of art and terror—'this leap from security, from what's ordinary, from life'—may be poor consolation for inhabitants of Manhattan who have lost loved ones, or now feel desperately insecure. However, his weird outburst touches on something deep. Why is it that, since the modernist revolts of the early twentieth century, composers and improvisors have continually shouted noise, crisis and violence?

The crucial point is that art is an attempt to tell the truth about the world, the whole world, not simply to provide baubles for those in the comfort-zone of privilege. The economic pressures and national conflicts that create world wars and mass starvation and genocide are still in operation. The operations of global capitalism mean that the inhabitants of Burundi, Beirut, Belfast, Baghdad and Belgrade (I use alliteration to limit the list) have long suffered the terror and chaos which the suicide hijackers brought to Manhattan. Edgard Varèse brought the noise of sirens and bombs into music in the

1920s, a response to the horrors of World War I. His 'Hyperprism' anticipated the terror of the Blitz, when civilian populations first became long-distant targets of military hardware. Unlike his 'objectivist' follower Xenakis, he bent the shapes he heard into organic ovaloids which speak for the suffering ear. This is why, of all the pre-war orchestral composers, only Varèse has a non-*salon*, yet humanist ruggedness: a realism that moves the blood and shakes the entrails. Sonically, Varèse can stand comparison to Coltrane and Hendrix, who provided lasting testimonials to a different noise: a struggle against racial oppression in America and genocidal war in Vietnam.

These moments of musical truth weren't easy to achieve, nor were they facile, attention-seeking stabs at ugliness or excess. According to his wife Naima (talking to C.O. Simpkins, his best biographer), Coltrane studied scales from all over the world, and tried to pack every musical system into his music. If the results sound ugly, that is because you are too wedded to your partial musical identity, to your comfort-blanket of familiar harmony: heavenly universality sounds like hell to closed-in ears. For his part, Hendrix was intensely loyal to classmates who had been drafted to Vietnam. Reaching an anti-US position was painful and slow, yet by 'Machine Gun,' it happened. His rainbows of audio-feedback revelled in spaces which brought pain to the repressed and rigid: in the ears of GIs, they were incitements to immediate pleasure, to disrespect for authority, and to outright mutiny ('fragging').

Coltrane and Hendrix did not invent this dialectic between musical shock and political liberation. It was the major theme for Beethoven and his followers. Romantic music was a call to revolution that now languishes under the idiot term 'classical'. The exhilarating *allegri* of the symphony—the hoofbeats, the jangling bridles, the crack of loading muskets—are not about hunting, as Roger Scruton fondly imagines. They are about bourgeois revolution—'to arms, citizens!'—discovering common aims, seizing the castle keep, liberating the prisoners, letting in the light of reason, sweeping away the cobwebs of feudal reaction. After 1848, when the bourgeois class made its historic pact with state power and landed interests, the excitement turned sour. In March 1871, the French state slaughtered the Communards in thousands, and drove the voice of universal truth and reason underground. In Wagner, massive chromatic transitions invoke myth and fate: surrender to the madness of the stock market as to a natural force. By Mahler, the revolutionary *allegri* are hollowed-out, febrile, a nostalgic memory.

By rationalising Wagner's brain-bending chromaticism, Schoenberg and Webern forged a music whose freedom of note combination rejected the respectable, bourgeois world of repression and exchange. Their negation of tonality in Twelve Tone, born through logic, is painful; its parallel in the Blues, itself born through pain, is alluring. These twin attacks on the tempered system stalked each other through the twentieth-century, fighting, aiding and abetting, fusing and swapping places (see Muhal Abrams, Frank Zappa, James Blood Ulmer). The struggle for authentic music resembled political resistance to war and inequality and mass starvation. Its history is likewise fugitive and unofficial: stark glimpses of a different order in a black night of violence and lies. When Mark Sinker [*Wire* 211] worried that the offensive volume of rock can be employed to confirm conservatism, he needed to pay more attention to its economic base. Noise organised for extraction of surplus value isn't noise, but silence at high volume: rock as spectacle blocks its liberating essence, its democratic release and insurrectionary energy (hence Punk etc).

However, just because musical truth sounds violent and unacceptable to the *status quo*, it doesn't follow that devastation and violence are art. Stockhausen's enthusiasm for the Trade Center attack could just as well be Marinetti praising war ('the world's only hygiene'). Stockhausen combines Baader-Meinhof's elitist idea of spectacular political action with neo-Wagnerian megalomania: he doesn't realise that art and revolution are not a physical force, a firestorm (despite the images prevalent in free-jazz criticism), but powers mediated via human intellect and will. In other words, the 'power' of great music is its truth content, its proposed relation to the totality, not brute force. Music is not real violence, but a discourse of affective states, one that creates opportunities for judgment about feelings. The split between intellect and emotion is transcended, the very terms warped. This can't be done with a bludgeon (Trotsky's critique of Narodnik terrorism still stands).

Varèse—and his handful of authentic orchestral inheritors, namely James Dillon, Simon H. Fell, Iancu Dumitrescu, and Ana-Maria Avram—make music which short-circuits merely intellectual appreciation (the tight shape of a Haydn Quartet or a pop song), and at moments speaks directly to the body. It maps out the flow of blood, the rustle of nervous synapses, the creak of bone. Yet it doesn't neglect the intellectual thrill of graphing such biological realities, nor twinges of anxiety and guilt. This emotional science steels the brainpan, giving us the resolve to regard the world in its true colours. The political corollary is not aesthetic awe before the actions of suicidal hijackers, but comprehension. Terrorism is inflicted by the desperadoes of suffering populations. They have no plan beyond revenge on the civil populations of dominant states. Unfortunately, their actions invoke the logic that led to the bombing of retreating Iraqi troops on the road to Basrah, and deaths in tens of thousands.

Violence as conflict between national or religious blocks is a species of psychic repression, akin to conceiving sex in terms of individual gratification, or music in terms of a quantitative measure ('genius,' 'outreach,' 'sales'). It obscures the international dynamic of capital and production (*mangetouts* from Kenya, silicon chips from South Korea, the multi-coloured metropolis), naturalising Anglo wealth and Afghan poverty. By facing the horrors of an unbalanced world, by making us experience its terror and violence and sorrow, radical music offers the satisfaction of truth rather than the blandishments of comfort. It arms the psyche for reality. This will become increasingly necessary as the weaponry and trade-deals sold by the First World to the Third send us their refugees, their anger and their despair. The grief-stricken should be allowed to bury their dead in whatever manner they wish, but sombre hymns and TV-studio candles are not the final word: only a courageous assessment of global realities—musical and political—will allow us to shape a future worth hearing.

INDEX

[Some instances of names and recordings mentioned in passing have not been indexed—Ed.]

Abrams, Richard, 33, 106, 209
Acuff, Roy, 99
Adorno, Theodor, 8, 58, 80, 153; *The Jargon of Authenticity,* 128; *Sound Figures,* 95–97
Adritti, Irvine, 63
Agren, Morgan, 72
Aimand, Laurant, 26
Akchoté, Noël, 125
Alabama 3, 192
Albright, Madeline, 144
Allan, Marshall, 51
Allen, Geri, 175
Alternative TV, 192
Amin, Ali, 57
Ammons, Gene, 8
Andriessen, Louis, 66
Antheil, George, *Bad Boys* (also with Leo Ornstein and Henry Cowell), 65-66; *Sonatas for Violin and Piano, 1923, 1948,* 65–66
Armstrong, Louis, 24, 146, 161
Armstrong Twins, 90
Army, Brain, 97-98
Army of Ghosts, *The Horror,* 97–98
Art Ensemble of Chicago, 101
Ascension, *'LP',* 69–70
Astronauts, 192
Aural Guerilla, 193
Autism, *The Comforts of Madness,* 98–99
Avram, Ana-Maria, 209
Ayler, Albert, 34, 159, 172

Bailey, Derek, 34, 35, 40-41, 69, 85, 86, 111, 113–114, 125–126, 138, 162, 167; *String Theory,* 126; (with Anthony Braxton) *Moment Précieux* 54-55; (with Vertek Ensemble) *Departures,* 125–126
Baker, Newman, 48
Ballard, J. G., 205
Bang, Billy, 24, 164 (see also El'Zabar, Kahil)

Bangs, Lester, 201

Barker, Thurman, 21, 165

Baron, Joey, 40

Barrett, Syd, 199

Barry, Margaret, 123

Bartok, Bela, 116

Bashful Brother Oswald, *Don't Say Aloha,* 99–100

Bassholes, *Blue Roots,* 85–86

Bates, Dylan, 120

Baugher, Carl E., *Turning Corners: The Life and Music of Leroy Jenkins,* 100–102

BBC Radio, 7

Beck, Jeff, 120

Beckett, Harry, 110, 159

Beckett, Samuel, 30

Beebe, Roger, Denise Fulbrook, Ben Saunders (editors) *Rock Over the Edge: Transformations in Popular Music Culture,* 127–129

Beenie Man, 152

Beethoven, 153, 165, 208

Benjamin, Walter, 10, 137

Bennink, Han, 113–114

Beresford, Steve, 82

Berg, Alban, 104

Berio, Luciano, 19

Berman, Marshall, *All That is Solid Melts into Air,* 79

Bernas, Richard, 31

Berne, Tim, 119, 172

Bernstein, Leonard, 41

Betsch, John, 22

Beuler, Marie-Angélique, 190

Bey, Ronnell, 38

Bikini Kill, 143

Bingenheimer, Rodney, 201

Birdyak, 197

Birtwistle, Harrison, *Antiphonies for Piano and Orchestra,* 60

Black Artists Group (BAG), 33

Black, Jimmy Carl, 86, 92; with Richard Ray Farrell, *Cataract Jump,* 71; (see also Eugene Chadborne)

Black Flag, 143

Blackwell, Ed, 187

Blake, Andrew, *The Land Without Music: Culture and Society in Twenti-eth-Century Britain* (book), 79–81

Blake, Peter, 189

Blast (publication), 37

Bleyle, Jody, 144

Blindman, David, 106

Blues Birdhead, 147
Bluiett, Hamiett, 56
Blum, Eberhard, 67–68
Blythe, Arthur, 56, 161, 168; *Spirits in the Field,* 11-12; *Lenox Avenue Breakdown,* 12;
Boehmer, Konrad, *Aspekt, Cry of This Earth, Apocalipsis Cum Figuris,* 18–19
Bohn.Chris, 8, 191
Bolton, Richard, 120
Bonds, Gary 'US', 104
Bono, Sonny, 14
Boulez, Pierre, 19, 24, 41, 59, 83, 163, 195; *Sonata for Flute and Piano / First Piano Sonata / Dérive / Mémoriale / Dialogue de L'Ombre Double / Cummings Ist der Dichter,* 26–27
Bourdieu, Pierre, 153
Bourelly, Jean-Paul, 33
Bowie, Joseph, 81–82, 119
Bowry, Carl, 189
Bradford, Bobby, 161
Braxton, Anthony, 18, 54–55, 105–107, 154; *2 Compositions,* 27–28; *Duets Hamburg,* 28; *For Alto,* 119; *This Time,* 105; *Three Compositions of New Jazz,* 101
Brecht, Bertolt, 94
Breton, André, 152, 192
Brettschneider, Evert, 32
Breuker, William, *Kurt Weill,* 93–94
Bridgewater, Cecil, 38
Britten, Benjamin, 80
Brook, Michael, *Cobalt Blue,* 42; *Live at the Aquarium,* 42
Broonzy, Big Bill, 123
Brötzmann, Peter, *Machine Gun,* 113; *Nipples,* 113–114
Brown, Clarence 'Gatemouth', 120
Brown, Clifford, 164
Brown, George, 22
Brown, Kimbal, 121
Brueker, Willem, 18
Brooks III, Cecil, 11-12,
Brown, Charles, *Blues and Other Love Songs,* 46
Brown, James, 152
Brown, Tyrone, 38
Bruno, Giordano, 86
Bryars, Gavin, 111; *Sinking of the Titanic,* 61, 165
Bubbling Over Five, The, 147
Burroughs, William, 26, 30, 76, 169–172, 176–177

Cage, John, 28, 32, 86, 90, 116, 117, 153, 155, 156, 161; *A Firenze,* 63–64; "Freeman Etudes," 63; "Music for Amplified Pianos," 64; "Music for Trombone," 39; "Ryoni," 63; "Sixteen Dances," 61; "Two," 64; "Winter Music," 64

Campbell, Ken, 204

Can, 35

Captain Beefheart, 35, 142, 178–179, 183, 200

Cardew, Cornelius, *Piano Music,* 28–29

Cardini, Giancarlo, 63

Carman, Jenks 'Tex' ("The Dixie Cowboy"), 89–90

Carmeli, Boris, 20

Carter, James, 119

Casale, Jerry, 148-149

Cashian, Philip, 189–190

Catling, Brian, 205

Cauty, Jim, 205

Centipede, 111

Ceramic Hobs, 192, 193

Chadbourne, Eugene, 9, 122; *I Hate the Man Who Runs this Bar,* 157; *Insect Attracter* and *Jungle Cookies,* 86–87; (with Jimmy Carl Black) *Pachuco Cadaver,* 71; (with Vertek Ensemble) *Dimsum, Dodgers, and Dangreous Nights* (125–126)

Chadborne, Lizzie and Molly, 86

Chailly, Riccardo, 83

Chambers, Joe, 38

Chance, James, 48, 81

Chantry, Art, 143

Charlemagne, 156

Charles, Denis, 82

Charles, Ray, *Genius + Soul = Jazz,* 16-17; *Genius Hits the Road,* 16; *Soul Meeting,* 16

Cherrier, Sophie, 26

Cherry, Don, 82, 187

Cho Wen-Chung, 83

Chomsky, Noam, 144

Clash, 143

Clayson, Alan, *Backbeat,* 115; *Edgard Varèse,* 114–116

Cleaver, Gerald, 90

Clinton, President Bill, 144

Clinton, George, 47, 50

Clyne, Jeff, 111

Coasters, 147

Cobbing, Bob, 197

Cohodas, Nadine, *Spinning Blues into Gold: Chess Records, the Label that Launched the Blues,* 129–132

Coke, Alex, 94

Cole, Nat, 32
Coleman, Anthony, *Selfhaters,* 72–73
Coleman, Denardo, 30, 170, 175–178, 181, 188
Coleman, Ornette [incl. Prime Time], 11, 17, 32, 48, 109, 159, 172–188; *Chappaqua Suite,* 30; *Colors,* 175; *Dancing in Your Head,* 30, 175, 176, 180; *Free Jazz,* 175; *Naked Lunch,* 29–31, 169–172, 176–177, 181; (with Pat Metheny) *Song X ,* 36; *Sound Museum,* 175; *Tone Dialing,* 171–172, 175, 179–180, 185
Coleman Steve (and The Five Elements), *Rhythm People (The Resurrection of Creative Black Civilization),* 17–18
Collins, Bootsy, 50
Coltrane, John, 15, 106, 152, 153, 156, 172, 174, 186, 196, 208; *Live in Seattle,* 53–54
Connors, Red, 174
Contortions, 179
Cook, Richard, 7, 8
Cooke, India, 51
Cooper, Howard, 121
Corbett, John, 27
Corner, Philip, 33
Corso, Gregory, 179
Cosmonauts Hail Satan, 190
Count Basie Orchestra, 16
Coxhill, Lol, 173–174, 197, 202
Cramps, The, 8
Crayton, Pee Wee, 23
Creative Construction Company, 101
Cronenberg, David, 30, 169, 176–177
Crouch, Stanley, 82, 104
Crystals, The, "He's a Rebel,"14
Cunningham, Merce, 61
Curran, Alvin, 39; *Crystal Psalms,* 61
Curry, Ron T., 146
Cyrille, Andrew, 90

Dada and Surrealism, 151–152; *Dada: Art and Anti-Art* [Hans Richter], 8
Damiens, Albert, 27
Daniel, Ted, 82
Darwin, Charles, 154, 195
Davis, Anthony, 145
Davis, Miles, 14-15, 172; *Birth of the Cool,* 14; *Bitches Brew,* 15
Day, Morris, 50
Dead Kennedys, 143
Deane, J. A., 164
Debord, Guy, 8, 105–107, 203
Debriano, Santi, 22

Debussy, Claude, 189
Deckwitz, Franz, 18
De Bellis, Bob, 106
De Gennato, Matt (with Alastair Galbraith) *Wire Music,* 102–103
DeJohnette, Jack, 145–146
DeLaurenti, Christopher, *N30: Live at the WTO November 30 1999,* 117–118
De Leeuw, Robert, 66
della Monica, Francesca, 63
Deleuze, Gilles, 195
Denyer, Frank, 40
Derrida, Jacques, 47
Descartes, René, 192
Desnos, Robert, 59
Deupree, Jerry, 21, 35
Devo, *Hot Potatoes: The Best of Devo; Q: Are We Not Men? A: We Are Devo/Devo Live; Oh No! It's Devo/Freedom of Choice; Duty Now for the Future/New Traditionalists,* 47–48
Dewey, John, 155
Diehl, Kevin, 121
Dietzgen, Joseph, 86
Dillon, James, 83, 209; *East 11th Street,* 31–32
Diry, Roland, 27
DJ Olive, 103
Dockery, Wayne, 22
Dohnanyi, Christoph von, 61
Dolphy, Eric, 27, 84, 172
Dorsey, Jimmy, 24
Douglas, Dave, 126
Dr. John, 46
Drake, Nick, 200
Dresser, Mark, 153
Drew, Kenny, 25
Drummond, Bill, 205
Drummond, Tim, 14
Drury, Stephen, 153
Duke, George, 18
Dulfer, Candy, 50
Dumitrescu, Iancu, 83, 209
Dunn, Blind Willie, 24
Dusapin, Pascal, 20
Dylan, Bob, 122, 123

Easton, Sheena, 50
Eaves, John, 159
Eden, Peter, 159

Edison, Sweets, 23
Ehrlich, Marty, 33
Eicher, Manfred, 8, 113
Einstürzende Neubauten, 206
Eisler, Hanns, *Deutsche Symphonie,* 93–94
El'Zabar, Kahil (with Billy Bang) *Spirits Entering,* 132–133
Eldridge, Toy, 23
Elisa, 50
Ellerbee, Charles, 48, 180
Ellington, Duke, 25
Emerson, Lake and Palmer, 111
Eneidi, Marco, 172
Eno, Brian, 9, 42, 47, 61
Ensemble 10:10, 188–191
Ernest, Max, 82, 194
Escott, Colin, 88
Eshun, Kodwo, 79
Evans, Gil, 15, 164
Evil Dick, 152

Fabbriciani, Roberto, 63
Fafchamps, Jean-Luc, *Short Works from Italy,* 61
Faithfull, Marianne, 93
Favors, Malachi, 90–91, 145
Feathers, Charlie, 87–88
Feigin, Mischa, 87
Feldman, Mark, 62
Fell, Simon, 136, 138, 209
Ferrari, Luc, *Petit Symphonie, Strathoven, Presque Rien Avec Filles, Het-erozygote,* 18–19
Fillon, Jacques, 105
Finnegans Wake [Joyce], 8
Finnissy, Michael, 29
Fish Brothers, 192
Flo & Eddie, 44
Fonda, Joe, 106
Forsyth, Lucy, 106
Foucault, Michel, 192, 195
Fowley, Kim, 201
Freud, Sigmund, 196–197
Frisell, Bill, 34, 35, 40-41, 153
Frizell, Andy, 190
Fry, Roy, 110
Fugazi, 143
Fulkerson, James, 40
Fuller, Buckminster, 184

Funkadelic, 152

Galbraith, Alastair (see Matt De Gennaro)
Garland, Peter, 153
Garrett, Don, 53
Garrison, Jimmy, 22, 53
Giddens, Gary, 104
Gilbeau, Phil, 16
Gilbert, Bruce, 205
Gillespie, Dizzy, 23
Gilliard, Roddy, 189
Gilmore, Dave, 18
Ginsberg, Allen, 171, 176, 179
Gjerstad, Frode, 8
Glenn, Lloyd, 23
Glover, Tony, Scott Dirks, Ward Gaines, *Blues with a Feeling: The Little Walter Story,* 133–135
Goebbels, Heiner, 61
Goldstein, Malcolm, 103, 185; *Sounding the New Violin,* 32–33
Grapelli, Stefan, 24
Graubard, Allan, 165
Grauerholz, James, 176
Green, Grant, 34
Greenburg, Clement, 152
Greene, Ann, 101
Griffiths, Bill, 204
Gruber, H. K., 124
Grundy, Bill, 143
Guralnick, Peter, 88, 89
Guy, Barry, 109–110
Gyaatees, 199
Gysin, Brion, 176

Haden, Charlie, 40, 186
Hall, Jim, 34
Hamilton, Andy, 64
Hanson, Martin, H., 65
Harriot, Joe, *Abstract,* 159
Harris, Beaver, 22
Hartley, David, 30–31
Haslam, George, 109
Hassell, John, 9
Havel, Vaclav, 45
Hawkins, Coleman, 13, 25; 'Picasso,' 119
Haymakers Square Dance Band, 123
Hearst, Patty (Tania), 158

Hedqvist, Rolf, 72
Hegel, G. W. F., 129
Hejinian, Lyn, 151
Hell, Richard, 143
Hemphill, Julius, *Blue Boyé,* 119; *Fat Man and the Hard Blues,* 33
Hendrix, Jimi, 9, 21, 32, 34, 49, 152, 156, 208
Heraclitus, 86
Herrington, Tony, 8
Hession, Paul, 138
Hi-Fi News (magazine), 7
Higgins, Billy, 187
Hindemith, Paul, 116
Hinteregger, Helge, 98
Hirsch, Shelley, 194
Hobsbawn, Eric, 80
Hodges, Johnny, 32
Holiday, Billie, 200
Holland, Dave, 18
Holzmann, Meike, 190
Home, Stewart, 193
Honneger, Arthur, 19
Hook, Peter, 148–149
Hooker, John Lee, 14
Hooker, William, *Mindfulness,* 103–105
Hopkins, Fred, 48
Hopper, Dennis, 14
Houtkamp, Luc, 86
Hughes, Henry, 117

IRCAM (Institut de Recherche et Coordination Acoustique/Musique), 20,
    26, 31
Iris, 10
Irving, Tony, 70
Ives, Charles *A Set of Pieces*, 60
Izenzon, David, 176

Jackson, Alan, 109
Jackson, Milt, 16
Jackson, Shannon, 85, 178
Jacobs, Little Walter (see Glover, Tony, et al)
Jajouka Musicians of Morocco, 176
Jarman, Joseph, *Calypso's Smile* (with Don Moye), 34
Jaworzyn, Stefan, 70, 110
Jenkins, Adam, 121
Jenkins, Billy, <*sadtimes.co.uk*> , 119–120, 192

Jenkins, Leroy (incl. Revolutionary Ensemble), 100–102, 105; *Forty Years of Discovery, 1954–1994,* 102
Jorn, Asger, 106
Joujouka Musicians of Morocco, 30
Jaworzyn, Stefan, 10
Jenkins, Leroy, 24
Joans, Ted, 22
John Motley Singers, The, 38
John Wilkes Booze, *Five Pillars of Soul Vol.1 Melvin Van Peebles; Five Pillars of Souls Vol. 2 Tania Hearst; Whisky and Pills,* 158–159
Johns, Jasper, 117
Johnson, Lonnie, 24
Johnson, Lyndon, B., 199
Johnston, Daniel, 199
Jones, Elvin, 53–54
Jones, Philly Joe, 102
Jones, Steve, 143
Jones, Wizz, 122
Jordan, Louis, 147
Jorn, Asger, 8, 108
Joyce, James, 30, 144
Justine [De Sade], 19

Kagel, Mauricio, 20, 188
Kaiser, Henry, *Lemon Fish Tweezer,* 43
Karajan, Herbert von, 79–80
Kaye, Lenny, 86
Kazuhisa, Uchihashi, 98
Keenan, David, 9
Keller, Alex, 117
Kelly, Thad, 120
Keneally, Mike, 92
Kenny Process Team, 179
Kerouac, Jack, 171
Kieffer, Aldine, 147
Kimbrough, Junior, 89
King, B. B., 15
King Oliver's Creole Jazz Band, 146, 161
Kircher, Athanasius, 102
Kitchener, Lord, 122
Klee, Paul, 82, 194
Klemm, Joachim, 27
Knapp, Daniel, 191
Koenig, Gottfried, 19
Kofsky, Frank, 103, 157
Kopf, Biba, 8

Kopinski, Jan, 17, 175
Kostelanetz, Richard, 142
Kozick, Frank, 143
Kraabel, Caroline, 85, 136–137
Krause, Dagmar, 19
Kronos Quartet, 7
Kubrick, Stanley, 19
Kühn, Joachim, 175

Lacy, Steve, 164
La Faro, Scott, 109
Laing, R. D., 199
Lake, Oliver, 33, 91, 119
Lam, Bela (and his Greene County Singers), 147
Lang, Eddie, 24–25
Langdford, Jon, 43
Lanois, Daniel, 42
Laswell, Bill, 84
"Late Lunch with Out to Lunch" [radio program], 10
Lawson, Terry, 121
Léandre, Joelle, 84
LeBlanc, Keith, 43
Leeds Other Paper, The, 8
Lennon, John (and Yoko Ono), 44
Leo, Ted, 144
Leslie, Esther, 10
Levy, Isaac, 20
Lewis, George, 153
Lewis, Wyndham, 8, 30, 37, 115, 203
Ligeti, György, Chamber Concerto, 58
Liggins, Joe, 17
Litweiler, John, 176; The Harmolodic Life, 185
Lloyd, Al, 122
Logos Duo, 43
London Improvisers Orchestra, the hearing continues. . ., 136–138
Loose Tubes, 8
Loriod, Yvonne, 60
Los Paralyticos, 198
Lovano, Joe, 35, 36
Lowe, Frank, 36, 165
Luca, Loas, 93
Lucas, Gary, Gods and Monsters, 43
Lutoslawski, Witold, Chain 3 / Novelette, 58
Lygeti, Gyorgy, 207
Lymon, Frankie, 51
Lyons, Rachel, 189

M'Boom (Max Roach group), 38
MacColl, Ewan, 122, 123
MacDougall, Jim, 193
MacGregor, Joanna, 60
Mackness, Vanessa, 194
Macomber, Curt, 185
Maddox, Rose and the Strange Creek Singers, 90
Maderna, Bruno, 19
Madness, 193
Mahler, Gustav, 41, 208
Malcolm X, 152
Mallard, 43
Malli, Walter, 86
Malthus, Thomas, 156
Maneri, Joe, *Dahabenzapple*, 73–74
Maneri, Mat, *Fever Bed*, 73–74
Mantilla, Ray, 38
Manzarek, Ray, 93
Mao Tse-Tung, 155
Marcus, Greil, 105, 200
Mariano, Charlie, 111
Marinetti, Filippo, 209
Mark P, 197, 202
Marriott, Steve, 120
Marsalis, Wynton, 27, 164
Marsh, Dave, 201
Martin, Andrea, 190
Martin, Ben, 174
Martland, Steve, 66
Marx, Karl, 79, 154–155, 195
Mathewson, Ron, 110
Maurizi, Marco, 196
McBee, Cecil, 74
McCartney, Paul, 188–189
McGregor, Chris, 169–170
McGriff, Jimmy, 16
McLaren, Malcolm, 121, 193
McLaughlin John, 19, 109; *Extrapolation*, 55
McLean, Jackie, 159
McLuhan, Marshall, 155, 156
McPhail, Pete, 17
Mefano, Paul, 20
Messiaen, Olivier, 19, 139, 163, 195, 196; *Oeuvres pour piano et orchestre*, 60
Metcalfe, Hugh, 197–198, 201

Metheny, Pat, 36
Metzmacher, Ingo, 61
militantaesthetix.co.uk, 10
Miller, Emmet and His Georgia Crackers, 24
Miller, Harry, 160
Miller, Max, 189
Miller, Mulgrew, 15
Mingus, Charles, 186
Minton, Phil, 19, 194
Minotto, Paul, *The Prime-Time Sublime,* 139–141
Mintzer, Bob, 92
Mitchell, Roscoe, *The Day and the Night,* 90–91
Moby Grape, 191, 200
Moffett, Charles, 164, 176
Moffett, Charnett, 170, 175, 181, 188
Moholo, Louis, 160
Moncur II, Grachan, 22
Monk, Meredith, 150
Monk, Thelonious, 25, 30, 87, 110, 176
Moods of the Day (four CDs of Indian Ragas), 77–78.
Moore, Thurston, 9, 103
Morgenthaler, Walter and Hermine Ferndriger-Marti, *Ein Geisteskranker als Künster,* 196
Moröder, Giorgio, 149
Morricone, Ennio, 39, 43, 59
Morris, Butch, 133, 136, 161–169
Morris, Joe, *Flip and* Spike, 34–35; *Human Rites,* 21; *Sweatshop,* 21;
Morris, Wilber, 82, 161
Morrison, Van, 44
Motian, Paul, *Motian in Tokyo,* 35
Moye, Don, *Calypso's Smile* (with Joseph Jarman), 34
Muddy Waters, 15
Muffin Men, 92–93, 188–191
Murail, Tristan, 31
Murray, Charles Shaar, 10, 157
Murray, David, 32, 33, 104, 163, 164
Music of Captain Beefheart Live, The (Various) 71–72
Music Revelation Ensemble (James Blood Ulmer), *In the Name of...*(56-58)

Naked City, 7
Nancarrow, Conlon, 43
Napalm Death, 69; *Utopia Banished,* 36
Negativland, 143
Nelson, Oliver, 121
New York Dolls, 143

Niebergal, Buschi, 113–114
Nirvana (incl. Kurt Cobain), 142–143
Nitzsche, Jack, *The Hot Spot*, 14–15; *Performance*, 14; *One Flew Over the Cuckoo's Nest* [film], 14, *Blue Collar*, 14-15
Nix, Berne, 180, 186; *Alarms and Excursions*, 48–49
Noel, Ray, 97–98
Nono, Luigi, 19
Norfolk Jubilee Gospel Quartet, 147
Norton, Kevin, *For Guy Debord (In Nine Events)*, 105–107
Nucleus, 111
Nutters with Attitude, 192
Nyman, Michael, 32, 139

Oliveros, Pauline, 32
Ornstein, Leo, *Danse Savage*, 65
Ortiz, Travis, 150
Osborne, Mike, *Outback*, 159–160
Otis, Johnny, 152
Oulette, Fernand, 115–116
Oxley, Tony, *4 Compositions for Sextet*, 111–112; *The Baptised Traveller*, 111, 159; *The Tony Oxley Quartet*, 54-55
Oz (magazine), 7

Page, Jimmy, 80
Palermo, Ed, *Plays the Music of Frank Zappa*, 92
Palm, Siegfried, 109
Palmer, Earl, 14
Palmer, Robert, 176
Panter, Gary, 124
Parker, Charlie, 57, 172, 174, 181–182, 200
Parker, Evan, 9, 76, 111, 113–114, 136–137
Parker, William, 103
Parkins, Zeena, 103, 165
Parlan, Horace, 22
Patton, Mike, 154
Pedersen, Niels-Henning Orsted, 25
Person, Houston, 46
Petit, Chris, 203
Philips, Barre, 30, 176
Pickering, Mike, 120
Pine, Courtney, 169
Pinski Zoo, 17, 186
Plato, 156, 195
Poole, Ted, 122
Pop, Iggy, 8, 47; *Naughty Little Doggy*, 75–77; *Zombie Birdhouse*, 76
Pope, Odeon, 38

Popeil, Lisa, 149
Posseur, Henri, *Scambi, Trois Visages de Liège, Paraboles-Mix,* 18–19
Pound, Ezra, 65
Prazsky, Vyber, 45
Presley, Elvis, 198
Previte, Bobby, 33
Prévost, Eddie, 109
Priestly, Brian, 22
Prime, Michael, *Micoplazma,* 107–108
Prince, *Batman,* 50; *Black Album,* 49–50; *Dirty Mind,* 49; *Graffiti Bridge,* 50–51; *Under the Cherry Moon,* 51
Prince Buster, 194
Prinzhorn, Max, 194
Puschnig, Wolfgang, 124

Raitt, Bonnie, 46
Ramones, 76, 143
Red Hot Chili Peppers, 152
Regis, George, 187
Reich, Steve, 58, 60, 66, 150
Reich, William, 142
Reichert, Carl-Ludwig, *Frank Zappa,* 141–142
Reid, Jamie, 193
Reisinger, Wolfgang, 124
Renaldo, Lee, 103
Revell, Graham, 196
Reynols (incl. Miguel Tomasin), 199, 200
Ribot, Marc, 62, 153
Richman, Jonathan, 199
Richmond Starlight Gospel Quartet, 147
Richter, Hans, 8, 117, 152
Rico with Kuubo & The Rare Riddim Crew, *Rising in the East,* 66–67
Riel, Alex, 25
Riley, Howard, *Angle,* 109–110; *The Day Will Come,* 110
Rivera, Nick, 121
Rivers, Sam, 56
Roach, Max, *To the Max!,* 38
Roach, Maxine, 38
Roanoke Jug Band, 147
Robair, Gino, 87
Robinson, Orphy, 137, 169
Robinson, Toby, 125–126
Rochester, Cornell, 57
Rogers, Chris, 191
Rolling Stone, 200, 201
Rolling Stones, 14

Rollins, Sonny, 172, 186–187
Ronson, Mick, 120
Rooks, Conrad, 176
Root & Branch 2: 'Everybody Swing,' 122–123
Rosenboom, David, 154–156
Ruckus, 143
Rudd, Roswell, 22
Rüegg, Mathias, 124
Rundell, Clark, 190
Rushton, Alan, 110
Russell, Ray, *Dragon Hill,* 110–111, *Rites and Rituals,* 111
Rutherford, Paul, 111
Ruttman, Walter, *Weekend,* 75

Salonen, Esa-Pekka, 59
Salzinger, Helmut, *Swinging Benjamin,* 142
Samuels, Dave, 92
Sanders, Mark, 138
Sanders, Pharoah, 53–54, 176
Satie, Erik, 124
Scanner, 204
Scelsi, Giancinto, 43, 87; *Bot-Ba,* 39; *Music for Cello,* 39
Schenkel, Cal, 189
Schnittke, Alfred, 62; *Concerto Grosso,* 58
Schoenberg, Arnold, 116, 188, 209; *Pierrot Lunaire,* 194
Schuller, Ed, 74
Sconadibbrio, Stefan, 63
Schott, John, 153
Schroeder, Marianne, 39
Schwitters, Kurt, *Ursonate,* 67–68
Scofield, John, 34; *Grace Under Pressure,* 40
Scratch Orchestra, 28
Scruton, Roger, 208
Sex Pistols, 143, 193
Sgt. Pepper cover, 189
Shankar, L., *Touch me There,* 44–45
Shankar, Ravi, *Chappaqua Suite*, 177
Sharp, Elliot, 48, 103
Shepp, Archie, *Freedom; I Know about the Life; I Didn't Know About You,* 22-23
Sheppard, Andy, 8
Shore, Howard, 30, 169, 176–177
Shull, Carrie, 87
Shultis, Chris, 19
Signorelli, Frank, 24
Simmons, Gene, 148–149

Sinclair, Iain, 192; *Downriver* and *Radon Daughters,* 205; *London Orbital,* 203–205
Singh, Talvin, 51
Sinker, Daniel (ed.), *'We Owe You Nothing' Punk Planet: The Collected Interviews,* 142–145
Sinker, Mark, 209
Size, Roni & Reprazent, 169
Slingsby, Xero, 159
Smith, Bessie, 152, 173
Smith, Harry, *Anthology of American Folk Music,* 122, 146, 201
Smith, Jimmy, 17
Smith, Leo, 101, 105; *Reflectivity* and *Golden Quartet,* 145–146
Smith, Paul
Smith, Stuff, 24
Smith, Winston, 143
Soloff, Lew, 164
Solomon, Clifford, 46
Sonic Liberation Front, *Water and Stone,* 121
Sonic Youth, 143
Sparkling Four Gospel Quartet, 147
Spearman, Glenn, 103
Spence, Alexander, 199; *Oar,* 200
SPK, 196
Stanley Brothers, 85
Staples, Mavis, 51
Steinberg, Sebastian, 21, 35
Steinmo, Siri, 191
Stern, Mike, 92
Stevens, John, 180
Stewart, Bob, 12
Still, William Grant, 101
Stockhausen, Karlheinz, 19, 28, 195, 197, 206–207
Stooges [see also Iggy Pop], 143
Strauss, Richard, 32, 84, 116
Stravinsky, Igor, 41, 188, 189
Sun Ra (incl. Arkestra), 104, 138, 164, 168, 173; *Pleiades,* 51–52
Sutherland, Roger, *New Perspectives in Music,* 117

Tacuma, Jamaaladeen, 21, 120, 180
Takemitsu, Toru, *Visions,* 41–42; *Waves / Water-Ways,* 59
Taylor, Cecil, 85, 110, 119
Taylor, Little Johnny, 50
Tenney, James, 32
Thomas, Luther, 119; *BAGin' It,* 81–82
Thomas, Pat, 55, 137, 162
Thomas, Richard, 10

Thompson, Barbara, 110
Thompson, Chris, 191
Threadgill, Henry, 11
Thunders, Johnny, 143
Thunes, Scott, 148–150
Toledo, Joey, 121
Toop, David, 9, 79; *Guitars on Mars,* 110
Tosches, Nick, 10, 88
Transient v Resident, *Broken to be More Beautiful,* 54-56
Tripp, Art, 201
Trischka, Tony, 86
Trotsky, Leon, 155, 209
Tubize Hawaiian Orchestra, 147
Turnage, Mark-Anthony, 80, 168
Turner, Joe, *Stormy Monday,* 23
Turner, Roger, 98, 138
Turner, Tina, "River Deep, Mountain High," 14
Turriff, Jane, 122
Twombly, Cy, 139
Tyndall, John, 102
Tyner, McCoy, 53
Tzara, Tristan, 67

Uitti, Frances-Marie, 39, 153
Ulmer, James Blood, 35, 56–58, 173, 186, 209; *Harmolodic Guitar with Strings,* 56; *Tales of Captain Black,* 185
Ulrich, Thomas, 106
Underdog [punk band], 198
Universal Congress Of, 186
Uptown String Quartet, 38

Van Hove, Fred, 113–114
Van Peebles, Melvin, 158
Varèse, Edgard, 31, 60, 114–116, 155, 189; 191, 207–209; *Arcana,* 150; *The Complete Works,* 83–84
Veacher, Rachel, 99
Vendrame, Romeo, 43
Venuti, Joe, 24–25
Vercerk, Volcmar, 86
Vertek Ensemble (Vadim Budman and Ron de Jong), *Departures* and *Dimsum, Dodgers, and Dangerous Nights,* 125–126
Vienna Art Orchestra, *The Minimalism of Erik Satie,* 124
Vinson, Eddie Cleanhead, 23
Virginia Roots: The 1929 Richmond Sessions, 146–147
Voice of God Collective, 192
Volvox, 200

Wadling, Freddie, 72
Wagner, Richard, 32, 208, 209
Waikiki, Rudy, 99
Walley, Denny, 72
Wand, Matt, 55
Ward, Alex, 87, 136, 167
Ware, David, 104
Warhol, Andy, 117
Warwick, Dionne, 104
Washington, Reggie, 17
Watson, Johnny 'Guitar', 120
Watts, Charlie, 93
Watson, Bobby, 17
Watson, Johnny 'Guitar,' 15
Weaver, Chris, 10
Webber, Andrew Lloyd, 155, 168
Webern, Anton, 209
Webster, Ben, *There is No Greater Love,* 25
Weill, Kurt, 93–94, 124, 155; *The Seven Deadly Sins,* 93
Weir, Judith, 80
Werner, Ken, 22
Weston, Calvin, 120
Weston, Veryan, 136, 197, 199, 201
Wheeler, Kenny, 111
Wheeler, Onie, 99–100
White, Andrew, 33
White, Clarence Cameron, 101
Wictor, Thomas, *In Cold Sweat: Interviews with Really Scary Musicians,*
    148–150
Wild Man Fischer, 200–202
Wilkinson, Alan, 159; *Seedy Boy,* 119
Williams, Frank 'Squirrel', 121
Williams, John, 19
Williamson, Aaron, 205
Williamson, Steve, 169
Willis, Ike, 44
Wills, Bob (& the Texas Playboys), 123, 174
Wilson, Andy, 206
Wilson, Cassandra, 13, 18, 167
Wilson, Peter, 28
Windo, Gary, 93
Wire, The (magazine), 7–9, 22, 47, 64, 79, 108, 191, 206, 209
Wobensmith, Matt, 144
Wölfi, Adolf, 196
Workman, Reggie, 90

World Saxophone Quartet, 33, 119
Wyatt, Robert, 29
Wynette, Tammy, 32, 173

Xenakis, Iannis, 83, 109, 208

Young, Neil, 14, 47
Young, Rob, 8, 206

Zappa, Frank, 8, 9, 47, 62, 92-93, 114–116, 120, 124, 141–142, 148–150, 154, 164, 189–191; 200–202, 209; *Burnt Weenie Sandwich,* 190; *The Grand Wazoo,* 189; *The Perfect Stranger, 190; Playground Psychotics,* 44; *Thing-Fish,* 189, 191; *We're Only in It for the Money,* 189
Zappa, Moon and/or Dweezil, 47, 149–150
Zorn, John, 7, 8, 51, 87, 139, 140, 164, 165, 168, 172; (ed.) *Arcana: Musicians on Music,* 150–157; *Kristallnacht,* 62

ABOUT THE AUTHOR

BEN WATSON is the author of *Frank Zappa: The Negative Dialectics of Poodle Play*, *Art, Class and Cleavage: Quantulumcunque Concerning Materialist Esthetix*, *Derek Bailey and the Story of Free Improvisation*, and the novel *Shitkicks and Doughballs.* He is also a poet and a visual artist. He lives in London.